COW TALK

The Environment in Modern North America

Cow Talk

Work, Ecology, and Range Cattle Ranchers in the Postwar Mountain West

MICHELLE K. BERRY

University of Oklahoma Press : Norman

Publication of this book is made possible through the generous support of
The Charles Redd Center for Western Studies at Brigham Young University and
The Kerr Foundation, Inc.

Library of Congress Cataloging-in-Publication Data

Names: Berry, Michelle K., author.
Title: Cow talk : work, ecology, and range cattle ranchers in the postwar Mountain West / Michelle K. Berry.
Other titles: Environment in modern North America ; v. 8.
Description: Norman : University of Oklahoma Press, [2023] | Series: The environment in modern North America ; volume 8 | Includes bibliographical references and index. | Summary: "A history of ranching in the U.S. from 1945 to 1965 showing how the issues and hardships faced by cattle ranchers brought about a new ranching culture in the Mountain West through the use of a language—'Cow Talk'—that allowed ranchers to maintain a sense of community and identity as leverage against the efforts of government agents and other perceived enemies"—Provided by publisher.
Identifiers: LCCN 2022034422 | ISBN 978-0-8061-9178-2 (hardcover) | ISBN 978-0-8061-9191-1 (paperback)
Subjects: LCSH: Ranchers—Mountain States—History—20th century. | Ranchers—Public relations—Mountain States. | Cattle trade—Government policy—Mountain States. | Cattle trade—Environmental aspects—Mountain States. | Cattle trade—Management.
Classification: LCC SF196.U5 B54 2023 | DDC 636.2/010978—dc23/eng/20220822
LC record available at https://lccn.loc.gov/2022034422

Cow Talk: Work, Ecology, and Range Cattle Ranchers in the Postwar Mountain West is Volume 8 in The Environment in Modern North America series.

For Anne, who nurtures my imagination and keeps me balanced.

This book is as much yours as it is mine. I love you.

Here's to the next adventure.

Contents

Acknowledgments

Writing a book, in many ways, is like running a marathon. And like any arduous athletic undertaking, the athlete needs commitment, stamina, and a world-class support network. I often ran out of the two former requirements, but thanks to the latter I was able not only to finish the race but to become a better person in the process. First and foremost, I thank my partner Anne. She was unwavering during times when I was certain that the decision to continue this project was the wrong one.

This book is derived from a dissertation that I wrote while attending the University of Arizona, but it likely began at The Colorado College when I was an undergraduate studying with Anne Hyde and Doug Monroy. Their mentorship and nearly thirty years of friendship inspired me to seek graduate education and lean into my natural tendencies of "egg-headedness." When I arrived at the U of A, I was fortunate to have access to a faculty that was inspirational and patient. Linda Darling gave to me a historiographical foundation for which I continue to be grateful. Reeve Huston would eventually expose me to an amazing world of labor history. While we could never quite find a way to have him serve as an official member of my committees, he has had as much effect on my scholarship as anyone. Thanks, too, Reeve, for always being someone who understood that play was just as important as work! Doug Weiner's intellect and passion for environmental history were always present and powerful.

Immediately upon embarking on the MA at Arizona, I found a committee of "power women" who would become my most inspirational mentors. Karen Anderson, I was scared to death of you when I first sat in that colloquium in 1998. You have since become someone who I have tried to emulate in scholarship, teaching, and life. I especially appreciate your humor and your unabashed enthusiasm for the sport of basketball! Sally Deutsch, when I first met you I had never encountered anyone whose mind moved so quickly and whose spoken dialogue was just as fast! I never thought I would successfully absorb all you had to share. I probably never have, but I benefited immensely from the little bit I could imbibe. Thanks, too, for always being so supportive of me, my teaching, and my scholarship. I'm not even sure what to say about and to Katherine Morrissey. Certainly, I would never have become the scholar I am without your guidance and your high standards. You of anyone deserved to see this book published and probably had lost faith that it ever would be. Thank you—I hope I've done you proud.

The book wouldn't exist if it weren't for those who believed in the importance of the stories told here even as political climates and scholarly priorities shifted. (Leisl Carr-Childers and Michael Childers, I'm looking at you!) I also remain grateful to the University of Arizona Department of History and the financial support and professional development they provided me over the years. I am in debt to those institutions that were kind enough to offer me research fellowships, including the Huntington Library (and Peter Blodgett for his ceaseless enthusiasm for my cow work), the Montana Historical Society, and the Charles Redd Center at Brigham Young University. Thanks to all the readers who made this work stronger through their thoughtful engagement with it. And thanks to Gender and Women's Studies at U of A for giving me a home and a space to continue to advocate the importance of learning about the more than human beings in our midst.

Last, but not least, I have so many dear friends and family to thank. The list is endless and could require another book! Thanks to Adam Geary, who read every word; Megan Mulligan, who always listened; Chris and Em and Kelly and Scott, who kept me committed to continuing my life as a scholar; MZ and Amy, who care about the West as much as I do; Leslie, for stories that took my mind off history; Emily Wakild, who is my scholarly, writing, and general life muse. My friendship with you means more than I can say! To Chinle and Zindy—fur babies who napped through the entire revision and publishing processes. Just their presence made the whole endeavor more fun. And, of course, to all my students former and future.

You inspire me. Thanks to the fam—especially Kay and Rich, my big bro Mike, Kathy, Tim and Cuz, and of course my awesome nephews, Mark and Matthew and their better halves (Katie and Elisa)—you guys are the best and I love you. Thanks also to Mom and Dad. Thanks for teaching me to love to learn and to always think critically—and thanks for knowing a thing or two about cows!

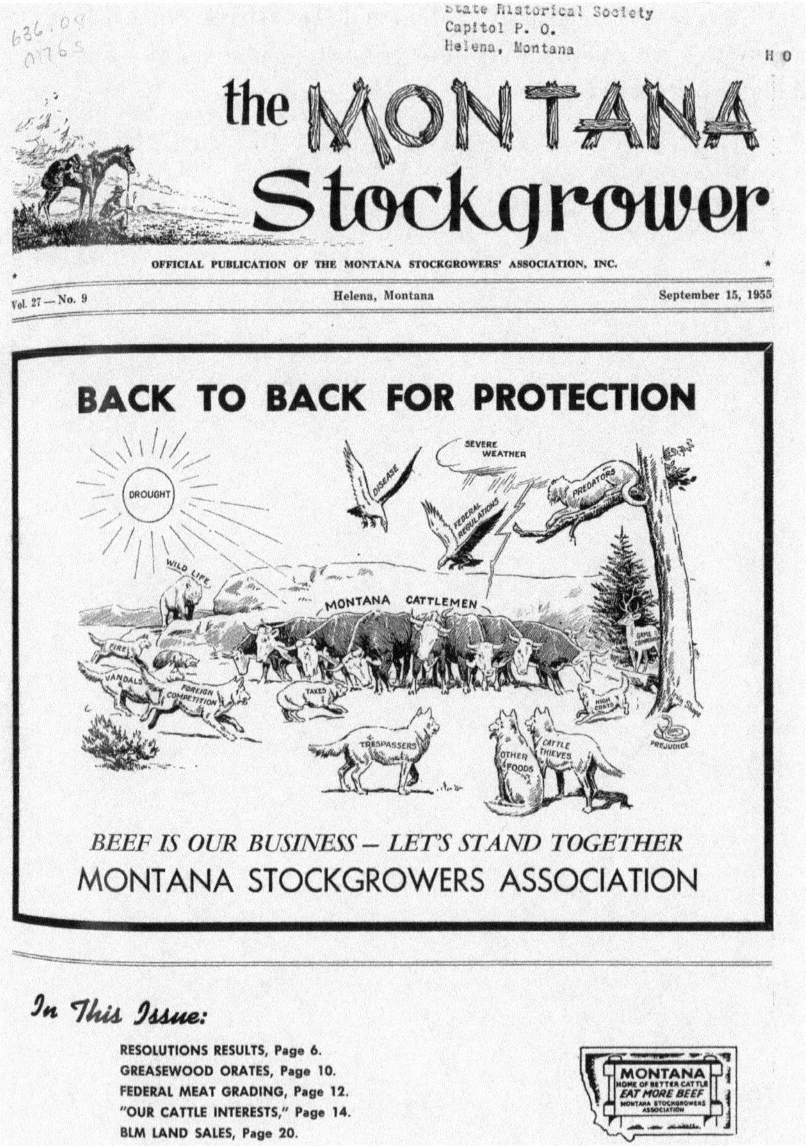

State Historical Society
Capitol P. O.
Helena, Montana

the MONTANA Stockgrower

OFFICIAL PUBLICATION OF THE MONTANA STOCKGROWERS' ASSOCIATION, INC.

Vol. 27 — No. 9 | Helena, Montana | September 15, 1955

BACK TO BACK FOR PROTECTION

BEEF IS OUR BUSINESS – LET'S STAND TOGETHER
MONTANA STOCKGROWERS ASSOCIATION

In This Issue:

RESOLUTIONS RESULTS, Page 6.
GREASEWOOD ORATES, Page 10.
FEDERAL MEAT GRADING, Page 12.
"OUR CATTLE INTERESTS," Page 14.
BLM LAND SALES, Page 20.

MONTANA
HOME OF BETTER CATTLE
EAT MORE BEEF
MONTANA STOCKGROWERS ASSOCIATION

Figure 1. Cover of the *Montana Stockgrower*, September 1955. MHS Research Center Archives, Helena.

Building Fence

Constructing the Parameters of This Project

> Communities are to be distinguished not by their falsity/
> genuineness, but by the style in which they are imagined.
>
> —Benedict Anderson, 1983

In September 1955 more than four thousand Montana cattle growers found an issue of the *Montana Stockgrower* in their mailboxes (figure 1).[1] As autumn descended on Big Sky country, the ranchers who gazed at the artistic rendering of themselves herded together for "mutual" protection must have nodded knowingly. The image caricatures an industry strong yet suffering and a community in need of "back-to-back" protection. The image is, of course, also a kind of advertisement for the Montana Stockgrowers Association (MSGA) as it suggests that Montana cattle ranchers were *already* united behind the business of beef through their trade associations. Back-to-back, the ranchers, embodied as cattle, face particular threats with heads lowered and horns at the ready. Note how the image depicts them as a single breed. This portrayal of cattle ranchers as all being of a single kind is emblematic of ranchers' attempts to overcome division, discord, and diversity during the postwar decades. During these years they spent considerable energy reinforcing their insularity and connectedness. The image also suggests how ranchers viscerally apprehended the threats running rampant in range country. As they faced the threats, they joined forces.

This work offers an analysis of how they united. It is also a cultural history of a political special interest group—namely, the owners and operators of range cattle ranches in the states of Montana, Wyoming, Colorado, Arizona, and New Mexico across the mountain West from 1945 to 1965.[2]

1

During these two decades ranchers joined forces in unprecedented numbers and worked tirelessly to protect a way of life they believed was under
attack. Rather than taking for granted the permanency of their political,
economic, and environmental power in the postwar decades, ranchers
came to fear for their place in the West, and they used that fear to gather
ever more tightly into collective organizations. This increasing unity ultimately enabled them to present to the nonranching public an image of a
cohesive cultural group.

As someone who grew up in rural western Colorado, I have long been fascinated by the ranching community. As I began my work as an environmental historian, I realized that there was no history solely focused on that group
of agriculturalists in the middle of the twentieth century, and it seemed like
there should be in light of their disproportionate power in western politics
and culture. In particular, I was fascinated with the growing discord associated with the Sagebrush Rebellion of the 1970s and 1980s, but as I studied
the history of the twentieth-century West, few explanations for the growth
of that militant movement seemed to exist. So I dove into the archives to get
a sense of ranchers' ire and to see if it stemmed from the immediate postwar years. My research did not unearth political demagoguery of the sort
we have become accustomed to in the late twentieth and early twenty-first
centuries. But what did emerge from the archives was abundant evidence
of ranchers trying to make sense of a newly complex world by sharing their
lived experiences with one another. The repetition of stories of triumph
and hardship, of common enemies and shared allies, of benevolent environments and fearsome ecologies seemed to serve as a kind of incipient cultural
glue. In short, we can think about the ranchers' sharing of information and
experiences during these years as an important first spark to an ideological
fire that would eventually rage nearly out of control.

This study uses ranchers' personal papers, ranching publications, and
cattle growers' association records to shed light on the mindset and identity formation that emerged from ranchers' lived experiences with work.
This investigation is important for a couple of reasons. First, it lends new
insight into the culture, work, and politics of an incredibly powerful group
of agriculturalists that has been understudied. Second, it helps shed light
on the concerns that emerged from ranchers in the latter quarter of the
twentieth century. The context and concerns would eventually inform

the strident and defensive politics that ranchers in the region seemed to adhere to after the period under study.

As they sought to make sense of their lives in the immediate postwar decades, ranchers engaged in group communication that had consistent elements across the mountain West, transcending the size of the ranch, the breed of cattle raised, and even the diverse ecological biomes in which the ranches were located. I soon realized that very specific vernacular and iconography characterized this communication, and both were grounded in labor with cattle as practiced in the environs of the ranch. The language and iconography ultimately created a symbolic universe that ranchers used for a cultural practice that I have termed "cow talk" (a play on the phrase "shop talk"). It became obvious that cow talk allowed ranchers to unify around a set of collectively created dominant cultural narratives. Cow talk shows up in articles in association periodicals, in private letters between ranchers, and in cartoons drawn for and by ranchers, and it was expressed at events where ranchers convened to share information and enjoy one another's company. Cow talk, much like industrial shop talk, relied on occupationally specific understandings of cattle ranching to communicate ideologies and values. Thus, cow talk included the topics of ranchers' work with cattle and the environments of the range as well as the unique slang and tropes ranchers used to articulate their identities to one another.

Perhaps a few concrete examples of the different manifestations of cow talk will help to further explain this central concept of the work. The president of the MSGA engaged in cow talk in 1958 when he explained in a convention address: "We cowmen are a pretty scarce breed. There are not enough of us to swing much weight in this country unless we are strongly organized." His reference to ranchers as a "breed" exemplifies one kind of cow talk. When Dan Fain, a rancher near Prescott, Arizona, wrote an article for the *Arizona Cattlelog* (the periodical of the Arizona Cattle Growers' Association [ACGA]) about his experience with cottonseed meal-salt mixture in keeping cattle alive and thriving, readers of the article consumed cow talk. Fain wrote: "One day I rode over into a pasture where about 300 head were bunched into a corner. They were drawn bad." Only those who had experience with cow work would understand his description of cattle being "drawn bad." In 1946 cattlewoman Lucille Anderson engaged in cow talk when she wrote a poem that showed up on the cover of the *Arizona Cattlelog*. In it, she likened the one-year anniversary of the *Cattlelog* to a yearling calf. She wrote, "I was born kinda small Tail, hide an' a bawl / But I've come a long way I'm a yearlin'." The dropping of the ending consonants to suggest rural slang and the bovinization of the periodical itself, as well as a drawing of a calf kicking up its heels next to the poem, provide another taste of cow talk. And, of course, the image that opened this chapter is a prime example of cow talk. The many manifestations of cow talk, then, are the focus of this book, because as I delved into the ranchers' archives it became obvious that cow talk served to unite them in commonality despite any differences of experience or opinion they had.[3]

This book explores four main themes that highlight the most common instances in which ranchers leaned on cow talk to connect with one another: how cow talk was used to demonize human and nonhuman threats that jeopardized the ranch community and its way of life; how the practice heroized a rural, masculinist heritage that was deeply gendered; how ranchers used shared language to reinforce collective values of labor and hard work; and how they used cow talk to claim and seek economic and environmental control and expertise.

To create and fortify their power and belief in their way of life, ranchers produced and shared cow talk. The archives are littered with countless images and stories that reinforced their conviction that they were united in an urgent mission to persist despite the new world that seemed to be quickly emerging from the ashes of Hiroshima. Ranchers then used their collective culture to justify claims to political power. While many histories of range ranchers focus on their political activities surrounding the Taylor Grazing Act of 1934 and their relationships with outsiders (specifically the federal government) after the onset of the Sagebrush Rebellion in the 1970s, this study focuses on ranchers' understandings of themselves and each other in a formative period that has gone mostly unexamined by historians—the immediate postwar decades of 1945–65.

The overt simplicity of the image in figure 1 belies the complexity of real life on the range in the mid-twentieth century. No ranch was the same. Some ranches held large numbers of deeded acres, others were rather small; some ranches existed in high-altitude country and in valleys surrounded by mountains, while some were located on the Great Plains, surrounded only by shrubs and a sea of grass; some ranchers had access to water while others did not; some utilized hired labor, while many relied on family labor to make their way; and some had large amounts of capital, while others operated in the red much of the time.

The diversity within range ranching meant that each rancher had her or his own individual interests. In addition to a diversity of experience on the ranch itself, macropolitical and economic issues surrounding the industry were profoundly complicated and, at times, threatened to divide ranchers. Foreign competition, taxes, predators, and federal regulations (to name only a few examples) all involved complex systems (whether human or ecological) that ranchers could not manipulate easily. In the world of the post–World War II decades, ranchers had to decide how to react to each of the perceived threats to their livelihoods. They could have chosen to do that on an individual basis—quietly grappling with the everyday problems on their separate ranches in their own solitary ways. Instead, however, they increasingly joined their collective, representative organizations and reached out to one another for support.

Images like that in figure 1 performed important cultural work by reducing the complexity of range ranching to a vision of seeming accord. It is important to note here that while cow talk deemphasized diversity within the ranching community, it also rendered all those in the business of beef who were *not* range ranchers (whether feedlot owners, meat packers, or dairy operators) as Other—outside of and peripheral to the main herd of range ranchers. Clearly, this separation was arbitrary. There are myriad layers of the cattle business, and at times range ranchers did have dairy operations or "finished" their cows by feeding them in corrals rather than on the range. Still, for range ranchers, the range itself was what mattered most in the construction of their group identity. In addition to the ranchers' own characterization of the range as a unifier, it has historically been the range industry that has occupied the most space (geographically, politically, and imaginatively) in the mountain West. Range ranching is the aspect of the cattle business that is most closely associated in popular culture with the industry known as "ranching" and with the extreme politicization of ranchers like those involved in the Sagebrush Rebellions of the 1970s, '80s, and '90s. For those reasons, this book focuses exclusively on *range* cattle ranchers and the cow talk that united them.

The ranchers discussed in this work were all owner-operators of ranches, from small to large, in Montana, Arizona, Wyoming, Colorado, and New Mexico. I define "ranchers" as anyone engaged in the growing of cows *on the ranch*.[4] By owner-operator I mean the class of people who owned or operated the ranch (sometimes both) and engaged in raising cattle through grazing on range grasses. This definition includes the men and women who actually owned a ranch and ran any number of head and also those ranch folk who may or may not have owned part of the ranch but who were (as operators) crucial to its success.[5] I chose this broad definition because while the bulk of my sources comes from owners who were also operators, some material includes the voices of nonowner operators (waged labor and hired hands).

In the postwar years ranchers seemed to buy into the notion that they could find strength in numbers, but this had not always been the case. In the mid-nineteenth century ranchers began coming together in voluntary livestock associations to advocate for access to the grasslands of the West, but by the early twentieth century ranchers' involvement in those groups had declined. But from 1945–65 ranchers in the mountain West again began to swell the ranks of their collective associations by unprecedented numbers. By 1955 the main cattle grower associations in Montana, Wyoming, Colorado, New Mexico, and Arizona each could boast of having two thousand or more members. Membership rosters continued to grow into the early 1970s. These numbers had increased substantially from the lower numbers of the 1920s and 1930s. The New Mexico Cattle Growers' Association (NMCGA), for example, reported 400 members in 1939, but by 1960 that number was 5,500. Membership in the MSGA increased from 502 in 1929 to 4,587 in 1951. Other state associations reported the same kinds of increases in membership.[6] In most states, one in every three ranches had a membership in the cattle growers' associations—in some places, like New Mexico and Wyoming, it was one in two.[7] In addition to increases in membership in the main organs of the associations, thousands of ranch women joined the newly formed women's "auxiliary" of the livestock associations, the Cowbelles.[8] The MSGA image, then, captures the historically specific phenomena of ranchers' renewed unity. In the immediate post–World War II years, ranchers decided it was worth coming together in solidarity to offer one another "back-to-back protection." Using their labor to manage the nonhuman ecology of the range and their daily work with cattle, they fashioned the discourse I call "cow talk" to serve as the cultural glue that bound them.

Unlike most studies of ranchers, which have sought to understand only ranchers' relationships with the federal government, this work explores the day-to-day lives of ranchers at a critical historical juncture in their unique politicization. Other studies have focused on the actions ranchers took in response to the increasing presence of the federal government leading up to and after the Taylor Grazing Act, but this work is interested in a broader investigation of the lived experiences of ranchers as a class of environmental laborers in the immediate postwar era. Their experiences in these twenty years can help us connect the dots between studies like Leisl Carr-Childers's and Karen Merrill's foci on the first five decades of the twentieth century to the Sagebrush Rebels of the 1970s.[9] It is true and important that ranchers had to continue to adjust to the presence of new range management agencies (the U.S. Forest Service and the Bureau of Land Management [BLM]), but they were also reacting to a quickly modernizing world. Their day-to-day experiences with things *other than* the federal government inspired them to overcome great paradoxes in their lives and to work out tensions between one another. They did so by embracing their common interests, joining collectively into association, creating a labor-specific language, and advocating for their and their cattle's survival.[10]

The paradoxes and tensions took a variety of forms. Regarding federal policies, most ranchers hoped to maintain some sense of autonomy from government regulations, but they also expected the government to protect them from foreign competition and rescue them in emergency situations. Culturally, they prided themselves on their traditional, simple way of life, but they also felt the impetus to embrace modern technological innovations. As a group, ranchers honored their identities as individualists, but they increasingly understood that there was political and cultural strength in numbers. And, finally, where their cattle and ranch ecologies were concerned, ranchers debated ideas about range management and modern cattle growing even as they sought to celebrate traditional and time-honored cow work.

To address these paradoxes, ranchers ultimately came to rely on the common discourse of cow talk, and this study investigates how ranchers used specific cow-talk topics (such as the encroachment of outsiders, mechanization, technoscience, collective memory, cows, the nonhuman environment of their ranches, and even the market) to organize and to convince themselves that they were *all* experiencing the same terrible troubles and the same extraordinary triumphs. Cow talk, as a vernacular unique to them, gave ranchers their group identity and allowed them to feel politically, environmentally, and culturally connected.

This study is not only an in-depth social history of the everyday lives of ranchers; nor is it solely an environmental history, labor history, or agricultural history. Rather, it seeks to blend these methodologies into a general survey of a group of powerful environmental and political actors that, to this point, has received relatively little focus. In 2019 Lisa Brady and Mark Hersey wrote an article on new directions in environmental history for the Organization of American Historians.[11] There they call for more inclusion of labor, consumerism, gender issues, agrarianism, and technology into the field of environmental history. When I was being trained as an environmental historian at the University of Arizona in the early 2000s, I was fortunate to be intellectually mentored by scholars who encouraged me to think about the interventions that all kinds of historical fields could make in environmental history. I came later to the history of science, science and technology studies, and political ecology thanks to opportunities to teach in those fields. My awareness of the importance of blending these many fields of scholarship led me to survey this group of agriculturalists with a variety of analyses in mind. It quickly became clear that ranchers were workers who were embedded in a contentious and powerful social world that centered around range ecology and that led to a strong sense of identity.

Just as environmental history needs to be infused with increasingly complex transdisciplinary approaches, agricultural history would also benefit from cross-fertilization. Agricultural history does not tend to address agriculture from both labor and environmental perspectives nearly enough.[12] While environmental historians do need to begin to address workers outside of the traditional earth-dependent professions (e.g., farmers, ranchers, loggers)—as both Richard White and Gunther Peck have argued—there are still tremendous opportunities for more complex studies of these professions. From the nation's founding, agriculturalists, as a special interest group, have exerted enormous control over American ecologies, myths, and politics (whether it is water use and access, immigration policies, or health and safety legislation), and ranchers in the West are no exception.

While my training encouraged me to blend labor, gender, environmental, agricultural, and cultural histories in this work, they are also here because the archives insisted it be so. The material record left by ranchers intertwines these topics, and while historians have long separated these areas of study, ranchers themselves did not. Thus, this book seeks to bridge artificially siloed academic foci by analyzing ranchers' ecoculture to arrive at an environmental history that uses the methods of the history of labor, agriculture, gender, and politics to craft the first cultural chronicle of range ranchers' lives in the two decades following World War II.[13] To be honest, when I undertook this work, I had hoped to focus solely on the nonhuman world of range cattle ranching. But the archives presented to me a visual and textual record produced by and for ranchers that encompassed far more than just dilemmas over invasive species and overgrazing. To do the group justice, I had to include an overview of as much of that record as possible. My purpose, therefore, is not to detail the ins and outs of range policy or even to chronicle the shifting ecologies of the ranches from this period; rather it is to gain insight into dominant rancher experiences in these years so that we might have a better appreciation of how they understood themselves. The study uncovers the stories ranchers shared with one another about their lifeways, and in doing so, it highlights their daily lived reality and shines a light on the political community-making as it commenced in the decades just before things grew tense (and finally violent) with the Sagebrush Rebels.[14]

Seeking to understand ranching in the decades just before the Sagebrush Rebellion is one reason for focusing on the immediate postwar decades, but there are others as well. The economic boom that arrived at the end of World War II set up two decades that were both typical and atypical for ranchers.[15] As has always been true for ranchers in the states I consider, prices and precipitation fluctuated throughout the period covered here. The five-year period after the war was one of the most lucrative times in history to be a rancher in the U.S. West, but beginning in 1950 and continuing through 1957, ranchers hit some of the hardest times any of them had witnessed. Prices soared directly after the war but dropped precipitously in the early 1950s, and prolonged drought throughout the region accompanied the recession. Thus, the ebb and flow of cattle prices and range health, which generally can be characterized by extremes, was no different during this period.

The years 1945–65 were also, historically speaking, both the zenith and nadir of family ranching. Family-based ranching simply refers to ranches that are owned by family groups rather than publicly traded corporations (like present-day Monsanto or Con-Agra). From the late 1940s through the mid-1960s, the number of ranches in each state fluctuated but averaged between six thousand (in New Mexico) and ten thousand (in Wyoming).[16] During the immediate postwar era, the ranching industry was more family-based than any time in its history. The average rancher ran about three hundred head of cattle on approximately 3,500 acres during the years covered here. And while the number of ranches decreased (and the size of ranches increased) during the twenty years covered in this study, they were not gobbled up by large corporations (as was the case for citrus farms in California during this time), but rather by other family-owned ranches. The rise in membership numbers in the associations in these years, therefore, is especially interesting when compared to the decrease in the number of ranchers overall in the same period.[17] In the 1950s and '60s range ranchers, always a minority in the West, became increasingly aware of their precarious position and their need to assert a singular collective identity and purpose. Additionally, the huge spreads so common in the open-range era of ranching became economically unfeasible during the postwar decades for two reasons. First, the Great Depression had sapped capital from most ranchers. And second, the increasing need to feed (rather than graze) cattle during certain times of the year became essential due to grass shortages on the range. Thus, if ever there was a "democratic" era of ranching, an era that was relatively stable, and an era when family ranching appeared most vulnerable, 1945–65 was it.

I focus on the mountain West states for ecological and geographical reasons. While I chose to do a multistate study (and thus sacrifice microsocial for macrosocial historical inquiry), I still had to draw limits somehow. I selected the five states of Montana, Wyoming, Colorado, New Mexico, and Arizona because they experienced the historical context of the postwar decades similarly. They also are unified ecologically in interesting ways. While there are specific and diverse bioregions throughout the region, each state and ecological zone is linked by the spine of the Rocky Mountains, arid conditions, and the presence of grasslands and plains. Of course, the species of grasses in each state vary—not just between state lines but within state borders. Thus, eastern Arizona has as much in common with western New Mexico as it does with western Arizona. Similarly, southeastern Colorado is situated on the Great Plains and so shares the traits of shortgrass country with eastern Wyoming, Montana, and New Mexico and has very little in common with the high country of west-central Colorado. In short, ranchers in each of these five states lived in bioregions that pay little attention to the arbitrarily drawn political demarcations of state borders. While any given rancher may have had much in common ecologically with others in her or his state of residence, that rancher might also have had much in common with ranchers in a neighboring state, at least ecologically. This transcendence of boundaries by grassland ecologies helped ranchers transcend political borders and come together regionally in interesting ways.

Ranchers in this period also experienced similarly the radical socioeconomic changes the mountain West experienced more broadly. Association archives from across the region make it clear that ranchers understood those changes to be threats to their power. If we understand that all people have power that they guard jealously, we can begin to think about the ways in which resistance to these socioeconomic changes became a vital aspect of the political mobilization of the ranching industry after World War II. We might be surprised to consider a well-connected, politically powerful, and historically privileged group of people such as range cattle ranchers as "resisting." But a narrative of resistance did culminate in the postwar West as ranchers shared stories of victimization and fear that were grounded in evidence they believed proved they were under attack from those wishing to steal their way of life (whether that was public lands managers, encroaching urban residents, or radical environmentalists). What we see in these years between the Taylor Grazing Act and the Wilderness Act is an agricultural group working diligently to maintain their access to political power so they could maintain their ecological and cultural dominance in the region. Their quest was to hold on to what they believed was their historic and righteous ascendency over the land, their cows, and particular sets of Others (which included other humans but also other organisms as well). The resistance ranchers practiced in these years not only appeared in their manipulation of the larger structures of economics and public lands policy but also in the relentless workings of the everyday. This is a book about the latter.

In addition to demonstrating some of the cultural strategies ranchers used to unite in political solidarity, this work also asks us to think about the power of the ranches' nonhuman world to create the settings in which ranchers found themselves. Jane Bennett, a professor of political theory at Johns Hopkins University, urges us to consider how matter (nonhuman organic and nonorganic entities) assembles in specific moments and places to exert power over human activities. The most recent example of this is the outbreak of COVID-19 in the spring of 2020 and the changes it wrought to everyday life across the world. But the phenomenon of vibrant matter dictating the cultural and political beliefs and activities of groups of people applies also and perfectly to the range spaces of the mid-twentieth-century West.

Ranchers kept bumping into matter that forced their hands in particular ways. Their ceaseless quest to control their lives and livelihoods required continuous and conflictual relationships with bacteria, coyotes, grasshoppers, and renegade plant life. Grass once planted innocently enough grew invasive. Predators that once seemed everywhere became overhunted, leaving only herbivorous mammals to compete with cattle for grass. A critical component of this book centers on the conversations ranchers had among themselves about those organisms and about how those organisms forced ranchers to adopt certain cultural practices and procedures. While the human context of the post–World War II American West was growing more complicated, so too were the natural and technological contexts of range spaces becoming ever trickier. Ranchers' shifting relationships with science and technology (topics often presented to them by the ever-more-powerful federal government land managers positioned as experts) forced them to interface with knowledge and practices that were both promising and terrifying. While the tools the experts advocated were sometimes helpful, they often were not as the nonhuman organisms evolved in unpredictable ways.

Creating knowledge about those tools required ranchers to engage in conversation with one another—across ranges, regions, and identities. Whether it was the high country of Colorado or the dry desert grasslands of Arizona, ranchers worried not just about a swiftly changing human landscape of federal government control and New West residents but also about an uncontrolled (and perhaps uncontrollable) range environment. The ecological dilemmas brought on by vibrant matter allowed ranchers to cultivate an ecoculture of both defensiveness and pride. They did so by transforming their everyday experiences and work with their cows and the nonhuman world of their ranches into resistance narratives that promoted unity and strength that they increasingly came to believe was vital to their survival in a changing modern West.

Before going much further, it is important to provide a bit more ranching background. For many, the most romantic moment in cattle ranching came in the mid to late nineteenth century—the era of the cattle kingdoms and the so-called heroic cattle kings. This era of cattle ranching has traditionally captured the collective imagination surrounding the American West. The notion of "cowboys and Indians" eking out a living in a harsh land and pursuing the American dream of life, liberty, and property has captured much of the popular imagination about the West over the long twentieth century.[18] This heroic, progressive, and triumphalist narrative of the open range is, of course, painfully inaccurate and incomplete, but it is an enormously important foundation upon which the Anglicized myth of the American West rests. Until the mid-twentieth century historians promoted this myth of the late nineteenth century. The broader preoccupation with Frederick Jackson Turner's interpretation of the frontier in Western U.S. history compelled historians to focus their early studies of cows and their caretakers on the nineteenth-century cattle boom. The cattle kings were an integral part of the frontier age, and whether historians wished to celebrate or critique the era, many asserted that the cattle industry of the late nineteenth century was one of the most vital industries in the cultural, political, and economic emergence of the West.[19]

Ironically, despite the amount of scholarly and imaginative attention the years of the open range have received, the era was quite fleeting and only encompassed a few decades. The brevity of the phenomena of open-range ranching might well have been what has made it so interesting to so many. Ranching as we know it in the early twenty-first century, however, is nothing at all akin to the nineteenth-century industry. After the difficult winter of 1886–87 on the Great Plains, during which most ranchers lost upwards of 90 percent of their herds, cattle growers across the mountain West realized that an era had come to an end.[20] Beginning with the conservation of forested areas in the 1890s and gaining speed throughout the early twentieth century, fences began to dot the once open rangelands. By 1934 and the passage of the Taylor Grazing Act (which effectively closed the public domain in the West to sale), ranching had become fixed. The endless motion of vast herds across unfenced spaces from Texas to Montana had ceased. Certainly, cattle still moved from here to there—to market in trucks and railcars, and on hoof to and from winter pastures—but the days of a cattle baron grazing his (and they were almost all male) cattle on millions of acres of unclaimed lands were over forever.

Still, ranching persisted. Wallace Stegner once wrote that "ranching is one of the few western occupations that has been renewable and has produced a continuing way of life," but there are comparatively few studies of ranching following the passage of the Taylor Grazing Act and after World War II.[21] There are several searing critiques of range ranching in the late twentieth century, and these books do contain a chapter or two on the long-twentieth-century history of range cattle ranching, but none addresses the industry in a solely historical context focused on ranchers' own understandings of themselves.[22] By examining twenty years of this context from the ranchers' point of view, I hope to lend to the debate about ranchers' power and place in the twentieth- and twenty-first-century West.

Chapter 1 explores how the rise of the military-industrial-government complex brought an influx of social, cultural, and economic change to the West. New residents brought new demands on the open spaces of the region and threatened ranchers' place in the territory. Some form of these demands can be said to have culminated in the passage of the Wilderness Act in 1964. For this study, then, the year 1965 (the year the Wilderness Act took effect) represents a good ending point, since, for land use and environmental values in the West, it was a watershed moment.

During this era the mountain West ranching industry was still based in a ranch-work culture that focused on, well, range ranching. Feedlots became more common, but they did not come to dominate the region in the immediate postwar years (as they did in California and even Texas to some degree) so that cow-calf and steer operations still reigned supreme.[23]

Weather (including temperature and precipitation), grass species, topography, wildlife, and soil types all varied immensely from one ranch to another, but ranchers still engaged in common labor—the growing of cows for sale or breeding.[24] In short, all ranchers in these five states had one uppermost goal—to grow fat, healthy cattle in disparate and diverse ecological niches; thus they were able to ground both their culture and their politics in this environmentally based labor. Ranchers' labor with cows (what I call "cow work") and the social relationships that that labor maintained are central organizing concepts throughout the book because ranchers themselves used their labor with cows as a unifying trope in their cow talk. We will examine this cow work and the social relationships that existed because of it in chapter 2.[25]

Cow work did not simply orbit around domesticated ungulates but also relied on nonhuman matter, including rain, grass, soil, microbes, and wildlife. This vibrant matter made ranch work specifically what it was. Thus, in addition to discussing cows and privileging ranchers' labor with bovines in order to come together collectively, ranchers also utilized the wider environment of their ranches to talk shop. Importantly, all ranchers had ecological challenges to overcome and ecological knowledge to share. These stories are simultaneously about control and helplessness, triumph and hardship. Chapters 3 and 4 explore ranchers' ecological labor and its manifestation in cow talk.

It will come as no surprise that one of the topics that dominated ranchers' cow talk was the power they sought in economic solvency. The archives are full of examples of strategies used by members of the range industry in their efforts to maintain access to both economic and environmental power as they articulated their group identity. Specifically, the role of the market occupied important ideological space in rancher discussions and imaginings. Chapter 5 examines the market and consumerism as they combined with cow work to promote ranchers' identities and staying power.

In chapters 6 and 7 I investigate more closely the variety of paths ranchers took to perfect their cultural confidence and belief in themselves. I will not uncouple political power from cultural identity, as they inform one another. In this case, the former gathered strength from stories about the latter. Importantly, power existed not just in ranchers' formal political activism and official positions on politicized topics such as grazing fees and tariffs but also in the cultural texts that they created for one another about their work and their social and ecological worlds.[26] Chapter 6 specifically looks at the role collective memories had in supporting ranchers' claims to entitlement and power in the mid-twentieth century, while chapter 7 investigates the hard work of organizing undertaken by ranchers and association staff to provide ranchers formal opportunities to solidify their affinity for one another and their lifeways.

To noncattle folk of the twenty-first-century West, the image of ranchers as a cohesive group fighting angrily for their rights smacks of the familiar. Many westerners and even some western-oriented easterners are well aware of ranchers' zeal for protecting what they refer to as their "way of life." Since the 1970s folks in the arid West have been reading about (and, in some cases, talking with) ranchers who are taking a stand—against developers, against the federal government, against undocumented immigrants.[27] In some circles these stances are viewed sympathetically and serve to shore up what journalist Brian Calvert calls the "political power of the cowboy."[28] And when leaders approve of these strident positions, as former president Donald Trump did when he pardoned some Oregon ranchers for setting fire to public land, the political power of the cowboy grows. That power has very real implications for the lands and resources of the West, and this book shows the ways in which that power was shored up between 1945–65 when range ranchers came together to learn from one another and share their hopes and fears.

After long days of battling human and nonhuman threats, engaging in cow work, and curating ecologies that most benefited them, ranchers engaged in cow talk. Cow talk allowed them to discuss the best new machinery and whether they could afford it. It allowed them to share stories of droughts, blizzards, and bugs. But they did not just talk. They also anted up the annual dues for their associations (about 50 percent joined their state associations; many more joined their local associations). They redesigned their official publications to make them more modern and iconographic. They increasingly attended their collective meetings (state conventions, local association meetings, etc.) to learn about technologies and scientific ideas that might make their work easier and the environment safer, at least for their cows. They joined together every week, and every day, at auctions, government hearings, and picnics to listen to one another and discuss the state of their economic and environmental lives. And as they did this, they created the discourse of cow talk in their private and public texts, a creation that had larger patterns and noteworthy concurrences.[29] This book focuses on those patterns that would, by the 1970s, turn into a singular bond that was culturally unmistakable and politically volatile.

CHAPTER 1

Hunters and Highways

The Postwar Context of Ranchers' Lives, 1935–1965

It seems like progress always seems to destroy something in its wake.
—Abbie Keith, Arizona Cattle Growers Association, 1956

People never want anything so badly as when they think it is about to disappear.
—Farrington Carpenter, 1935

The image shown in figure 2 was tucked away discreetly in the back of one of two hundred or so boxes in the papers of the WSGA housed in the American Heritage Center at the University of Wyoming in Laramie. The illustration is undated and unsigned. It had not appeared in *Cow Country*, the WSGA's monthly periodical. With the way it lay seemingly unclaimed in the box, it appeared to be an image for which the WSGA record keepers cared little. Perhaps its haphazard placement in the historical record was related to its slightly sad air. It does not celebrate a youthful rancher looking ahead to a limitless future, and it does not depict an old but proud cattle baron of the nineteenth century. Rather, the rancher seems aged, somewhat weak, uncertain, and befuddled by the sparkling new hat he holds. The rancher's face expresses dismay at the shape and texture of the headgear, and his gaze seems tinged with bewildered fear.

The tough, masculine air so prevalent in conceptualizations of the "cowboy" stands in stark contrast to the rancher in the drawing. Instead of exuding an aura of confidence and strength, the wide-eyed rancher seems perplexed or even angry at the appearance of the new hat, and while many

Figure 2. Drawing of an old rancher holding a new hat. Artist unknown. WSGA
Papers, Box 192, no folder, American Heritage Center, UW.

cultures, including perhaps the dominant culture of the United States,
celebrated modernity and progress, ranchers in the mid-twentieth century
confronted modernization as the depicted rancher seems to—with profound uncertainty.[1]

Modernization, which accelerated during World War II and continued
throughout the Cold War years (and beyond), affected ranchers unevenly.
Even the term "modernization" could have multiple meanings depending
on a rancher's individual circumstance. To one rancher becoming modern
may have meant having to decide whether to add another tractor to his
fleet of fifty. For another, it may have meant buying the first fossil-fueled
vehicle the family had ever owned. For some ranchers modernizing meant
deciding to purchase an electric washing machine, while for others it meant
purchasing an airplane. Modernization may have meant interacting with
the federal government's grazing regulation agencies or deciding to sell
the ranch to capitalize on the high property values of the postwar West.
While the experiences of modernization varied tremendously for ranchers

across the mountain West, for *all* ranchers the process and possibility of modernization were evident in the everyday experiences of ranching.

The specter of modernity revealed itself through cow talk. Despite distance between operations, variations in ranch size, or diversity in breeds of cattle, the ranch community used modernization as an opportunity to converse about the possibilities and paradoxes inherent in the context I will set forth in this chapter and the next. New technology, mass produced, awaited ranchers at the feed store and in rural catalogs. Property values increased at a consistent rate, often because outsiders descended on range spaces in search of summer homes, rural retreats, and weekend recreation. Federal and state land managers found themselves in increasing regulatory control of public space in the West. These trends did not originate in the postwar years, but their sheer depth and breadth was new. The Taylor Grazing Act of 1934 bolstered the increasing regulation of federal grazing land that began in the late 1800s with the creation of forest reserves. Peoples of all races and classes had been flooding the arid West for centuries, but in the postwar years the population of the region increased exponentially. Every rancher in the mountain West encountered some aspect of modernity during the years included in this study, and that modernity sets the parameters of this work. Many historians have considered the vast changes wrought in the West as a result of the World War II, and it is not my purpose in this chapter to reconstruct the ways in which the Old West became the New West.[2] Instead, in order to lay a basis for what follows in this book, I use this chapter to highlight the broader postwar context of ranchers' lived experiences as they grappled with that context. Regardless of whether ranchers welcomed it, modernity arrived in the New West in what seemed to many old-timers to be the blink of an eye, and it demanded intellectual, emotional, material, and political responses that ranchers achieved by creating and sharing cow talk.

The term "modernization" connotes a process that includes multiple and interrelated phenomena that are historically specific. I deploy the term to outline several ways that ranchers experienced changes in their lifeways due to the material and cultural context of the post–Taylor Grazing Act and the postwar world. Definitions of modernization abound, but for ranchers from 1945–65, I have found that modernization encompassed two main elements. First, there occurred a new degree of close interaction between "outsiders" in the New West and range ranchers. Increased state regulation of range spaces, new consolidation of space via the building of roads, and the increasing presence of tourists in the form of recreationists and hunters all brought newcomers nearer to ranches and added pressures to everyday life for ranchers. Second, unprecedented mechanizing and technologizing occurred on range ranches due to the widespread industrialization of agriculture. The process of modernization for ranchers, then, included changes in the social makeup of western spaces as outsiders descended as well as changes in the ways ranches operated.[3] In this chapter I focus on the first aspect of modernization—the changes in the social makeup of range country and how those changes reordered ranchers' lived experiences and ultimately affected their collective ideologies. I turn to the operational changes in chapters 2, 3, and 4.

The changing West brought an influx of outsiders into ranchers' worlds that forced them to begin to think about their communities in increasingly defensive ways. In dealing with these outsiders, ranchers created a vernacular of trade-specific localism that was an essential component of cow talk. This vernacular was grounded in their sense of rural identity as cow folk and was place-based, allowing ranchers to claim local knowledge that positioned them in conflict with an increasing population of newly arriving extralocal Others. In a way, ranchers began to view themselves as a political faction in opposition to those who could not possibly understand ranching or the ecologies of the arid, mountain West. Confronting political, environmental, and social change enabled ranchers to believe they were experiencing common troubles and that they could overcome these troubles, at least partially, through camaraderie with one another.[4]

The modernization ranchers experienced in the late 1940s, '50s, and '60s was presaged by events in the mid to late 1930s and early 1940s. In particular, the year 1934 changed ranching in the West permanently when the federal government passed the Taylor Grazing Act, thereby profoundly increasing the regulatory control of the state over range resources. The previous year had witnessed severe droughts, and the 300 million grazing acres in the western United States were in terrible condition. The 1933 droughts had hit the southern Great Plains the hardest, but ranchers all over the mountain West experienced the pain of low moisture and low prices. The drought of 1934, however, according to ranchers like J. D. Craighead in southeastern Colorado, "was a heartbreaker."[5]

By 1934 the federal government, under the leadership of New Dealer Franklin Delano Roosevelt, knew that something needed to be done to assist rural Americans economically. To get agriculturalists back on their feet, New Deal scientists, buoyed by the new science of grassland ecology, believed the land needed a chance to recover. The ideal of recovery motivated government ecologists, western cattlemen, and federal congressional representatives to urge the passing of regulatory legislation to monitor grazing on the public domain; in response Congress and Roosevelt passed the Taylor Grazing Act.[6]

In its early years the Taylor Grazing Act was popular within many sectors of the livestock community.[7] Part of the popularity of the act in the West may have rested in the fact that it was organically grown by a western rangeman from Colorado. Representative Edward Taylor recognized that the soil in most range areas was badly depleted and needed time to rejuvenate. The act, however, like most New Deal environmental legislation, was much more concerned with the health of human beings than with the nonhuman world. In typical anthropocentric prose, Taylor wrote the act to "stabilize the livestock industry dependent on the public range."[8] According to the act, the secretary of the interior had legal discretion to create grazing districts and charge graziers a small fee for use of the public domain. Additionally, the act provided for the creation of local grazing boards and the U.S. Grazing Service. After Congressional amendments, the Taylor Grazing Act brought 146 of the 165 million acres of open grazing lands in the West under the control of the Grazing Service (which became the Bureau of Land Management [BLM] in 1949). Without necessarily ending grazing activities on those acres, the act "represented a radical solution to the grazing issue by injecting federal management into the administration of lands that previously had been virtually ignored."[9] Many ranchers welcomed the management as long as it remained locally controlled and was conservationist (versus preservationist) in nature.[10]

Taylor's grazing act did reignite controversy among many ranchers as it brought renewed attention to long-held notions that the federal government was the ultimate outsider in range country. That ideology had been woven into ranch culture since conflicts began in the late nineteenth century around public domain and the U.S. government's sovereignty. The antigovernment sentiment experienced a lull in the 1930s, when ranchers needed help, only to resurface fervently in the 1940s. The conflicts continue to this day and are the focus of much of the history written on the western range industry. Indeed, historians such as Karen Merrill, William Graf, William Rowley, and Nathan Sayre have discussed at great length the causes, conflicts, and outcomes of federal control and the incursion of scientific management of grazing spaces.[11] For our purposes, however, it is not necessary to recount all aspects of those issues. Suffice it to say that while the creation of the Grazing Service in 1934 was the culmination of four decades of policy debates, it was also a beginning, as it brought the federal government into the world of range cattle ranching in new and intensive ways, thus creating one of the most salient aspects of modernization for ranchers.

In the five states under consideration here, about one in four ranchers had grazing permits either on Forest Service or Grazing Service lands, so seemingly this aspect of modernization did not affect every rancher. That would be true if by "modernization" I meant only direct, daily interactions with government regulators over specific permits. But even those ranchers who did not have permits often owned property near Grazing Service or Forest Service lands and thus potentially faced interaction with government officials. Furthermore, at any point, a rancher could purchase land (and thus any permits that went with it), so it behooved ranchers to be aware of grazing regulations. ·

By the late 1930s ranchers' association periodicals were attempting to keep ranchers apprised of legislative changes in grazing regulations. That constant and fluctuating regulations and ever-changing rules preoccupied ranchers is evidenced not only by the amount of copy devoted to understanding the regulations but also through cultural cow talk such as the poem printed beneath a reiteration of the changes in the range code in an issue of the *Montana Stockgrower* in 1938. In the poem, Ralph Miracle, a rancher and eventual executive secretary of the MSGA, explicated the problems of dealing with so much regulatory complexity:

Looks like the folks back in Washington
Are swingin' an awful lot of rope.
A good hand
Can shake out quite a loop
And hang it where he wants.
But there's a limit.
Too much rope
Can tangle up your own hoss.
And that's the way it looks back there.
It's damn risky
To stretch out a long twine
Tied to the horn
When you ain't an expert.
A short rope
With a dally
Might be lots safer
And then
If you miss, you can gather it up
And have another try.

Miracle used cow talk to draw an analogy between roping (a time-honored cowboy skill) and regulation. Too much regulation (just as in the case of too much rope) could trip up a person's "hoss" (horse). Note the reference to folks in Washington not being experts and thus being incapable of understanding what too many regulations might mean for an expert herdsman. Miracle's poem suggests that many ranchers believed the government moved too quickly with their regulations and had not left "a dally," or a way out of their policies. The poem appeared at the end of a reprint of a letter from Farrington Carpenter, the director of the Grazing Service, and illustrates well how the modern incursion of the federal government into range regulations affected and promoted a particular kind of cow talk among ranchers.[12]

Ranchers' worries about the heightened consolidation of power in range agencies prompted congressional representatives such as Frank Barrett (R-Wyo.) and Patrick McCarren (R-Nev.) to lead early fights against the Grazing and Forest Services. These representatives, responding to the outcry from the livestock interests, conducted public hearings throughout the mountain West from 1942–49 trying to force lenient, locally controlled range policies. In 1946–47 ranchers even suggested that federal range lands should be sold to their respective states with possible private dispersal to follow.[13] These attempts were never legislatively successful, but they were powerful cultural and political symbols. Ranchers capitalized on tensions with outside government regulators to create opportunities for cow talk. And while national news outlets covered the stories in ways that made ranchers appear to be reactionary and self-serving, ranchers represented themselves as conscientious experts who were being oppressed by clueless meddlers.[14]

The relative newness and increase of federal rangeland regulators represented one kind of extralocal presence in range country after World War II, but other forces encroached on range spaces and represented threats that were equally (if not more) impactful to ranchers' way of life. By the end of the war the federal government and private enterprise had joined forces to create the military-industrial-scientific complex for which the West became famous in the postwar decades. Thus, land agencies were not the only federal presences that increased in the postwar years.

The U.S. military was one such entity that increased its presence in the region throughout the 1940s and '50s. In these years western states joined eastern states in spearheading military development. California was the leader in this realm, but the mountain West states also underwent intense militarization. New Mexico, for example, experienced an influx of funding (almost $1 billion) from the War Department (in 1947 renamed the Department of Defense), which contributed to the rise and continuation of research and development institutions such as those at Los Alamos and the University of New Mexico.

In New Mexico ranchers came into direct conflict with the U.S. military as it demanded access to range spaces for testing new atomic technology. Beginning in 1945, for example, hundreds of acres were "condemned" by the War Department to create the White Sands Proving Ground. Ranchers across the four-thousand-square-mile Tularosa Basin, where the government eventually located the missile testing site, felt the effects of this militarization directly. Some, like Robert Boyd, felt the effects more acutely than others.[15] In an emotional appeal to his senators and to the secretary of war, Boyd explained that he hoped it was not "presumptuous" to appeal

to the political powers regarding the loss of his home to the White Sands
Proving Ground. The government had, according to Boyd, seized title
to the most important part of his ranch, namely his ranch headquarters
(meaning the family's home) and the ranch's only permanent source of
water. Boyd explained, "The land that I am losing is my old home where I
grew up, and is where I have anticipated spending the declining years of
my life." He tried his best to understand the government's need to acquire
his property, but he just could not make sense of its need to own eight
hundred acres on the west side of the Organ Mountains.

Although he tried desperately to assure the federal powers-that-be that
he could be "reconciled" to the loss of his land if it meant the "protection" of
the country, losing his home and his water left Boyd feeling vulnerable and
attacked. To defend his power, which he located at least partially in his local
autonomy, he enlisted the support of the NMCGA, telling them in a letter
that he "knew from past experiences" that the group would assist him. Even
the NMCGA was relatively powerless in the White Sands issue, however,
and nothing in the record tells us whether Boyd successfully maintained
ownership of his property. The outcome is not as important for this story as
the conflict itself because the incident provides insight into the modernization of ranchers' worlds in the postwar years.[16] In his dealings with the War
Department, Boyd, like so many other New Mexico ranchers, encountered a
powerful force with which, only a few years earlier, he had had little contact.
The militarization of south-central New Mexico transferred control of the
range spaces from local residents to an extralocal power, and ranchers felt
keenly this transformation and sought to maintain not just their property
rights but also their sense of autonomy.[17] In the minds of many ranchers, the
intrusion of the military into range spaces, like the incursion of the Forest
Service in the early 1900s and the Grazing Service in the 1930s, brought yet
another federal presence against which ranchers had to defend themselves.
They wrote letters to their friends and their communities to find solace and
support. This manifestation of cow talk often resulted in sympathy alone,
as the U.S. military was far too powerful for ranchers to oust from range
spaces. Their shared experiences are what interest us. With each story of
victimization, ranchers' sense of potential catastrophe grew.

The building of White Sands, like the construction of any military unit
(twenty-two were established during World War II and the Cold War in

the five states studied here), did more than bring the federal government's domineering presence to the West. The bases, and the concomitant growth that occurred in the West due to the rise of the military-industrial complex, brought vast numbers of people as well.[18] Seven million people passed through the West at various times during the war, and, upon its end, many of these people became permanent residents. Most of the newcomers settled in western cities, and the majority did not work in the agricultural sector. Even though the relative productivity of agricultural sectors (like ranching) increased, the numbers of people working in agriculture, as well as the amount of land under agricultural production, declined rapidly. For example, in 1950 Wyoming and Arizona had several counties where at least 20 percent of wages and residents' income came from farming. By 1970 no counties in either state had more than 20 percent agricultural production.[19]

As agricultural space in the West declined, the demand for land ensured that property values increased across the region.[20] This elevation in property values did not affect the region monolithically. Populations in warm-winter states like Arizona and New Mexico grew more exponentially than the cold-winter states like Wyoming and Montana.[21] In Colorado property values for pasture rose from $11.86 per acre in 1945 to $33.70 per acre in 1965. Colorado experienced the highest jump in land values of the states under consideration here, while Wyoming experienced the lowest. Still, Montana, New Mexico, Arizona, and Wyoming each experienced at least a 35 percent increase in pastureland values during the postwar years.[22] Land that had irrigation rose more steeply in value than land that had no water improvements. And land located next to federal grazing lands or that came with grazing permits also increased more in value than land that did not have public grazing access.[23] In addition, rural areas located around urban centers (like the Salt River Valley surrounding Phoenix) tended to experience inflated property values more quickly than more remote areas, but the influx of newcomers created a ripple effect in which land became an increasingly scarce and sought-after commodity. Ranchers could benefit from this new land regime, but only if they sold the ranch. If ranchers wanted to remain ranchers, the exorbitant land prices could spell trouble. For example, smaller ranchers found it increasingly difficult to add to their land holdings, and for many small- to midsized ranchers, this reality of the

postwar real estate market in the West spelled death to the dream of climb-
ing the agricultural ladder.

Take, for instance, J. D. Craighead's experience in southeastern Colorado
in the early 1950s. In 1950 Craighead received a letter from the owner of
320 acres Craighead had leased for many years. J. F. Gauger, the owner of
the land, had received an offer from some businessmen who wanted to buy
the pastureland to speculate for oil. Gauger offered Craighead, his longtime
friend and business relation, the first chance to buy the land at the same
price the businessmen had offered, $11 an acre. Despite good cattle prices in
the late 1940s and early 1950s, Craighead, like most ranchers, did not have
access to that kind of disposable cash, but he also knew that he could not
afford to lose the 320 acres of pastureland since the grass was thin on all
pastures due to a painful drought that was gripping the region. After much
haggling about the value of the ground and after securing a loan from the
Production Credit Association of La Junta, Craighead purchased the acreage
from Gauger for $10 an acre. In a tart letter Craighead explained to Gauger
that "the people from whom I am accustomed to borrow think the price you
offered to take for this land is much too high. I think so too, but I need the
grass." Lest Gauger not believe Craighead about the local drought situation,
Craighead explained: "The papers have been minimizing the effects [of the
drought around here], but parts of a number of days have been so you could
not see very far and could not work outside [because of dust storms]. An
unusual thing is the lack of water in even the older canals. The result is we
have not been able to plant much crop nor irrigate what we have planted.
Some cattle have been moved out and a lot have been sold."[24] Craighead's
desperation about the scarcity of available land with good grass is palpable
in this anecdote. On the one hand, he knew that he needed the 320 acres of
grazing to keep his cattle alive. On the other hand, he knew full well that he
could not afford to purchase the land with his available capital. Craighead's
position as the president of the La Junta Production Credit Association
meant he had better accessibility to lines of credit than many ranchers, but
like Craighead, ranchers across the mountain West recognized a decline in
the use of land for grazing. Census statistics bear this out. Whereas in 1880
there had been 883 million acres of land used for grazing, by 1930 that number had dwindled to 437 million, and by 1954 only about 353 million acres
were being used by graziers.[25] Grazing land, for ranchers, *is* power, and as

land accessibility declined, so too did ranchers' power and their perceptions of that power.

An increase in urban spaces in much of the West compounded the increase in land value and the decrease in agricultural land. From 1945 to the end of the twentieth century, metropolitan areas in the West grew phenomenally in area as well as in population. Between 1950 and 1990, for example, Phoenix added 402 square miles to its municipal boundaries. In 1940 the five states under consideration here had three metropolitan areas (defined by the Census Bureau as a "core city of at least fifty thousand inhabitants plus its contiguous suburbs"). Denver and Pueblo, in Colorado, and Phoenix, Arizona, were the only cities that could be quantified as metropolises before the beginning of World War II. By 1990 each of the five states could claim at least one metropolitan area.[26] In addition to the sprawling metropolitan spaces, urban populations of the West increased from 11.8 million in 1940 to 63 million by 1990. This process of urbanization was, of course, gradual, but its noticeable acceleration in the immediate postwar years accentuated the sense of loss felt by the declining rural population. Phoenix residents, for example, grew from sixty thousand to five hundred thousand in the two decades following the war. Denver and Albuquerque both doubled in population.[27] Nathan Sayre has posited that "what unified rangelands is thus not so much a biophysical or natural characteristic as a social one. Just as they are residual in classification . . . rangelands are peripheral to other, more lucrative types of land and the people who inhabit and use rangelands are often . . . socially marginalized as well."[28] Certainly ranchers felt increasingly marginalized as the demographic and land-use patterns in the postwar West shifted toward more modern uses.

City folks living *in* the city were one thing. But when those folks ventured forth into the range spaces of the West, ranchers really became concerned. One of the most direct ways ranchers experienced the flood of newcomers was through increased tourism and recreation. The presence of these "dudes" (as ranchers disdainfully referred to any nonrancher) was a continual source of conflict and cause for cow talk in postwar mountain West range country.[29]

The proliferation of road building during World War II and the postwar years increasingly led ranchers and tourists to come face-to-face. The Interstate Highway Act of 1956 poured millions of dollars into a federal road system whose purpose was to link forty-two state capitals that encompassed 90 percent of the nation's population. The act provided extra funds to build roads on federal property, including that occupied by Native nations, national parks, and Forest Service lands (the bulk of which were in the West)—ostensibly allowing people a safe escape in case of a national catastrophe (including nuclear attack). The new federal emphasis on automobile infrastructures changed the face of transportation in the West in ways not felt since the completion of the transcontinental railroads in the 1860s and 1880s.[30]

Ranchers experienced this aspect of modernization in mixed ways. Of course, new, more passable roads meant that ranchers could transcend the boundaries of isolation both economically and socially. The new roads—built by the Forest Service, the BLM, and the various state highway departments—took both ranchers and their beef to town. The road building came in fits and starts for ranchers, especially in states with few urban centers (such as Wyoming and Montana). In 1953, for example, the average distance Wyoming ranchers traveled to a trading center of any kind was fifteen miles, and they traveled over unpaved or barely improved roads. In the early 1950s, 52 percent of Wyoming ranchers traveled over ten miles to get their cattle to market and themselves to town.[31] In the Southwest ranches were a little better connected with the broader world, but in 1950 Arizona ranchwomen were still bemoaning the isolation that came with poor transportation routes. Rancher Evelyn Perkins, whose ranch sat in the Chino Valley in Arizona, told others at the Seventh Annual Country Life Conference that "a sign appeared on our road . . . apparently placed there by some wayfarer who didn't appreciate our boulder-and-dirt *highways*. It read: 'This road is not passable [by humans]; it isn't even jackass-able.' . . . We have more and better roads today, but still the family and workers on a cattle ranch are thrown close together . . . [and] even today on many of the . . . isolated cattle ranches mothers [have to] teach their children [at home]."[32]

Ranchers continued to experience isolation from mainstream society well into the 1960s, but they also increasingly became aware that paved and improved roads were bridging their separation from the outside world and that, in some ways, they could take advantage of these new linkages as the construction of highways could help them to communicate with one another. These new roads not only allowed ranchers to take beef to market but also transported them faster and more easily to feed stores, to sales and auctions, and, perhaps more importantly, to their association meetings, conventions, and social events. In fact, this aspect of modernization could account, at least partially, for the high numbers of ranchers who attended the state cattle grower conventions in the postwar decades—a topic I will examine in chapter 7. It is safe to say that transportation improvements encouraged and facilitated cow talk.

Despite some enthusiasm for and reliance on highway construction, this aspect of modernization was not without its problems, and for many ranchers road building was nothing but a nuisance. The archives are filled with evidence of conflicts ranchers encountered as highway crews descended on range spaces. Most of them were minor scuffles, but their relative significance did not diminish ranchers' belief in their magnitude. Take, for instance, the experience of J. E. Magnum in the early years of New Mexico state road building. In 1947 he wrote the NMCGA to complain about ranchers' situations regarding the incursion of state highway builders. Magnum explained that his situation was "the case of most of the New Mexico ranchers."

Magnum's family had arrived to start a ranch near Bloomfield, New Mexico, in 1904. There were no bridges or roads at that time, so they made do until 1916 when a makeshift bridge was built. In 1945 that changed. The highway department asked Magnum to cede right-of-way on a section of his land to enable the state to build a highway nine miles south of Bloomfield. Magnum obliged and then the trouble began. His unique style makes a rather lengthy direct quote worthwhile as it is a prime example of cow talk. Not only did Magnum write phonetically while using a ranch vernacular, he did so by reaching out to his community of ranchers as represented by the NMCGA. According to Magnum:

> First the contractor with one of the dump trucks run over a $500.00 reg. bull i had to kill him. [I assume he means the bull, not the contractor.] . . . [Then he] tore my telephone down put it intirely out of use and it is still out of use cut fences as they come to them that i had spent a lifetime putting up. . . . They are still down [I assume he means the fences] as i am not able to do hard work and cant hire a man for love or money. . . . Burnes me up [when] some people thinks

we should just step aside when see the outsiders comeing and give
them what we have got the hard way but they wouldn't go through
what we have for the world. . . . Then to finish up the road story now
we have a fine road from the san juan river to Albuquerque . . . a fast
road . . . so fast that acuple days ago some one run over my fine stal-
lion. worth $1000. . . . i had to kill him . . . now what we need is good
5 wire fence on each side of highway for at least 7 miles. . . . i would
like you to use your influance to have this done before we have alot
of recks the cattle is still on the summer range but i will bring them
down in november then they will be in great danger of being run over
as they will be crossing this road everyday i have wrote the Highways
Department but i have very little [confidence in them].[33]

Magnum's letter, in grand style and ranch jargon, suggests ranchers'
frustrations at dealing with an impersonal and encroaching state. Additionally, Magnum hints at many ranchers' sentiments that road building
could be quite welcome in ranch country: note the way he describes the
road as a "fine" road. The moment, however, that fine road threatened
his property (in this case his livestock), Magnum became irate. Note that
his solution was not to tear up the road but rather to have the state install
a fence to keep his cattle off their highway. Magnum accepted modernization and the coming of outsiders, but he expected to be compensated
for that acceptance, and he appealed to the larger community of cattle
growers (namely the NMCGA), through cow talk, to help him persist in his
ranching business despite structural changes occurring in the increasingly
modern western spaces.

In Arizona relations between the state highway department and ranchers were a little better, but not much. In March 1956 E. C. Aguirre, whose
ranch sidled up next to Highway 84 in northern Arizona, had a hundred
acres of pasture accidentally torched by an Arizona Highway Department
crew that was burning unwanted brush alongside the highway. Just as
Magnum had almost a decade earlier, Aguirre wrote to his stock growers'
association hoping it could do something to stem the problems appearing
from the tide of blacktop rising near his ranch. Aguirre wished the highway building would stop immediately so that he could stop worrying about
his cattle, but failing that, he hoped that something could be done to avoid

such flammable disasters in the future. In the correspondence about the incident, Aguirre represented himself as an innocent victim of an uncaring state that was acting on behalf of ignorant tourists. Abbie Keith, upon receiving the correspondence from Aguirre, wrote to the highway department and reminded the department that cattle ranchers across Arizona had cooperated with the association to have cards printed to circulate amongst tourists in rural towns urging them to be careful not to start wildland fires. As Keith reminded the state agency, highway department personnel had even helped distribute the cards to the would-be firebugs. Even so, fires continued to be ignited, and both Keith and Aguirre were growing tired of the constant diligence required of the ranchers by the newly passable roads. While Aguirre never received compensation for his one hundred acres, William Willey, the state highway engineer, admitted his department's culpability and promised that "extreme care will be used in all future burning of brush along the highway."[34] Still, the conflagration between ranchers, agents of the state, and newly arriving hordes of outsiders continued to blaze.

The shared mindset shown in the anecdotes about road construction is representative of ranchers who considered themselves to be under attack from a newly modernizing world order. These ranchers believed that their livelihoods, to which they were entitled, were being threatened by modernization—an impersonal process impervious to ranchers' "rights" to access soil, grass, and acreage. In ranchers' minds, the lands being used and changed by agents of modernity did not belong to the public but rather to the rancher who worked the land. Modernization undermined the control over western spaces that ranchers believed were rightfully theirs. Thus, an aspect of modernization that in some ways served to connect ranchers to towns, markets, and nonranchers also served to further unite ranchers socially as they took on a common enemy that threatened to render them powerless. In seeking to deal with the new forces that adversely affected them, the land, and their cows, ranchers sought help, restitution, and sometimes even retribution. To do so, they turned to one another using cow talk.

Although road building was mostly intended as a national security measure, its result was to increase access to western scenic spaces for Americans seeking respite from a Cold War world. The roads that brought problematic agents of the state into range spaces also served to bring dudes whose values often conflicted with those of the ranch community. As men in gray flannel suits sought to recover their masculinity and June Cleaver housewives craved an escape from Levittown-type suburbia, camping, fishing, and hiking—wholesome, largely middle-class outdoor adventures—enjoyed a renaissance.[35] As Hal Rothman and other historians have shown, this recreational impulse began, for the West, in the 1920s as automobiles became more available to more people and as industrial society increasingly inspired an escapist culture, and this recreational-based tourism only increased in the post–World War II era.[36] In the words of historian Richard White, by the postwar years "more and more metropolitan residents viewed the land not in terms of the resources it produced but rather in terms of the experiences it could provide."[37] Like encroaching floodwaters, urbanites and suburbanites seeped out of the metropolises for weekend trips and summer vacations, and these folks preoccupied ranchers as they sought to maintain their relative isolation from the outside world.

Perhaps the recreational group who most inspired ranchers' fury was sportsmen (i.e., recreational hunters and fishers—and they were mostly men). No one can know exactly how many men and women ventured onto ranchlands in the postwar decades and intentionally poached wild animals (and in the process inadvertently killed domestic cattle or "accidentally" cut ranchers' fences in their zeal to access recreational space), but based on the avalanche of paper in the archives dealing with these very topics, it is clear that the intrusion of recreational hunters on the private property of ranchers was an aspect of modernization that occupied a great deal of ideological space for ranchers and their cow talk.[38]

The tension between ranchers and recreationists—especially the "game interests"—is an interesting mid-twentieth-century continuance of conflicts over natural resources that had long been occurring in the West. As historians have illustrated, those conflicts became especially pronounced in the nineteenth century when Anglo colonists attempted to rob Indigenous peoples of their traditional hunting and fishing grounds.[39] Louis Warren and Karl Jacoby have shown that game management, hunting, and conservation became sites of contestation over access to natural resources and the power to define proper use of those resources. In New Mexico in the early twentieth century, ranchers had joined forces with conservationists to define game as private property. Despite protests from Indigenous peoples, impoverished locals, and some progressive bureaucrats like Aldo Leopold, federal and state governments set up wildlife refuges on private ranches across the state supposedly to conserve game. The result was a privatization of game in the European tradition that came from and exacerbated "complicated racial and ethnic politics."[40]

Similar to their relationships with highways, ranchers were of two minds when it came to hunters. On the one hand, ranchers worried that nonlocal (and especially out-of-state) hunters were a threat to game that ranchers claimed for themselves. On the other hand, ranchers welcomed those hunting game species that directly competed with their cattle for grass. But while ranchers were not wholly unified on the controversies of hunting, their discussions of it were important opportunities for cow talk. One of the narratives they repeated to one another most often in sharing cow talk about recreational hunters was their belief that ranchers played an essential role in propagating healthy game populations. In these versions of cow talk, ranchers told one another and the outside world that outside sportsmen threatened to upset that historic equilibrium.

Ranchers often took credit for the health and proliferation of game herds, arguing that the herds spent a majority of their lives on private land as they roamed in search of forage. In the mid-1950s one rancher wondered "how many people who buy hunting licenses know that the cow people furnish the water and salt for the elk, deer and antelope?" Another claimed that ranchers actually raised the game herds, who spent 100 percent of their time on private land. According to an incensed rancher writing in the *Montana Stockgrower*, ranchers who harbored game herds often lost up to $1,000 a year in grass, water, and salt for doing so.[41]

The question of how to manage those herds is where the debate arose. While herbivores such as a deer and antelope were sometimes seen as unwelcome competition for cattle, many ranchers feared nonlocal hunters more than the game itself. During the 1940s and 1950s, some ranchers turned to dude ranching to supplement their uncertain income (just as they had in the 1920s). Dude ranchers, whose main business was cattle ranching, relied on hunting to attract interested guests to their ranches. These ranchers often protested raising the fees for hunting licenses (especially for nonresidents) and found themselves constantly trying to convince

other cattle growers that tourists were essential to the financial success
of all ranchers in the mountain West. Paul Christensen, the president of
the Dude Ranchers' Association, was particularly vocal in the 1940s and
'50s about the need to "impress into" the minds of cattle ranchers that
"whether it's the automobile tourist or any other type," as long as "tourists
come to Montana they add a great deal to everyone's income."[42] Still, by
the 1950s cattle ranchers believed they were enveloped in an increasingly
uncontrollable hunting free-for-all, and they did not like it. They did not
seem to care how beneficial license fees were for the state or how useful the
influx of tourist money was for local towns, and they increasingly blamed
incoming tourists and recreational hunters for invading their private lands
in pursuit of public game.

Part of the ranchers' frustration with outside hunters stemmed from
the fact that ranchers themselves hunted regularly; thus, the regulatory
apparatus meant to control outside hunters also controlled ranchers. Many
ranchers relied on hunting to supplement their own families' diets; others
hunted predator species to protect their herds and often used the byprod-
ucts of such hunting (furs, for example) in various ways on the ranch. Perhaps more importantly, many ranchers used hunting to assert their control
over an often uncooperative, nonhuman natural world. And, just as in the
case of grazing numbers on public lands, they wanted to have local and
individual autonomy in deciding what was best for their area.

Ranchers claimed to like game and not to mind supporting reason-
able numbers of game species on their ranches. But if the availability of
resources pushed ranchers to privilege one species over another, they
would almost certainly choose their domesticated bovines. In 1951 a controversy erupted in Arizona that pitted a rancher against a rapacious elk.
Earl Van Deren, a Munds Park rancher, had found the elk in question rav-
enously devouring his grain field. The frustrated rancher took matters into
his own hands. Rather than waiting for the elk to get his fill, Van Deren
shot it (out of season and without a license). The state attorney general
prosecuted Van Deren and ordered that he pay a fine. The ACGA quickly
came to the defense of the Munds Park rancher, and John Babbitt, president of the ACGA, explained to the broader Arizona public in a letter
entitled "Cattle or Elk?" that "the true attitude of nearly all stockmen is
that they like game." The problem, Babbitt not so calmly explained, was

that ranchers had been very patient while watching elk herds take over the ranges. At long last, ranchers had decided to take matters into their own hands and defend their way of life. "What man, worthy of the name, will not fight for his living, for his family, for his home?" demanded Babbitt.[43]

His word choice in his letter, like so much of ranchers' language in the postwar decades, showed Babbitt believed Van Deren and ranchers like him were under attack—this time from native fauna. To protect themselves, ranchers would (and, Babbitt implies, should) defend themselves both physically and discursively. Importantly, this defense of their way of life depended on ranchers' ability to maintain control over the ecology of the ranch, whether the enemy was predator or prey. Rancher periodicals used cow talk to celebrate any successes in organized hunts for predators (such as rattlesnake hunts—especially in the Southwest—and mountain lion and coyote hunts). Ranchers wrote the association publications with heroic tales of defending their family (by which they often meant their cows) from any invading presence—both human and non. The stories of successful hunts allowed ranchers to believe in their own agency and ability to control a world spinning out of control.[44]

The same could be said for having to abide by tag limits that ranchers believed should apply only to nonlocal hunters. They expressed frustration when outside forces (land agencies, game departments, and the like) made the environmental context in which they lived even more complicated. Ranchers knew through experience that they could never completely control predators and game populations, but they also knew such control would be even harder to achieve if they also had to battle regulations they believed to be set arbitrarily by faraway bureaucrats. Extralocal officials (judicial and land management officials) seemed to ranchers, as we see in Babbitt's communication, to be offering them little or no help. If the state game boards were not going to increase licensure and extend hunting seasons, then ranchers would do what they had to do to win the contest for grass and maintain their way of life.

The tensions and negotiations over hunting inevitably centered around the notion of scarcity. In the postwar years it became apparent to many that there simply was not enough space to go around. Despite the call for "multiple use," a policy priority that was given legislative mandate in the Multiple Use and Sustained Yield Act of 1960, there were too many users with varying priorities for every group to get exactly what it wanted. As Louis Warren has noted, game is a tricky entity to define and own because it moves. The discussions between sportsmen and ranchers in the 1940s, 1950s, and 1960s, therefore, centered on when a deer was public property and under the jurisdiction of the state and the public, and when it became private property under the jurisdiction of private property owners.

Many hunters believed that when they had a license in hand, it invested them with the power to trail the object of the hunt wherever the hunt led. Unlike human beings, deer, elk, and antelope do not acknowledge the private or public categorization of land. In trying to escape a hunters' scope, an animal could very well move across boundaries. Hunters followed—often taking on predatory characteristics that kept them from respecting land demarcations in their quest for their prize. There were instances of fence cutting and moments when hunters, in their zeal, forgot to shut gates and let cattle escape. There were times when a wayward bullet killed a rancher's favorite or most valuable bull. Perhaps more important than the numbers of these occurrences, however, was ranchers' obsession with sharing tales of these occurrences with one another because such sharing reinforced a common sense of threat and harm.

Ranchers engaged in cow talk via letters to one another and in articles in the pages of their association publications to share ideas for addressing the problem of invading, dim-witted hunters. Placing large signs on ranches urging hunters to ask permission to hunt on the property was one strategy ranchers employed. Posting notices threatening legal prosecution of trespassers was another. One particularly clever example of cow talk was kept in the WSGA papers (figure 3).

The artist intended the image to depict humorously the level of intelligence of the average hunter, but it also communicated a common experience that ranchers were being subjected to by the influx of the recreational public.[45] H. A. Porter, an Apache Creek, New Mexico, rancher, answered a call in the *New Mexico Stockman* for stories about ranchers' experiences with state agents and hunters. He wrote two pages about Forest Service bureaucrats but saved his real vitriol for the "present day so called 'sportsmen.'" He suggested that hunters *could* help with the problem of herbivore competition if modern hunters were worth their salt. Instead, according to Porter, "the majority of them [hunters] come into the country . . . well

Figure 3. Cartoon of a hunter, a rancher, and a cow. Drawn by Melvin Miller, 1959. WSGA Papers, Box 192, American Heritage Center, UW.

heeled with liquor and ammunition, drive up and down the highways for three or four days hoping to kill their buck in some rancher's wheat field— if unsuccessful in this they drink their liquor and expend their ammunition on ranchers, turkeys, livestock, water tanks . . . and depart. A far cry from the type of hunter we used to know who came after his buck and got him."[46] Not all hunters were bad, according to ranchers' cow talk on the subject, just the new, modern hunters. These hunters incurred ranchers' disdain because ranchers believed they had no knowledge of the range, no etiquette, and no skill.

In the early 1950s, in another example of ranchers sharing cow talk, the WSGA issued a questionnaire to its members regarding the negative outcomes of the presence of game on ranches. The hope behind this survey, according to the WSGA, was that the numbers would help the association's fish and game committee to more easily convince the state's Fish and Game Commission that ranchers were being materially harmed by intruding and rude hunters. The questions are illustrative. Some questions are indicative of too much game on ranches (such as the one that asks how much tonnage of feed loss ranchers had experienced due to game). But the more usual questions (five out of seven) deal with property losses at the hands of "hunters or sportsmen." How many gates were left open by hunters, the questionnaire demanded. How many head of livestock were killed or damaged? How about human death and injuries? Other damages the questioners wanted to know about included "mail boxes, fences, insulators, windmills, etc."[47]

Unfortunately, the archive holds no results of the survey, but by the late 1950s, the problems ranchers believed they were having with hunters had not subsided, and the WSGA had, in coordination with the Izaak Walton League, the Wyoming Fish and Game Department, and the Farm Bureau, completed an educational movie intended to promote amicable hunter-landowner relations. The language used in the film was conciliatory and was meant to help outsiders and newcomers learn the ways of the ranching West. The film is told from the viewpoint of a rancher who describes his interactions with a bank teller "in town" who had come west "because he likes the out-of-doors." The rancher decides to take Joe, the teller, fishing on the ranch, and as they approach the land, they see a gate has been left open. The rancher/narrator explains to the viewer that "this is kind of thing that causes a lot of folks to put up a No Trespassing sign. Those cows of mine might have gotten into an alfalfa field and bloated. I can't afford to have my cows dying." The rancher/narrator proceeds to take credit for the health of fish and game in the state because he is conservationist in his land use. He then explains to poor, naive Joe that only the "carelessness" of some irresponsible hunter was cause for the poor relationship between ranchers and sportsmen. Only through communication among recreational hunters and ranchers, the film explains, could there be any hope of keeping the land of Wyoming "a wonderful place to live" and of sustaining the state's "beauty and the natural wealth." In the course of the postwar years, the guardians of the grasslands had become caretakers not just of the grass but of the grasslands' wild animal inhabitants as well (at least in their own imaginations).[48]

The relationship and tension between ranchers and hunters occurred in almost every season on the Bell Ranch in east-central New Mexico. George Ellis, the Bell's manager, worked tirelessly to share information and come up with solutions that would protect his ranch from outsiders seeking to harm native game. The Bell Ranch, because of its size, location, and well-known tradition, was a popular place for hunters in the postwar years.[49] The ranch had ample crops of quail, antelope, and other game animals.

Like many ranchers in these years, Ellis had to decide how many hunters he would allow access, and this meant interacting with game wardens as well as the hunters themselves.[50] The 1949 antelope season saw Bell welcoming twenty-five permitted hunters on its property. This number was arrived at through careful negotiation between Ellis and the state game commission. The landowner (Ralph Keeney) reserved five of the permits for personal friends (reminiscent of the early twentieth-century privatized game preserve mentality that Louis Warren found in his study).[51] The other permittees were all town folk. Three permittees hailed from Santa Fe, four from Albuquerque, five from Tucumcari, two from Springer, and the rest from other small towns. Ellis knew some of them, but certainly not all twenty.

It was not, however, the twenty permitted hunters who concerned Ellis and inspired him to inquire at the NMCGA office regarding the association's intent to publish notices to the public specifying off-limits ranchlands. The notices set clear boundaries across which nonpermitted hunters were not welcome. Any hunter who ignored the printed and posted notices would be prosecuted according to the law. The notices were to be posted at any gate Ellis sensed the interloping hunters might use and were to be published in several regional publications. Ellis believed that such notices were not just useful but essential, and he relied on the support of the larger body of ranchers to protect his range from unwanted outsiders. He also encouraged ranchers to talk with one another about their experiences so that they could better hone their strategies to keep unwanted tourists out of range country.

The existence of a concerted, collective effort on the part of the larger body of ranchers to keep trespassers off their lands suggests how owner-operator ranchers defined the modernization trends in the rural West as threats. Others were trespassing on their world in ways they had not done previously. Ranchers across the mountain West were quite aware of the changes occurring around them, and they increasingly built ideological and physical fences to keep those changes at bay. That defensiveness became a kind of reactive consciousness around which ranchers constructed their cow talk and their collective identity throughout the postwar decades.

Ranchers in these decades bought and sold land, cattle, feed, and water just as they had since the ranching enterprise began in the late nineteenth century. By the mid-twentieth century, however, operating a cattle ranch in the mountain West became more complicated than the simple transformation of grass to flesh. In these decades ranchers found themselves embroiled in a modern and modernizing historical context. They increasingly encountered outsiders interloping on range spaces. They had to consider the presence of the federal government in a way they had not had to do before 1935, the year the Taylor Grazing Act went into effect. They witnessed intense economic and geographic trends that brought highways, hunters, tourists, and new, more urban residents to their rural spaces.

Hunters and highways and government agencies all brought to range country and cattle ranchers some of the most widely concerning developments of modernity during these decades. Another aspect of modernity also occupied ranchers on nearly a daily basis: the arrival of technological modernity. New technologies and scientific tools arrived on the range at an almost dizzying speed in the immediate postwar years, and their presence required ranchers to consider changing their operations and their approach to ranch labor. The potential this new technology and mechanization held for shifting the means of production threatened the social world of work that had traditionally defined the collective identity of ranchers. Thus, adopting that modern technology was not a decision any one rancher took lightly. Ultimately, they had to make those decisions individually, but they did not do so before sharing information and learning from their fellow ranchers through robust community gatherings and endless hours of cow talk. I turn to this world of mechanizing cow work in chapter 2.

CHAPTER 2

"Be Shure to Fix the Fence"
The Social World of Mechanizing Cow Work

Cow Work means all of the work that must be done at a certain time of the year.

—George F. Ellis, New Mexico rancher, 1973

Yet the very vulnerability under certain circumstances of traditional forms of production points to the importance of processes through which those forms are reproduced.

—Harriet Friedmann, 1978

Chapter 1 shows how ranchers experienced modernity as a kind of unpredictable and uncontrollable occupation of range spaces by Others. The anxiety and stress that ranchers felt due to the presence of recreationists, government agencies, and urban residents arose largely because these entities carried with them the possibility of a disruption to the central purpose of ranch life, the work of growing cows. In this chapter, I examine a further aspect of modernity—mechanization—and the ways in which technology both threatened and reinforced the broad contours of traditional cow work. I investigate how the everyday lived experiences with cows dictated work rhythms for range ranchers: experiences that could be both helped and hindered by the adoption of new technologies. I also focus on labor relations among the various workers on ranches in these years and analyze the kinds of work that were celebrated in public cow talk as ranchers strove to reproduce not just their cows but also their identities as members of a timeless and masculinist work culture.

As George Ellis explains in the epigraph above, cow work was just that: work with cows that occurred during certain times of the year. Cow work encompassed different tasks and goals, but in its essence, it was simply the growing and reproducing of cattle. Cow work could include the quest to put meat on the bones of those animals destined for slaughter or sale, and it could include the goal of reproducing a better heifer or bull for future breeding. In either case, the components were the same. Cows needed to eat—preferably rich grasses. They needed to have ample water, and they needed to be protected from the diseases that consistently threatened both their lives and their ability to flourish. To supply those needs, ranchers had to engage in work they believed required great skill, experience, and dedication. As the postwar decades wore on, the definition of "skill" began to shift, creating uneasy tensions between owner-operators and hired hands as technology threatened to utterly redefine what it meant to be a rancher.

Take as an example the 1959 *Cow Country* image shown in figure 4, which suggests how modernizing could radically alter life on the range. In the image, cows sit around an antiquated chuckwagon, the kind that ranchers would have used since the days of the open range, enraptured with an image on a television screen. The image pokes fun at the frivolity of some of the mechanization that was occurring the 1950s and 1960s, but it also suggests that all aspects of the ranch, from the cows to the cowboys to the equipment, were affected by the new technological contexts in which ranchers lived. Note that the cows are captivated by the TV and are lying lazily in front of it. There are no cowhands anywhere nearby, yet the TV seems to have everything (namely the cows) perfectly under control. Traditionally, the wagon would have served ranchers and any waged workers their meals during roundups and branding sessions. The chuckwagon cook, like most male workers engaged in cow work, held idealized power in ranching culture. In this image the artist suggests that the cook and all the cowhands were being rendered invisible and unnecessary by the new technology. This would have been deeply upsetting in a culture where cow work, steeped in tradition and masculine endeavor, was venerated. Technology and its concomitant social ramifications seemed poised to upset every traditional relationship in the world of ranch work in the postwar decades. Even though by 1959 few ranchers owned chuckwagons (let alone

Figure 4. Drawing of a "modern" chuckwagon equipped with a TV. Artist unknown. WSGA Papers, Box 192, American Heritage Center, UW.

electrified chuckwagons), ranchers during these years were all experiencing radical shifts in their working world. In this image the cowboy does not even need to be present to perform his most important job—overseeing the cows. Like so much of the modernizing postwar world, mechanization and new technological options served as both threat and opportunity for ranchers.

To reproduce their cultural way of life, ranchers had to employ certain technologies to complete the all-important goal of growing healthy cattle. We often think of technology in the form of objects that we use to do certain tasks. Certainly, this kind of technology existed for ranchers in these years. They might use hand tools to rid the range of noxious plants. They might use tractors to dig ditches to deliver water to thirsty cows. They might use syringes to deliver medication or vaccines. They certainly used barbed wire and other fencing technologies to keep their cattle where they wanted them. But I encourage us also to think about

technology in a different way. The word comes from two Greek words—
"techne" and "logos." The former loosely means skill, or the method or
manner by which something is done. The latter means an expression or
word. Viewed this way, "technology" means the words or discourse describing how things are accomplished. This definition is important for this
study because throughout the archives, ranchers showed how their use of
technologies made up the essence of much cow work and their discourse
about those machines was one of the most important elements of cow talk.
In the mid-twentieth century the increasingly industrialized approach to
agriculture offered ranchers a chance to conceptualize of cow work in new
ways, but the potential for new methods of production was both inspiring
and wearisome. Through the sharing of cow talk, ranchers demonstrated
the ramifications that decisions about mechanization had on their culture
and their relationships with one another and their cows.

Historians have long documented how new agricultural technologies revo-
lutionized yields while simultaneously undermining the common farmers'
ability to compete.[1] By the postwar years, thanks to wartime innovations,
increasingly sophisticated technology and expanding modernization in the
form of breeding practices, synthetic and manufactured fertilizers, herbicides (such as 2,4-D) and pesticides (such as DDT), range management
innovations in water capture and sequestration, and various kinds of auto-
mation had become available for ranchers. This modernization created the
need for intense capital outlay, something many ranchers could not provide. The cycle was a vicious one. To remain competitive, ranchers needed
technology to increase their productivity. To get the physical technology,
they needed capital, a resource they often had to borrow. Just as they
implemented one form of mechanization, another option would present
itself, and the cycle would continue. Ranchers feared that the endurance
of their ranches was one tractor purchase away from being unattainable.

Technical modernization was not just about buying new materials to aid
in production, however. Knowledge about how to use those materials was
also a consideration. All operators on the ranch needed to be trained in
any new techniques that were adopted, and owners often felt that they had
to give up power when they brought in experts to educate themselves and
their workers. This concerned them.

To maintain a form of production that allowed owner-operators to preserve their positions as household-based commodity capitalists atop a social hierarchy, they had to make sure that they maintained, at a minimum, certain control over the structures and technologies of labor. Technology threatened to upset that hierarchy by undermining ranchers' claims to expertise about and control of the methods of production on the ranch. This in turn meant that ranchers had to selectively adopt only certain technologies to maintain traditional relations of production on the ranches. The archives are rife with evidence of ranchers' discourse about the ways in which technology decreased their need for waged labor, made knowledge of cow raising more difficult to access, and, ironically, led to at least a perceived decrease in skilled ranch labor, which in turn led to even further mechanization. If it was hard to find a "real" cowboy to tend the cows, then putting a virtual one on TV would have to do, but this was rarely done without considerable agonizing over the effects such technology would have on the ranch itself and the relationships thereon.

Ranchers did indeed adopt technologies and their corresponding knowledge bases, and labor and life on the ranch did change as a result of such adoptions. Despite the shifts, however, ranchers worked hard to ensure that the relations of production on range ranches were not seen to change completely. They knew if traditional cow work disappeared, then the owners' cultural world and rural identities would also cease to exist. This chapter looks at how mechanization informed the labor relationships that existed in the social world of production of the ranch and how cow talk about technology provided material space for ranchers to promote their established values regarding orthodox cow work.

By the 1930s ranchers realized that the political and ecological environment would no longer allow them to remain simple pastoralists. As the twentieth century progressed, ranchers knew themselves to be increasingly steeped in a complex system of mechanized and politicized labor. The ever-increasing demands of industrial agriculture forced many ranchers to consider investing in agricultural technology in order to remain competitive in the post–World War II livestock industry, but they did not do so without grave misgivings. Ranchers were accustomed to relying on their own experiences and their own understandings of nature to succeed in raising cattle. Nature *was* culture for ranchers, and technology implied reliance on outsiders who may not have understood or valued the nature and culture of the ranch environs.

Take J. D. Craighead and his wife Leonora, for example. They confronted difficult decisions about mechanization on their southern Colorado ranch throughout the 1940s, '50s, and '60s. Like ranchers across the mountain West, the Craigheads enjoyed the boom of the 1940s. By 1939, thanks largely to government relief programs and a slight improvement in the weather, cattle ranchers in Colorado, New Mexico, Arizona, Wyoming, and Montana had survived the droughty 1920s and 1930s. Their ranches had become slightly larger in acreage, and the numbers of ranchers remained relatively constant.[2] When World War II began, range cattle ranchers in the mountain West were ready and willing to reap the profits of a wartime economy. And, according to the price of cattle, which soared by 1943, they did so. Just as ranchers were getting used to the good times, however, the drought of 1950 hit. All over the mountain West, the year had been unusually dry. In southeastern Colorado it marked one of the driest years on record and thus hit J. D. Craighead's ranch in La Junta particularly hard.

Craighead was aging, and he could not decide whether the dry year was an omen telling him to sell the ranch and get out of the business altogether or whether it was just one more rough spot. He had seen some awfully dry years; the worst had come in 1934. His land lay in the shortgrass country of the southern Great Plains, and he had many of the same Dust Bowl experiences chronicled in such epic histories as Donald Worster's *Dust Bowl: The Southern Plains in the 1930s* and Paul Bonnifield's *Dust Bowl: Men, Dirt, and Depression.*[3] In many letters to friends and family, Craighead recalled the dust storms, dying cattle, low prices, and the desperation that had existed nearly constantly for seventeen years on Craighead Ranch (1921–38). In 1943 Craighead wrote to a friend in Kansas about those long years:

> From early in 1921 until 1928 we simply slowly starved. Cattle went down, crops failed, taxes piled up, the irrigation company got into financial difficulties by reason of farmers being unable to pay assessments until the whole situation seems hopeless. 1927 was a good crop year, prices were better, 1928 even better and 1929 was fine. Everybody thought they were going to get on feet again, when blooie, everything blew up. . . . Then about 1933 crops got good and we thought again

our section and people would get on better. Then the droughts [of the mid 1930s] struck.[4]

The long periods of little or no rain meant dry pastures and minimal green grass for grazing cattle. In fact, Craighead had witnessed the cyclic droughts come again and again, but always he had stayed. He supposed the main reason he did so was because he knew "nothing else," and in 1950 he decided to stay and ride out the dust storms one more time. But he knew his own muster would not be enough in a changing ecological and economic context, so Craighead mulled over adopting a variety of technologies.

Like Craighead, ranchers knew their decisions about which technological advancements to utilize on their ranches could make or break them financially, especially because the technology was connected to a larger market economy in which ranchers were tightly bound. Tractors, electricity, automobiles, household appliances, pesticides, herbicides, grass seed, water improvements (such as drilling wells), and the latest disease vaccines were just some of the technological developments that, if adopted, would require ranchers to lean on outside experts to use effectively. The cost and increasing dependency on outsiders worried owner-operators. This was why, in early 1950, Craighead wrote to the Wyatt Manufacturing Company in Salina, Kansas, to inquire about a piece of equipment that he thought might be beneficial to his operation. Craighead explained to the sales representative that he had met a fellow rancher at the Denver Stock Show who thought that "the Jayhawk hydraulic loader was now made attachable to Ford Ferguson or Ford tractors."[5] Craighead owned two Ford tractors (that he had purchased in the lucrative years of the mid to late 1940s), and, since he now had to grow hay as supplemental feed for his purebred Herefords, he knew that if he could get a hydraulic loader for a new hay crane, his labor and that of his hired hands would be greatly simplified (and perhaps reduced, lessening the need for expensive ranch labor).[6] Craighead explained to the machine dealer that his was a midsize ranch, that "had to pay for itself," and he could not afford the equipment if its cost was astronomical. In the end the equipment was too expensive to be justified, and Craighead decided to forego its purchase, but his decision was surely not easy, since the efficient growing of supplemental feed would have been especially urgent in a year of profound drought and little range growth.

As Craighead's story illustrates, not all ranchers invested in every available machine, but the majority did modernize in some ways. The purchase of technology and the adoption of modern ranching techniques (including vaccination, reseeding, and so on) surged and dipped according to cattle prices throughout the postwar decades. According to surveys conducted by the USDA, by 1960 ranchers were spending approximately twice the amount on machinery costs as they had in the 1930s. The expenditures incrementally increased throughout the postwar decades and indicate a consistent growth in the numbers of ranchers who were adopting (at least limitedly) ranch machinery.[7]

Importantly for this study, the mechanized component of modernity and the knowledge required to understand it brought ranchers together in commonality and spurred the sharing of cow talk. The archives are full of ranchers communicating publicly and privately about whether to mechanize. In addition to serving on committees and listening to reports on research at conventions, the pages of the association publications are filled with articles and letters relating to new technology and its potential usefulness (or destructiveness). Ranchers wrote across miles and miles of ranch country to aid their fellow ranchers in the difficult decision making about technological adaption. In 1951, for example, numerous letters arrived in Abbie Keith's mailbox regarding whether it was worthwhile to invest in branding tables. Mrs. Ott Dixon of Buckeye, Arizona; Georgia Baker of Young, Arizona; and Frank Krentz of Douglas, Arizona, were just a few of the ranchers who wrote to claim that a branding table was a worthwhile investment. These letter writers were responding to Keith's call in the ACGA newsletter looking for information about ranchers' experiences with the new technology. Krentz reminisced that "the old way was—we were in the dirt, the calf was in the dirt, dust was flying and everybody was worn out long before the end of the day."[8] Mrs. Dixon explained that she and her husband had used a calf-branding table for a number of years and had let neighbors borrow it to see if they liked it. They did. "We just wouldn't be without one," the experienced ranchwoman exclaimed.[9] Georgia Baker not only advocated for the adoption of a branding table but explained that she and her husband had "bought" into modernization by getting "the whole works." They had purchased "a squeeze chute, Howe Scale (a mechanized scale), a sprayer to keep the bugs off the cattle, and a Jeep which puts the burro to shame."[10] The letters illustrate not only an intense engagement with mechanization on the part of the ranchers but are also part of a broader social discourse about modern ranch work that served to create points of commonality around which ranchers could gather. The appearance in the newsletter of a public call for knowledge from an anonymous rancher and the subsequent private responses from knowledgeable ranchers serve as examples of cow talk and show how shared knowledge of material experiences in turn created space for cultural connections.

Scientifically based management can mean many things, but in the minds of ranchers it mostly required that they increasingly come together to learn about new methods. In doing so they came to rely ever more extensively on one another to make sense of the ramifications of technoscientific cow work. In June 1955 the *Montana Stockgrower* printed two images side by side (figure 5). Whereas the first image, "As It Was," shows a lone cowboy doing his labor in an unfenced and technologically unsophisticated space, the second, "As It Is," shows several cowboys gathered in a corral using modern technological tools to complete the task at hand. One can see electric power assisting with the branding. A telephone pole to the right tellingly hints at the connectedness of this particular ranch to the broader world. The truck parked nearby suggests that the rancher and his cowboys used fossil fuels to conduct ranch labor as well as to communicate with others beyond the confines of the corral. The image also hints at a labor regime that was more than a simple, individualistic enterprise: the industry now required the use of new kinds of power that could mean new kinds of relationships with the cows and one another.

Some of those new relationships occurred within the cattle growers' associations. Thousands of ranchers served (without remuneration) on committees for the local, state, and even national associations to explore the possibilities and the pitfalls of modernization and mechanization of the industry. Each state had differing priorities. In the Southwest, cloud seeding to produce more rain held an importance that it did not have in the more mountainous regions of Wyoming and Colorado.[11] In the northern Great Plains states, research on the best ways to control brucellosis (see chapter 4 for more discussion of this disease) took precedence. But no matter the priority of research, ranchers could agree that research on the best modes of modernization and mechanization should be a priority of

Figure 5. Cartoon "As It Was . . . As It Is." Drawn by Ben Burnett. In the *Montana Stockgrower*, June 15, 1955, 18–19. MHS Research Center Archives, Helena.

ranchers' associations. George Ellis, on the Bell Ranch in New Mexico, was particularly involved with the research side of association life. He not only served on NMCGA research and development committees but also chaired the research committee of the American National Cattlemen's Association from 1957–59. Some of the committee's priorities in those years included helping ranchers create an administrative system for the poisons they were using for parasite control; "intensified study of the control of mesquite and other noxious plants by chemical means[;] further efforts to develop more productive varieties of range grasses and to improve methods of seeding"; and a "continued study of the use of antibiotics and growth stimulating hormones under range conditions."[12] Hundreds of letters in Ellis's personal papers reveal the regional (and even national) conversation in which ranchers engaged as they not only tried to make sense of new science but also tried to share knowledge.

The technical changes in cattle ranching in the postwar years meant the interpersonal dynamics of production in ranching were also subject to drastic change. Growing the herd by traditional methods was increasingly at risk, which meant that rancher identity was equally unstable, since that identity was so singly wrapped up in cow work. Owner-operator ranchers believed that they had reproduced an entire social world that was essential to maintain if they could be most successful at growing cows. Throughout

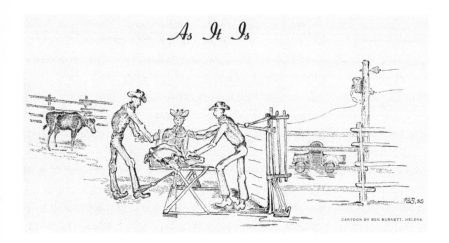

the archives, we can see ranchers, especially those who benefitted most from the maintenance of traditional cattle growing (the owner/operators), working very hard to culturally promote, value, and *reproduce* the social dynamics of production despite the mechanization in their midst.

The labor most cherished was that directly connected to the growing of cows with or without technological interventions. Ranchers (male and female) and even, at times, hired hands subsumed what might have been a contentious social world under a mirage of cultural unity reflected through an incessant veneration of cow work. The growing of cows and the cultural celebration of that labor were, therefore, two of the main cultural practices ranchers performed to create an appearance of rapport among all those who encompassed the world of work on the ranch.

To understand the cyclical nature of the cow work that held such tremendous cultural power for ranchers, we turn to one of the best sources we have for understanding that work—a 1973 publication called *Bell Ranch as I Knew It* by Bell Ranch manager George Ellis. By the time Ellis took over as manager of the ranch, in 1947, it had been subdivided and parceled out among several different owners. He managed the 130,000-acre parcel and developed it into one of the most prestigious ranches in the intermountain West. Ellis chronicled his time as manager on the Bell from 1947–60 in the book, and he focused almost entirely on what he referred to as "The Year's Work." We can use *Bell Ranch as I Knew It* as a window into the social world of work on postwar ranches because, although the Bell was a particularly large ranch, other, smaller ranches appear to have experienced a similar seasonal work culture that varied in scope but not necessarily in content.[13]

George Ellis explained that "work on the Bell was pretty well systematized and we usually did about the same things at the same time each year."[14] No matter where range cattle ranchers lived, how many head they ran, or how many acres they owned or leased, their lives revolved around cyclic, seasonal events.[15] Seasonal continuity (both short-term, annual continuity and long-term, generational continuity) provided one of the most important touchstones that ranchers used to relate to one another. The introductory sections of the book pay particular attention to the Spanish conquest and Mexican eras, when the Bell had been one of the largest land grants in the region. The land grant from which the Bell descended was originally "given" to Pablo Montoya from the Spanish government and consisted of land that varied topographically and included canyons, plateaus, and prairies. The land had ample water, a rarity in the arid region of eastern New Mexico, and was covered with rich grasses.[16] In chronicling the longevity of land use on the Bell, George's recollections assert the premise that the work on the land had been reproduced by its inhabitants for hundreds of years.[17]

Winter was the quietest time of the year around the ranches of Arizona, Montana, Colorado, Wyoming, and New Mexico. Ranchers in the winter months (usually December through February for the Southwest and October to March in the northern states) often needed to feed cattle to keep their weight up and to seek out cattle watering locales to break ice. Beyond this, ranchers attended to labor in the winter that they had neglected during the busy spring, summer, and fall. Repairing ranch technologies such as fence constituted the outdoor activities around the ranch in the cold months. Balancing books, catching up on correspondence, and generally taking stock of the business occurred year-round for ranch owners and managers, but managers and owners privileged these activities in winter months.[18]

Labor on a range cattle ranch accelerated in the spring. For Ellis on the Bell, "It all began March 1 when the new calves started coming." During the spring months, owners who could afford to hired seasonal hands to help with the round-up and branding activities. These seasonal workers remained on the ranch through early fall, and the larger operations kept a few hands year-round. Monitoring the calving and making sure that heifers did not need any assistance took up most of the labor until late spring or early summer, when branding and breeding season began in full swing. Ranchers herded cattle together, administered vaccines, branded new calves, and inspected older cattle to determine their overall health and to ascertain how well they had survived the winter. During this time, ranchers put the bulls with the cows to breed until the latter part of summer.

It was during the spring and summer months when women in the owner-operator class were most likely to "help out" with the cow work. Ranch-women's work was varied, interminable, and very often unremunerated, but they still had well-formed labor identities that were important to the larger cultural identity of ranching. Ranchwomen's identities centered on the importance of their domestic labor, especially for such ranch rituals as roundups and brandings. Ranchwomen, often with the help of one or two female employees, did the laundry, served meals, and made sure the cowhands had all the coffee they could drink before they began their work.

Women's work, however, extended beyond these domestic tasks. For example, Mattie Ellis often did the books for the Bell Ranch—and was espe-cially knowledgeable about the registered herd of Hereford cattle. She was the person in charge of welcoming the myriad guests who arrived monthly at the Bell. She rode the range with the crew and knew the contours of the ranch topography as well as anyone. She raised a garden, cooked for guests, raised two children, and still found time to write about her expe-riences as a ranchwoman, at least partially because the Bell hired other women to assist Mattie with the domestic labor.[19]

The archives are full of female testimonials about the ways in which domestic labor was critical to the production of the cattle. That is not to claim that ranchwomen did not recognize that there existed two gendered realms of work on range cattle ranches. Domestic labor was gendered female and separated from the outdoor work with cows, which was gendered male. Male owner-operators rarely if ever did the cooking or the laundry. Still, the creation of a commodity in a capitalist household economy (which most ranches were) depended, literally, on reproduction of the household—and ranchwomen knew it. While brewing coffee may not seem to us to be connected with bovine bloat or the eradication of intrusive weeds, ranch-women were keenly aware that sustaining male owner-operators and the hired hands physically so that they were able to confront those problems contributed directly to the growth of healthy cows and to the continuation of both the family business and the wider culture of ranching. While ranch-women culturally valued outdoor cow work more than their indoor work, they did not believe cow work to be separate from domestic work.

While male ranchers labored mostly in the outdoor environs of the ranch, a ranchwoman's workspaces included the range, the grass, the cows, as well as the house, the garden, and the yard. The following excerpt from Stella (Mrs. Cort) Carter's 1952 letter to the *Cattlelog* exemplifies how these women celebrated the multitasking that required them to balance difficult, outdoor labor with their more domestic tasks. She wrote:

> You know Cow Gals, how it goes on a ranch. . . . If through the day a horse gets into the fence, you think nothing of it—just go lift him out. BUT BE SHURE TO FIX THE FENCE. . . . Maybe when you get back to the house you find a hay truck suspended over your rock wall! You help jack the thing up . . . then pull the truck out with the trac-tor. . . . You turn to survey the damage to your favorite corner in the garden. A tree skinned; some shrubbery crushed . . . flowers smashed and trampled—why is it some men never watch what they're walking on? . . . Well, you tackle the mess with pruning shears, ax and pitch-fork dampening the ground with tears.[20]

Throughout the postwar decades, ranchwomen consistently penned articles and columns similar to Stella Carter's feisty rendition. Vast docu-mentation of women's direct involvement with cattle drives, stray round-ups, gardens, cattle diseases, and range issues fills the archives and depicts a group of women willing to extend their work identities beyond the home to the wider economic and ecological worlds of the ranch.[21]

Additionally, all ranchers tended to view women's labor as more flexible than men's labor, and dominant ranch culture expected women to step into outdoor cow work whenever necessary. For Marion Moore, the owner-operator of the CM Ranch (a dude and cattle ranch) in Dubois, Wyoming, the shortage of help in the spring of 1945 and the harshness of the spring weather meant that by mid-May she had barely "gotten the garden in" and fully expected "the seeds" would "do little more than shiver in their skins, these frosty nights" because she had been so busy attending to cow work.

Despite having gotten the "garden in," she felt overworked and still had the milking to do. As a result, she pleaded with Walter Nye, the secretary of the Wyoming Dude Ranchers' Association (DRA): "If you can, send a man to the CM, we would love you harder than ever—especially me, on account of the cows."[22] Her entreaty fell on deaf ears because there simply was not enough labor to go around.

Ranchwomen considered their presence on the ranch as "helpmates" to their cattlemen important, but in their private correspondence, I have found that they maintained their own identities as individual laborers who worried about the cows and refused to be subordinates in a masculinist ranch work culture.[23] Even those female owner-operators who loathed their lives on the ranch still seemed to understand their importance to it. Take, for example, Rosa Ronquillo Rhodes, who with her husband William Robert Rhodes owned the Diamond R Ranch near Redington, Arizona. Her diary entries for the postwar period often discuss the acute loneliness she felt as her husband "went to work as usual," and her children went about their lives. In particular, "women's work" held no glory for her. Her diaries intimate a sense of an ordinariness of daily life that was nearly suffocating. And yet she trudged on because she sensed the ranch would cease to exist if she did not.[24]

In the archives, then, it is abundantly clear that ranchwomen knew their labor to be vital to the overall success of the ranch and the industry as a whole. This "Jill of All Trades" mentality pervades the women's writing about their work culture. Many, if not most, ranchwomen prided themselves on their abilities to bake a cake *and* fix a water pump. Still, as Teresa Jordan has pointed out, men were expected to do outdoor labor, while women were allowed to, and ranchwomen lived under intense hegemonic ideas about the proper role of women in the postwar years.[25] While ranchwomen labored under these strict gender expectations, however, they also subverted them at critical junctures, and they did so through their work with cows.

In this subversion of the dominant gender paradigm, ranchwomen never abandoned their commitment to simultaneously identifying themselves and being identified as "true women" and "real ranchers." In her discussion of ranchwomen's labor, Arizona rancher Jo Jeffers explains: "Because she is sure of her innate womanliness, [the ranch woman] is not afraid to do a man's chores when she has to. She doesn't mind getting dust in her eyes, mouth and nose, having the wind knot her hair or wading in manure up to her ankles when necessary."[26] Jeffers and other ranchwomen believed that their individual identities as "real" women were durable enough to withstand the possibility that masculinized work would undo their femininity. Women's participation in the social world of production, then, was a significant part of cow talk and shows that cow talk was deeply gendered.

The domestic labor in which all ranchwomen had to engage was, of course, critical to the success of the ranch business, and ranchwomen acknowledged that fact, but even so they rarely centered those tasks in their public portrayals of themselves in cow talk. In most of the public sources, ranchwomen associate themselves with the cow-centered aspects of ranch life. Spring was one of the times of the year when labor with the cows took precedence over other kinds of labor. The heifers and cows were calving, and, for those ranchers who did so, the herds moved from the winter range to summer pastures (usually at higher elevations). Ranchwomen incorporated the cyclic, seasonal temporality of ranching into their own identity productions, thereby helping to reproduce the hegemony of the cow as being central to ranch life.[27]

Ranchwomen's chores would increase again in the fall, but first, spring morphed into summer and brought with it the grazing season, during which ranchers rode among the cattle. Summer months required due diligence on the part of the hired hands and the owners to assure cattle's wellbeing on the range. Like all seasons on the ranch, summer always brought surprises; while the cyclic nature of ranch labor often meant repetition, there were also new challenges to be overcome daily. As George Ellis wrote, "August and September were spent riding among the cattle. If you see cattle often enough, there is always something that needs tending to."[28] Eulalia Bourne, a female rancher who owned and ran her own operation, echoed George's comment, but she put a feminine spin on it. She wrote, "If you ride the range every day, you neglect your housework and other duties. If you don't ride, some cattle will go blind with pinkeye or otherwise be fouled."[29] Eulalia had no Mattie or Marion to take care of the other reproductive tasks while she rode the range, and so her sense of having something to tend to among the cows differed significantly from George's: nowhere does George mention neglecting his housework, because he had none to do.

Those women who lived on the ranch as the wives of ranch hands found spring, summer, and fall just as tense as did the women owner-operators, but for different reasons. For ranch hands' wives, spring, summer, and fall were the loneliest times of the year. During these months the hands were gone for long periods. They participated in the buying and selling of calves, heifers, and steers during these months, which required much labor. To ready the cows for market, ranchers and hired hands would round up the cattle and cut out the animals that were going to be sold. Concern about getting the cattle weighed at their heaviest weight marked much of the work. For example, assuring that the calves did not lose too much weight between being separated, weighed, and delivered to the buyer meant ranchers and hands had to decide the exact moment to separate the steers or heifer calves from their mothers. Because timing was crucial and the handling of the cattle vital to getting the best price possible for each animal, the labor crew—whether composed only of family members or of two hired workers or thirty—needed great cow sense and skill and deep commitment to the growing of cows. It also required that the hands be gone from the home ranch for days, weeks, and, sometimes, months at a time.

Language barriers and class biases served to separate the families of the owner-operators and their employees. The wives and daughters of male hired hands remained on the ranch with little recourse to leave, and they understandably often grew disgruntled. These women's work was mundane, routine, and isolated. Josefina Badilla, whose husband labored on cattle ranches across southern Arizona in the 1940s, explained her experience on the ranch as "lonely" and "depressing," largely because she was left at home doing tedious domestic labor while her husband rode the range and visited other ranchers and cowboys on neighboring ranches. Josefina explained: "I told my husband I don't want to be here on this ranch all by myself because a ranch . . . is a very hard thing, very depressing because . . . you see the woman stays on the ranch all day. . . . We women are just at the ranch. . . . [I would just] make dinner for my husband when he came home, wash and iron my clothes and all of his. . . . I would just pass the day all alone . . . [because] people lived very far away."[30]

As Josefina's memories indicate, the ranches' stereotypically gendered hierarchy relegated the wives of male ranch employees to "women's work." These women rarely if ever mention engaging in cow work, and thus their contributions to the ranch are rarely mentioned and never celebrated. As Josefina eloquently explained, the men, even those who were underpaid and underappreciated, got to partake in the exciting work and sociability of the cowboys. Their mobility and changing work routine stirred the monotony of daily life on a ranch and reinforced their sense of manliness and their claim to labor legitimacy. Both male ranch hands and male owner-operators, conversely, expected the hired hands' female family members to be immobile, isolated, and content in drudgery.

Technological modernization required male ranch hands to expand their skills during these years. Owner-operators who hired waged workers seemed to demand that hired hands have both traditional horse and cow skills as well as mechanical knowhow and the ability to operate and fix mechanized implements when necessary. These newly complex qualifications created conflict among ranchers and the waged labor force, and the two groups often viewed the social world of production very differently in the postwar decades. Take, for example, the decision of George Ellis to modernize the Bell Ranch's chuckwagon in 1957, when Ellis retired the old chuckwagon and replaced it with a mechanized vehicle.[31] Part of the reason behind the mechanizing of the wagon was that by the early 1950s George knew that the traditional wagon was outdated technologically. To mechanize, Ellis built a kitchen on a four-wheel-drive army truck: he added a butane cook stove, butane lights, running water from a tank at the rear, and sleeping quarters for the cook. Ellis's choice to mechanize the Bell chuckwagon was largely in response to the changing (and lessening) skills of laborers. He explained that the skills of cowhands diminished in the postwar years, and by the late 1950s it had become exceedingly difficult "to find a cook who could drive four horses."[32] He may also have found it difficult to find a cook who could fix a carburetor, but that skill was less important than the ability to drive a truck, and presumably that was easier to find by the late 1950s.

Jack Brenner, former president of the MSGA and owner of the Lazy E-4 Ranch, echoed Ellis's sentiment. Brenner remembered that in the 1920s and 1930s, he and his family had been able to raise a cow for $8 per head. By 1976 it took $85. In the pre–World War II years, Brenner believed it had been much easier to find "good," "skilled" labor. As the postwar decades wore on, Brenner remembered, mechanization forced a change from horse-driven ranch operations to complex mechanized outfits that simply added "labor and expense" to traditional ranch tasks, but he claimed that the shift had been necessary. Skilled cowhands simply did not exist on the range. When asked why he stopped using temporary labor, Brenner recalled, "[We] just ran out of them [workers]. Just couldn't get them anymore. . . . [The] old boys kind of wore out . . . and by golly [the new ones] don't know anything." If not knowing anything generally about a ranch was not bad enough, there was the ignorance of laborers when it came to upkeep and proper operation of the machinery. Brenner exclaimed, "Good lord the machinery! You've got $15,000 here, $20,000 there and you've got to have darn good men that know how to take care of that machinery." Trusting hired hands with modes of production that cost thousands of dollars, when it was not necessary to do so for the production of cows, did not seem worth it to Brenner. He did the mechanized work himself and called a mechanic when something went wrong. Still, he admitted that "if I had my druthers I'd settle for old system because . . . I was raised a horse man. And I did all my work with horses and I never did learn the mechanical part of it too well. I've got to depend on somebody else."[33] This quote is particularly interesting because it shows how technologies could make "old time" ranchers feel uncomfortably dependent and vulnerable. Having to rely on someone else meant sacrificing some of the values and traits associated with masculinity and surely made propping up that masculinity more important than ever before.

Shorty Wallins, a ranch laborer whose main skill was breaking cow horses, would have disagreed with Ellis and Brenner vehemently over the root of the problem with labor on ranches in the postwar years. Shorty, a prolific writer and amateur cowboy illustrator, roamed the mountain West looking for work in the 1940s and 1950s as an aging cowhand. He wrote regularly to Frank M. King, the associate editor for the *Western Livestock Journal,* and considered King, a former cowhand like himself, a friend and fellow old-timer. In his letters Shorty confided to King his extreme frustration with life as a cowhand on the mechanizing mid-twentieth-century range. In 1949, during the "Hunger Moon" (the seasonally slow time for hired help on ranches), Shorty wrote to King from Billings, Montana, where he was in between jobs. He explained to King (emphasis mine):

They [ranchers] are hirin less and less of us seasoned hands getting so a top hand can't get a job no more. Them half lost ranchers want

these gear farmers that'll milk cows, [and] jump on a tractor. . . . Its all
addin up to so much dung [so that] ranchers are a cross between barb
wire, tractors and hog lots. Yeah they call therselves ranchers [but]
them ranchers now days don't know what a saddle blanket is made
for. There is a few decent ranchers but the majority are half baked
imbeciles *who come out of nutte colleges an tractor factories.* Frank I wonder where all them old timers are that I used to know? . . . I say I stand
here on the sidewalk on a street alone no one to talk to. I'm alone.[34]

Shorty's frustration with modern ranchers is palpable in this prime
example of cow talk. In his opinion, the owner-operators had been produced by the technoscience elite and thus knew nothing of horses. These
developments had left him feeling isolated and alone. A few months after
he penned the letter above, Shorty was writing King again. He had relo-
cated several hundred miles to Dillon, Montana, was still looking for a job,
and was getting considerably more agitated. His lament to King is worth
quoting at length:

Well I'm in Dillon again in a shack cookin eggs. Lookin for a job again.
Things are not so good no more to many people. The big [guys ride]
rigs trucks jeeps tractors and bulldozers an all that stinkin inferno.
Them would be monkeyward cattlemen as they ride around there [their] *cattle in trucks.* They are loose in there ego an substitute the jeep for the
saddle horse. . . . Enough don't want to be bothered to rope horses
they would rather let the bulls an cows do the best they can. They run
there cow heifers, yearlings in chutes an squeeze the life out of them
till all the insides bust loose. They don't know what a rope or rope
horse looks like. . . . That's me but this all happens in most parts of
the range country. . . . Here is the joke frank . . . these monkeyward
cattlemen don't know nothing but fences and trucks. . . . They won't
buy saddle horses wont buy em don't want em around [cause] they
eat grass don't need riders wont hire em. . . . [But you] cant run cattle
with a car. He's got to have riders saddle horses rope horses ride the
range scatter them bulls to the cows and don't leave em all summer
with a few cows and let the rest go without bulls. . . . Of course these
rotten cattlemen wont own up to their ignorance.[35]

He equated the intermediary of the machine in the rancher-cow relation-ship to be downright dangerous. Other ranchers worried, too, that knowl-edge of the range would disappear if too much technology intervened in cow work. Shorty suggested that ranchers were "monkeyward"—a reference to Montgomery Ward, the department store—cowmen who did not know how to ranch. Compare this to George Ellis's and Jack Brenner's claims that good and properly skilled ranch hands were increasingly scarce, and a picture emerges of a classed and even generational tension among owner-operators and ranch hands. These three had very different opinions of the problems surrounding labor in the industry, but—and this is crucial—they all agreed that technological adaptations and technoscientific approaches to growing cows were creating problems.

Shorty's letters also indicate that waged tensions existed on the range. These tensions are evident as well in quantitative fact. Wage disparities among ranch laborers show a distinct class hierarchy and reveal one area in which divisions among ranch folk certainly existed—although these divi-sions did not make it into the pages of ranch publications but exist quietly in the personal papers of ranchers. In 1950, for example, the foreman on the Bell Ranch, Bill Yaqui Tatom, earned the most of all Bell employees (aside from George Ellis) at $135 per month plus room and board. His job was to oversee general operations of the cattle crew and to communicate with the manager (George) as issues arose regarding cattle health. The second highest paid employee, the bunkhouse cook, who cooked for the cowboy crew, earned $115 per month. A cowboy earned between $80 and $85 a month (plus room and board), while the sole female employee, Emily Esquibel, the cook for the Ellises at the main house, earned the least, $75 a month. George himself, as the manager of the ranch, earned approximately $350 a month. His wife Mattie's never-ending work went unremunerated.[36]

Comparisons with another ranch in New Mexico, George Godfrey's operation twenty-five miles south of Animas, show that wages there were consistent with wages on the Bell. In October 1951 Godfrey paid his most permanent hand, John Dallies, $150 per month; day laborers earned an average of $5 a day, which averages to about fifty cents an hour. In Mon-tana in the early 1950s, the wage picture was much the same. In 1955 Con Warren's ranch in Deer Lodge, for example, paid employees an average of just over fifty cents an hour.[37] Shorty Wallins wrote that while he was on a ranch in Wyoming, he was paid "200.00 a moon," and he received "a 100.00 bonus" if he would "tough her out 3 moons." Shorty gloried in this salary, and he was thrilled to report that "wages have never been so high and men are scarce as now."[38] It might come as a surprise that wages seemed so consistent throughout the region, but Jack Brenner suggested in his 1976 oral history that there existed a kind of moral economy among owner-operators and waged laborers regarding wage rates. Brenner explained that ranchers tended to not "play one rancher off against another" on wages. He said, "There was never any formal agreement or anything like that but everybody knew about what wages would be and that was it."[39] Here the owner-operator class is clearly, albeit informally, allied against the workers. Of course, if the wages paid by owner-operators were fair, this alliance was not contemptible, and hands often agreed that wages were fair. When they did not, they registered their distaste by quitting. In the cases when the hired hands had no recourse, the unspoken premise—that owner-operators should be (or should at least appear to be) united in economy and ideology and should sit atop the social hierarchy—inched toward price fixing, but owner operators and hands never discussed the wage system in those terms.

It might come as some surprise to learn that the labor of female employees does not appear to have been particularly undervalued. Approximately two out of ten waged workers on larger ranches were women, and generally women ranch laborers were married to one of the other ranch hands. As mentioned previously, the hired female employees tended to work in domestic labor. They often cleaned the main ranch house and the bunk houses or cooked for the crew, the manager, or the owner's family. Periodically, a female ranch hand worked with the cattle. No matter the kind of labor they performed, however, female waged laborers tended to be paid similarly to the male employees. Again, the Bell can serve as an example. Throughout the late 1950s and early 1960s, Mattie and George occasionally hired Carlos Blea's wife Cecilia to help with general domestic duties, especially cleaning the main ranch house before visitors arrived. Carlos was the fence foreman and one of the highest-paid employees at the Bell. He earned eighty cents an hour, while Cecilia earned seventy cents an hour for her work—which comparatively was a middling wage. Seferina Estrada, the main housekeeper for the Ellises, earned as much as Carlos Blea, $200 per month, and Lana Turner, the wife of the ranch foreman, who cooked for the crew, also earned $200 a month. Because female workers did not engage in cow work per se, it should come as no surprise that they did not make as much money as men who performed outdoor cow work. It is interesting, however, that owner-operators did recognize, at least partially, the importance held by women's domestic labor in continuing the form of production on the ranch.

While gender had less effect on the wages paid to ranch workers, a very real distinction in wages appears to have been based on race. Of Ellis's hired hands from 1951–67, just over half had Spanish surnames and at any given point earned nearly $100 less per month than their Anglo counterparts. In 1951 George Godfrey employed seven Anglo workers who earned an average of $165 per month and eight Hispanic workers who earned an average of $88 per month.[40] On the Bell and other southwestern ranches, it would seem, whiteness colored the wage-labor system. Gender characterized these wages of whiteness as well, but not in the way we might expect. In ranch business records, women of color do not appear to have earned substantially less than Anglo women.[41]

Owner-operators ostensibly paid ranch hands for the type of work they did and their ability to handle different technologies on the ranch. Each employee had a craft-like skill that fit into the larger systematized routine on the ranch. Within this systemization of labor, however, lay an unspoken cultural assumption about which work was most important. Common laborers, who were not as skilled with cattle or horses (an obvious technology in the working world of the ranch), generally received the least amount of pay even though their work might be critically important to the functioning of the ranch. For example, many common laborers were assigned work that seemed too easy to give to a more experienced or skillful cowboy. They fixed water pumps, changed the oil in the truck, or perhaps mended a fence. Many laborers, then, did noncow work on range ranches. They worked on the maintenance crew and often arrived to do seasonal and piecemeal work such as "windmilling" and welding.[42] Female employees, while making up a smaller proportion of overall hired labor, conducted crucial work on range cattle ranches despite not riding the range. Though crucial, these jobs often were undervalued monetarily and culturally.[43] What is clear is that owner-operators needed skilled laborers with an increasingly impressive skill set. These workers needed not only to excel in horsemanship but also to understand a variety of machines as they went about growing the cows.

As the above discussion has shown, the personal and more private sources in the archives reveal a wildly diverse world of skilled work happening on cattle ranches, but that diversity is not what took center stage in the public celebrations of cow work. Instead, owner-operators reproduced a culture that spoke to the importance of direct, productive, and usually unmechanized "traditional" work with cows. They chose to highlight that work because it was the labor most steeped in heritage, was the easiest labor to romanticize or at least heroize, and was the labor most important to the related goals of making a profit while persevering ranching as a permanent way of life. As changing land regimes, changing technology, and changing markets caused the traditional form of producing cows to become increasingly vulnerable, owner-operators sought to emphasize the traditional form of production (growing cows from grazed grass) by convincing themselves that it was the only work that truly mattered. In this situation the creation of a dominant culture and the sense of unique community repressed different kinds of experiences and views of ranch life. This claim to a special kind of community, I argue throughout this book, was then used by the cattle growers' association members and certain ranchers to underpin the political rhetoric of cow talk, which served to present an image of unity and power.

To read ranchers' cultural productions (verses the personal papers in which I found details about wages and labor relations), one would never know that not all of the people on a ranch were cowhands equally engaged in the production of cattle the old-time way.[44] Take, for example, the story of the "female cowboy" that made headlines in the ACGA publication the *Arizona Cattlelog* in 1946. The article, written by Lillian Riggs, owner of the Faraway Ranch in southeastern Arizona, reminisced about Riggs's decision to hire a woman cowhand in the early 1940s. The decision to write the piece and to publish it is interesting because the story does not necessarily bemoan the fall of traditional womanhood but instead celebrates the cow work that the young woman was able to learn and do well.

In 1943 Riggs hired a young woman from Chicago named Clover Kline. Clover had written a letter of inquiry to the ACGA office looking for ranch work. She explained in the letter that she "wished to make ranching" her life. Lillian worried about Clover's gender, her work experience, her urban upbringing, and her intentions. As Lillian wrote in the article, "If this girl were merely looking for a vacation on the ranch in the guise of asking for a job, we wanted none of her. . . . She would be expected to make a hand with the cattle work." Because it was 1943 and labor was "hard to obtain and good help had been an impossibility" due to the war, Lillian and her husband Ed decided to give Clover a chance. Clover ended up making an excellent hand, both "in the round-ups and in the branding corrals," and she succeeded in the cowboy craft by asking "intelligent questions" and figuring out "things for herself."[45] These kinds of stories about female cowhands are rare in the archives because owner-operators usually slated female employees for domestic labor if for no other reason than their gender, and when a woman "cowboyed" it made an interesting story. It is, however, more than just an interesting story. When the story left Lillian's pen and appeared in print in a ranchers' collective periodical, it began to perform important cultural work—to celebrate cow work—even for women. No stories in any of the publications celebrate a young ranchwoman learning how to do laundry.

We might expect male ranchers to propagate the idea that cow work was the only kind of labor that really mattered on a ranch, but ranchwomen also reified cow work as the most important work to be done. Jo Jeffers serves as a perfect example. She explained that the wives and daughters of owner-operators "may put on a pair of Levi's, go with her husband to doctor a sick cow, repair a windmill, mend a fence, put out feed or chop ice. She may don an apron and stay in the kitchen over a hot wood cookstove all day, preparing a meal for thirty men. . . . She may or may not like to ride horses, but she knows a thing or two about a cow and that is what is important on a cow ranch."[46] Apparently, having expertise with any number of technologies and having the technical knowhow to prepare a meal for thirty men was not what was important on a cow ranch. Rather knowing "a thing or two about a cow" was all that really mattered in the gendered cow talk of ranchers' cultural narratives

The heroization of cow work was not only evident in texts but also in the visual culture of ranches.[47] Images on ranchers' and association stationary, the images published in ranchers' collective publications, and the photographs kept in ranchers' papers almost without exception show a visual

Figure 6. The March 1955 cover of the Montana Stockgrowers Association publication, *The Montana Stockgrower*. MHS Research Center Archives, Helena.

record of ranchers engaged in work with cows, horses, and the nonhuman
world of the ranch. They show the ranchers out of doors, and little technology interferes with those relationships. Whether it was the covers of
association periodicals (figures 6 and 7), or personal ranch photos shared
with the ranch community in publications (figures 8 and 9), or images on
association and personal ranch stationary (figure 10), representation of
ranch culture visually privileged nonmechanized labor and cattle.

Figure 7. The February 1951 cover of the Wyoming Stock Growers Association publication, *Cow Country*. WSGA Papers, American Heritage Center, UW.

These images illustrate the kinds of representations ranchers valued and the kinds of covers that appeared throughout the postwar years. Ranchers' cultural iconography served to privilege cows and humans' (particularly male) labor with them in both public and private sources. The stationary also represents an important example of cow talk. Under these letterheads ranchers received news vital to their cultural and economic lives, and the inclusion of cow work (and the focus on the cow itself) on stationary matters because it was a critical way to give center stage to the masculinized, traditional, outdoor work in ranch culture.

Figure 8. Branding on the John David ranch in Montana. This intergenerational and male-centered image represents the primacy of masculinist cow work in so many ranch photos. John David Ranch Collection, PAC 76-45.20, MHS Research Center Archives, Helena.

In these examples, ranchers used both cow work (men atop horseback) or cows themselves (or both) as emblems to represent the ranch business.[48] No antibiotic tube or electric branding table achieved symbolic visibility in the most prominent and permanent visual culture of ranchers. Despite its importance in cow talk—at association meetings and in correspondence— and despite its increasing omnipresence in workspaces of the ranch, technology was visually relegated behind the more traditional physical human and nonmechanized labor of cow work.

Technology also allowed labor relations to appear perhaps more cohesive than they were. In privileging traditional cow work in cow talk, owner-operators also made sure to blur the divide between employees and employers, and they did this by making technology the bugaboo. The cohesion and unity owner-operators sought could be buttressed by their own experiences, both negative and positive, as laborers alongside their hired hands. In much of their cow talk, then, owner-operators revealed a dominant assumption in ranch culture: namely that all laborers (waged, family, skilled, unskilled) were essential to the overall success of the individual ranch and the industry as a whole.

A 1954 letter from Harry Day, owner of the Lazy B Ranch in southeastern Arizona on the Arizona-New Mexico border near Lordsburg, New Mexico,

Figure 9. The Rulan Jacobson children. Personal photos submitted to associations from ranchers showed the centrality of cows to ranch life. Submitted by the Jacobson family, the photo appeared in the WSGA's *Cow Country* in 1958. WSGA Papers, Box 190, Folder 3, American Heritage Center, UW.

serves as an example of this ideological labor inclusivity. Day wrote to Abbie Keith, the secretary of the ACGA, as he often did, to update her on progress on his high-grade Hereford ranch.[49] Day had been battling cockleburs. His battle to eradicate this particular invasive and toxic plant relied heavily on the modern technological weapon of herbicides—namely 2,4-D, a subject we will discuss more in chapter 3.[50] The risk of using toxic technology seemed worthwhile to Day, and his workers likely had little choice about whether to engage with it. Still, Day was there every step of the way and took the time afterward to write to Keith about how their difficult labor was paying off. Importantly, the use of technoscience (2,4-D) to manage the range did not absolve Day and his hired hands of performing manual, bodily labor against the weed. Day described loading containers of 2,4-D into the jeep, spraying it on the plants, and waiting for the plants to die; but afterward, "there

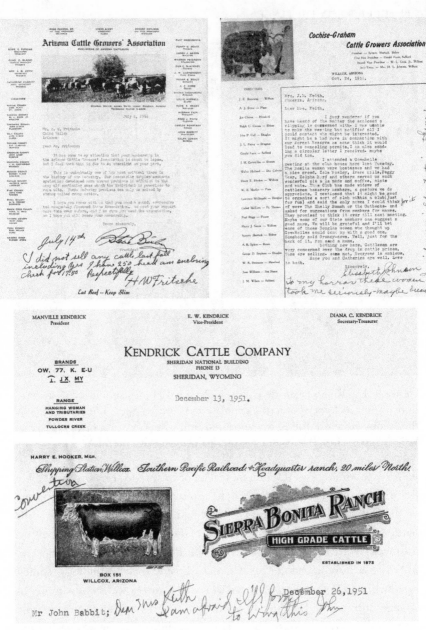

Figure 10. Examples of the centrality of cows on association and ranch stationary. From left to right and top to bottom: Arizona Cattle Growers' Association
stationary; Cochise-Graham Cattle Growers Association stationary; Kendrick
Cattle Company letterhead; Sierra Bonita Ranch letterhead. ACGA Manuscript Collection, Box 5, Folder 1, AHS, Tempe and WSGA Papers, Box 191,
Folder 13, American Heritage Center, UW.

remained scattered plants all up and down the draws so we pulled these by hand. I used all of my cow boys. *We* would spread out, like making a drive to round-up cattle, and walk up the draws pulling all of the cockleburs out of the ground, roots and all. My cow boys are now all complaining about having xanthiumitis (sore feet and an aching back) but *we* have nearly all the burs killed for this year" (emphasis mine).[51]

The hard soil of southeastern Arizona and the painful prickliness of cockleburs would certainly have made this particular ranch labor arduous. In addition, the time taken away from other ranch work, all for only one year of control, must have frustrated Day and the cowboys alike, but it was necessary to enable edible grass to grow, and Day clearly believed himself to be engaged as fully in the labor as his cowboys. He shared the work as well as the risk.

Day's letter goes on to illustrate how this labor experience could serve to connect him to his fellow ranchers. He wrote that he was "wondering what experiences other members have had with cockleburs."[52] After expending physical labor on the invader plant and engaging in risky use of toxic chemicals with his wage laborers, Day sat down to write Keith the letter from which he hoped not merely to gain knowledge but also to share his identity as just another laborer in the social world of cow production on the ranch.

In Day's letter and in much of the correspondence and storytelling about cow work, there existed an almost naturalized expectation that the labor came with injury and hardship, and *real* cowfolk were those who overcame physical challenges with masculine toughness. Note the injury complaints of Day's cowboys. Aching back and feet were just a few of the outcomes of harsh cow work, and indeed, the danger of cow work served as a binding element in the mythologized intimacy between the owner-operators and their hired hands. Interestingly, that danger seemed only compounded by technological adaptation. Toxic chemicals, heavy machinery, and mechanized tools were added to the health hazards of bucking horses, brutal weather, and uncooperative cattle. An article in a 1948 issue of *Arizona Cattlelog* chronicled fourteen-year-old David Valdez's learning of cow work on the Car Link Ranch near Redington, Arizona. What stands out in the article, in addition to the paternalistic depiction of Valdez's relationship to the owner King Smallhouse, was the description of the physicality and danger of cow work for a cowhand. David explains that the cowboys worked long hours (from 6 A.M. to 9:30 P.M.), and by the time he arrived home, he was more than ready to go to bed. At one point in the story, another cowboy's horse gets tangled in a rope, and David had to help free the horse so that the cowboy would not be bucked off.

Regardless of their gender or their job, ranch workers' health was at risk every day. Ranch cooks, for example, labored over hot stoves all day. In the Southwest they commonly worked with no air conditioning in summer temperatures well over 100 degrees. Other tasks around the ranch headquarters that required intense physical exertion included hauling water, tending the garden, feeding horses, milking dairy cows, and doing laundry (often without a mechanized washing machine). Cowhands rode long days on horseback, dealt with angry and strong cattle, and, as we heard from Harry Day, dealt with myriad kinds of pesticides and herbicides.[53]

Discussions about environmental conditions that led to occupational health hazards encompassed a more general concern with worker health on ranches that was a constant worry but was rarely spoken about in public publications. Agricultural accidents, although seldom discussed by ranchers, happened all the time. Sometimes a cowhand's work even resulted in death, as was the case in 1957 on the Bell Ranch when Buster Taylor died while branding cattle. George included the story in *Bell Ranch as I Knew It* because the death was "the greatest tragedy that had ever occurred there."[54] In July 1957 George wrote to Mrs. Keeney and her husband Ralph, the absentee owners of the Bell, to tell them of the accident, but it took him some time to write the letter because he had "never had anything hurt quite as bad as this." He continued, "I could not have thought more of Buster if he had been a member of the family. He was one of the finest people I have ever known and we had come to depend on him in so many ways."[55] Buster, Yaqui Tatom, and another cowboy had been branding a few calves that had been missed in the main work of branding that year. George explained the events to the Keeneys as they had been described to him:

> Buster roped one [calf] and started to drag him out to the fire. His horse must have got excited [because] he whirled and wrapped the rope around Buster. Before he could throw that off the horse . . . wrapped the rope around again. Buster was then jerked off with the rope around him and the horse kicked him in the head. I feel sure he was killed instantly although Yaqui and Mattie worked on him for

almost two hours until the Doctor got here. Doctor Hoover says he could not have saved him if he had been there when it happened.

George had been out of town when the accident occurred and so had gone straight to tell Buster's wife of the tragedy.[56] In Buster's case an occupational safety net, an insurance policy from the ranch, did exist, but thousands of ranch laborers across the mountain West put their bodily health at risk without such safety nets. Ironically, Ellis's solution to the grief and fear created by the accident was to put everyone to work again. He wrote: "Yaqui has taken the foreman's job and we will go right ahead. Everyone has felt so badly that I thought we needed to get real busy so there would be no time to think about it. So we have been busy. There is a new Federal regulation that requires that every ranch in the state test its cattle for Bang's Disease so we have spent the last week doing that . . . and it is a big relief to know we have a clean bill of health."

George believed that through tending the bodily health of cattle, the workers at the Bell (himself and Mattie included) could perhaps heal and achieve a "clean bill of health" for themselves.

Note how George included himself as one of the laborers and described the laborers as "almost one of the family." Such a viewpoint was not unusual in the mentality of the owner-operators. Rarely did an owner-operator discuss the work of the ranch as belonging only to someone other than themselves or as being only their own accomplishment. For their part, the owner-operators believed themselves to be part and parcel of the workforce. Economic success maintained both the owner-operators' class position and worker identity, and that identity depended on reproducing a labor culture that celebrated time-honored hierarchies, cycles, and skills. Cow work served as a crucial unifying element for the larger group culture and provided important material for the sharing of cow talk. That cow talk would serve as the foundation for owner-operator power even as they sensed their power starting to wane.

In this chapter I investigated the contours and seasons of cow work on mid-century range cattle ranches and outlined how technology could change that work. Despite classed, gendered, and racialized tensions, and despite fairly common (however reluctant) incorporation of new, mechanized work methods, dominant ranch culture continued to value traditional cow work above all other labor in public discourse and visual culture. A fear of losing traditional cow work drove much of the decision making, rhetoric crafting, and myth constructing, and it allowed owner-operators to gloss over tensions in the workplace and insist that theirs was a gloried industry that was striving valiantly to maintain its traditional work culture as much as possible. The laborers discussed here, no matter their position in the hierarchy and no matter their job titles, created the bodies of cattle from ecological resources. The common experiences with the nonhuman world involved in cow work served as a unifying point around which ranchers rallied and shared cow talk. In the next chapter I turn to more specific areas of cow work—specifically, to the world of ranchers' ecological economy—to explore how the nonhuman world played a significant role in further creating cultural affinity within ranching circles.

CHAPTER 3

"I Am the Grass. Let Me Work."

The Ecological Economy of Range Cattle Ranchers

"With the good comes the bad," that's what they say
It's a truth that outweighs all the lies
And it's a fact that for every birth on some warm Spring day
Somewhere, all alone, something dies.

—Virginia Bennett, Arizona rancher, 1997

There's a mark across the malpais
Where alfalfa's sudden green
Is alive with whiteface cattle—
Finest herds you've ever seen!
Where the level watered acres
Show what love and labor mean.

—John Frohlicher, 7 Lazy T Ranch, Camp Verde, Arizona, 1946

On a cool spring day in Florence, Arizona, in 1946, several friends gathered around the dinner table of Mrs. Walter Meyer. No doubt everyone was enjoying a perfectly cooked steak when Meyer turned the conversation to a debate that was being had across the state about whether the U.S. Department of Agriculture should introduce biological controls to stop the unwanted spread of the prickly pear cactus. Prickly pear (*Opuntia* spp.) is a plant native to Arizona, but it had been introduced in places like Australia, where it had become a nuisance. In the 1920s the Australian government had undertaken the most effective attempt to eradicate the cacti by using a species of moth (*Cactoblastis cactorum*) to control the plant.[1] In a letter to Abbie Keith, executive secretary of the ACGA, Meyer explained the discussion among their neighbors the Haydons and "Mrs. Lottie Haydon's cowboy, Jesus Encinas." Walter, Mrs. Meyer's husband, weighed in by saying that he thought prickly pear and cholla were two of the "best aids to erosion control" ranchers had. Jesus Encinas agreed and, in the voice of wise experience, explained, "There would be many an old cow die in this country in dry years if we didn't have the Prickly Pear and Cholla."[2] The small group was generally in agreement and seemed in step with ranchers across the state. Keith devoted sections in three issues of the *Cattlelog* to the biological control conversation, because she had fielded so much interest in the topic from ranchers all over the state. Seven out of ten came out against the importation of such a bug. As one rancher from Skull Valley explained, he had seen "them" try the "bugs down in Texas and they still have both the cactus and the bugs. We better let well enough alone."[3]

In general, the letters reveal an astute understanding of the ecology of the desert plant's role on the ranchers' operations. Not only is prickly pear decent feed for cattle (especially the fruit); it also provides shelter for forage grasses and protects against erosion. Its unique adaptation to the Sonoran Desert means that it is one of the few plants that can consistently withstand the droughts that ravage the bioregion every few years. For those around the Meyers's table, who were experiencing another drought cycle in 1946, the cactus provided "many an old cow" with feed in locales where other feed (especially grass) was not available.[4] The Meyers's dinner debate and its resulting appearance in the pages of the *Arizona Cattlelog* help to introduce us to the next element of cow talk that was so prevalent in ranchers' lives in the postwar decades. Chapter 1 introduced a plethora of strangers threatening the time-honored craft of ranching, and chapter 2 covered the role technology played in both easing and threatening ranchers' sense of their own power through labor. In both instances, modernity provided context and purpose for ranchers' sharing of stories, ideas, and frustrations. In this chapter and in chapter 4, I will investigate the role the nonhuman world played in ranchers' lives and explore how plants, animals, and microbes continuously engaged ranchers' time and consideration. When ranchers were finished with the cow work we learned about in the last chapter, they turned toward members of their own ranches and ranchers far away to consider strategies and approaches for combatting a chaotic but sometimes benevolent ecology.

The debate around the Meyers's dinner table is notable for few reasons. First, unlike other studies that insist the federal government occupied ranchers' every waking worry, the government is relatively absent in the conversation other than as the entity proposing to radically alter the ecology of the region by importing biological control agents to stop the spread of a native plant. Thus, the debate around the table is less about ranchers' relationship with the government and more about their relationships with the nonhuman ecology of their ranches. Second, the debate also shows that ranchers were thoughtful about the ecosystems on which cow work depended. Third, the debate is also an important example of ranchers' relationships with one another. Evident in the story are years of experienced cow work (which Jesus Encinas brought) and differing power relationships on the ranch itself (evident among Mrs. Meyers, her husband, and the hired cowboys). Last, and most importantly, the debate is a prime example of ranchers' cow talk. Of course, cow talk at the dinner table was important and noteworthy, but it was most powerful when it transcended the dinner table and made its way to the larger community of ranchers. Thus, the decision to write to the *Cattlelog* about the debate made the debate itself even more significant than if it would have ended with Mrs. Meyers's dessert. As they attempted to grow the healthiest cattle they could under difficult circumstances, ranchers realized they were part of a much bigger world. Of course, that world included the threats to their ways of life (see chapter 1) and the difficult decisions ranchers faced about technological approaches to cattle raising (see chapter 2). But by the 1940s that bigger world also included the broader community of ranchers. And that collectivity could bring solace, offer allyship, and inspire ideology.

The wider world also encompassed thousands of species that made up the ecology of the bioregion. Range ranchers—male and female owner-operators and hired hands—were intimately connected to an ecology that encompassed beetles, moths, cacti, cows, grass, rain, and soil. And ranchers needed to understand the interworking of these components if they were to be successful at their all-important cow work. The way that they sought that understanding was largely through cow talk.

From the archives, it appears that, perhaps more than any other single topic, ranchers were bound together through their knowledge of and their work with the nonhuman environments of the ranch. One decision by a far-off agency head to introduce an insect to eat away at *opuntia* could mean less fodder for cattle and more trouble for the ranchers. Just as ranchers came to distrust the presence of outsiders in range country and struggled with imperatives to mechanize, they also sought to control the ecology of their ranches. But this control, they well knew, had its limits.

Historian Linda Nash has suggested that environmental historians need to think more creatively and analytically about human beings as organisms dependent on their environment. As she and historian Tim Ingold have both argued, historians should move away from the idea that when humans engage in ecological activities, they confront only the external world in a removed way. Instead, these historians argue, it is "through practical engagement with the world, not disembodied contemplation" that humans most readily come to know and alter their biophysical contexts. This reconceptualization of humans' ecological relations can help us understand, in particular, one of the most important elements that drew range cattle ranchers together both culturally and politically in the immediate postwar decades. Ranchers were not operating *outside* of nonhuman nature—looking only to dominate or commune with it—rather they were working *within* it, in a variety of ways, to fatten their cattle, pad their pocketbooks, and ensure their cultural longevity.[5]

Ranchers and their employees, like Jesus Encinas, did not just contemplate the ecology of their worlds over juicy steaks; their opinions were formed through their work, which required them to have direct, physical involvement with the nonhuman world. After long days of hard labor and years of precarious living, ranchers came to inscribe cultural meaning onto those material and intellectual experiences. The prickly pear, as much as any federal bureaucrat, dictated what ranchers believed they knew and valued about their ranches. The defensiveness from the 1970s onward, which may seem overwrought to outsiders, was informed by the postwar environment—an environment that was changing not just politically and culturally but also ecologically.

In this chapter, I argue that ecological demands and constraints vied for equal importance with economic and political imperatives in ranchers' cow talk. This chapter and the next build on chapter 2 as they focus more specifically on the details of cow work in the wider environs of the ranch. In short, the cows had context—both human and not—and ranchers' work beyond what they did with the cows should be considered ecological labor that required ranchers to maintain a balance between environmental stability and economic production. At the end of the day, work with cows meant doing more than tending to the cow itself, and this reality built for ranchers a kind of ecoculture that they took great pride in. While ranchers certainly sought to alter ranch ecologies to fit economic expectations for growth, they also trusted nature in interesting ways. What is often overlooked in assessing ranchers of the twentieth century (and maybe even today) is their unique cultural identity as *both* economic and ecological actors.

Let us return to that conversation at the Meyers's dinner table. There, on that lovely day in March, the neighbors agreed that while it might be preferable to have more space for grass to grow, the native prickly pear played a pivotal role in ranch ecology, so its health and continuing presence had to be taken into consideration. Managing that resource carefully could mean the difference between a cow living or dying. In the collective understanding of the ranching community, every cow that thrived meant a ranch family lived a little better and ranch culture persisted a little longer. Sound economics, therefore, required the effective management of resources that naturally required ranchers' labor in the ecological systems of the range in ways that were not solely destructive.

This investigation of the ecological labor of ranchers contributes to the growing interest of historians in combining labor and environment. Most labor histories are interested in the formation of unions or the relationships between owners and workers, often in industrial settings to the exclusion of any investigation of the raw resources on which the labor is based. Richard White was perhaps the first to ask historians to take seriously the connections between the environment and labor in his seminal article "Are You an Environmentalist or Do You Work for a Living?"[6] White urged labor historians to not ignore the nonhuman world of work and urged environmental historians to not demonize or exclude those whose work affected the environments these historians were so keen on chronicling. Gunther Peck has similarly argued that there is a geography of labor in the U.S. West that links nature and humanity in endless concert and struggle.[7] Thomas Rogers has suggested in his agroenvironmental history of the sugarcane industry in Brazil that it was the sugarcane itself that created the human cultures that surrounded it.[8] In this same vein, Linda Nash has argued that if we listen carefully to the narratives that workers share, we may hear something that transcends the stories environmental historians tend to tell about labor's alienating effects on the nonhuman world.[9] Nash contends that environmental history tends to see humans as separate from the nonhuman, and she encourages us to rethink that false dichotomy. Indeed, the ranchers in this study seem to incorporate both Rogers's and Nash's perspectives. Ranchers saw themselves as embedded physically in the nonhuman world of the ranch. They experienced both control and desperate helplessness in that embeddedness. Their interactions with a variety of environmental actors such as grass, microbes, and even rain drove the identity and purpose of this rural culture. To suggest that ranchers were insensitive to the effects on the land of their labor is inaccurate.

By the postwar years (and realistically long before), domesticated bovines had become part of the natural order of range country. The cow has been in the American Southwest since the arrival of the Spanish as early as the 1680s. Domesticated ungulates consume grass, drink water, trample soil, and discharge feces, and in doing so they affect the microenvironments in which they live. This eating and processing of grass to flesh was all ranchers wanted cattle to do. But ensuring that cattle fulfilled those simple expectations could be a complicated biological task indeed, especially from the late 1940s to the 1960s. In particular, ranchers had to balance ecological reality with their dreams of utopian grasslands—a process clearly visible in the debate over controlling the prickly pear. In many circles today, ranchers are considered to be a force bent on environmental destruction. And indeed, cows are tough on the land. But this study reveals that the ways in which ranchers perceived their work led them to see their cows as part of the larger ecology, not as unnatural trespassers (unlike their opinions concerning many categories of human beings). Despite some of the bravado of bravery and dominance, ranchers recognized their own dependency on the biomes of their ranges.[10] The efforts by owner-operators trying to figure out how to best grow cows were, literally, grounded—in the soil and in the plants that grew from that soil. Of course, grass was the best-suited plant for growing healthy cattle, but ranchers knew an Edenic pasture rarely existed in the mountain West; to grapple with less-than-ideal range conditions required them to communicate with one another. The use of cow talk regarding grazing and range management facilitated ranchers' sense of themselves ecologically as well as their belief in their unique (and perhaps dying) culture.

To protect and promulgate their dominant culture, ranchers knew that they had to manage both their ranges and their public image—and they did both via cow talk. Take, for example, Con Warren's address to the members of the MSGA in 1951. Warren, the son of the cattle baron Conrad Kohrs, stepped up to the microphone to speak to ranchers from all over the state as they gathered in convention. Warren explained to his fellow ranchers what they all knew: "Grass is [our] principal crop. Without it all life would disappear from the face of the earth. Grass stabilizes our agricultural economy by using cattle and sheep to harvest it."[11] When Warren referred to "all life," he was perhaps overstating his case a bit, but in speaking to a ranch audience, he knew that the lives of their nonhuman bovines and their own way of life as ranchers would disappear without grass. Warren went on to explain that cultivation of grass was crucial to cattle ranching and to stabilizing cattle culture in the long run, and those in the audience would have known much about the various species of grass as well as the attempts to alter range spaces to protect their culture and their businesses.

The grasses ranchers knew varied depending on the bioregion, and the biodiversity and variations among the five states considered here are too vast to describe in any specific detail. Still, an overview about grassland ecology and how ranchers understood that ecology in the postwar years is essential for understanding the ecology in which ranchers in the mountain West lived and worked.

Grass occupies a venerated position in ranch culture because of its relationship with cattle. Grass is only digestible by certain herbivores. Human beings, for example, have difficulty digesting grass, and thus grass appeared to ranchers to be destined for grazing. The hundreds of species of grasses in the mountain West do not just transform cattle's bodies into tenderloins of beef for human consumption. Grasses are also crucial to local ecosystems because they stabilize soil through dense root systems and help defend topsoil against erosion. Part of the reason for the terrible erosion experienced in the Great Plains during the 1930s was because wheat farmers had plowed up and destroyed the web of native grass roots, loosening the topsoil. When the climate dried and the winds arrived, the soil blew away.

Like all plants, grass can create its own food using minerals, water, and sunlight. Across the mountain West, grasslands made up of annuals and perennials vary depending on rainfall, elevation, and soil quality. In the higher elevations, species of grasses change with every foot of rise. They vary depending on whether a slope is north-facing or south-facing and from season to season. No matter where they are located, however, annual and perennial grasses become more or less palatable to cattle depending on the time of year. In years of abnormal precipitation, the palatability and availability of grass varies radically and unpredictably. But at all times, grass is crucial for cattle growth.

The Great Plains comprises four grassland types. The central and southern parts of the region are dominated by four species of grass: big bluestem (*Andropogon gerardi*), little bluestem (*Schizachyrium scoparium*), red switchgrass (*Panicum virgatum*), and Indiangrass (*Sorghastrum nutans*). In the northern portions of the region the dominant grass is porcupine grass (*Hesperostipa spartea*). Central and western Arizona are characterized by grasses prominent in the Sonoran Desert scrublands and semidesert grassland biomes. These include mostly three-awns (*Aristida*) and side-oats grama (*Bouteloua*) in the Sonoran Desert scrub, various species of lovegrass (*Eragrostis*), and big galleta (*Hilaria rigida*) for the semidesert grasslands.[12]

Range ranchers depended heavily on these range grasses because they believed, as Wyoming rancher E. G. Hayward explained in 1951, that "ordinarily no weight" was gained by cattle during the feeding months of winter (when range forage was either lessened in the Southwest or absent altogether in the colder climes). Hayward was contributing his thoughts about grass to *Cow Country* just as Con Warren prepared his address to the MSGA. Hayward and Warren would have agreed that "the real growth of meat producing animals is made during the months when grazing is to be had."[13] Having palatable feed for their cattle was the foremost priority for ranchers in their ecological economy, and, ideally, that feed would come in the form of range grass supplemented by other kinds of feed (including cottonseed cake and alfalfa hay). As mentioned above, range grasses depend on decent soil, water, and adequate seeding, and all of those could exist naturally without human labor or involvement. But when time was of the essence, when a rancher was depending on the quick and adequate growth of a cow in order to ensure her or his economic well-being, the rancher hoped to hurry along the process of growth wherever and however possible.

Because of this temporal pressure, ranchers attempted to intervene in the growth of grass. By the postwar years ranchers were no longer, in their own minds, simply the guardians of the grasslands, passively watching the grass grow and then protecting it (by using it); rather, by the 1940s and 1950s ranchers were increasingly coming to see themselves as the developers of the grass, stimulating it with their well-informed, technoscientific management. Just as ranchers chose to sometimes mechanize operations on their ranches, they also considered a variety of scientific strategies for prodding along the vitality of the grasslands. Poor growth, invasive plants that hurt cattle or crowded out favorable species, and wildfires were among some of the threats that could be mitigated with new scientific approaches, and ranchers in the postwar decades often pondered the wisdom and necessity of engaging such approaches.

Consider the geography of the range from the viewpoint of a rancher. Whereas a modern visitor to range country may see wide-open, sweeping vistas worth preserving for their aesthetic value or a desolate nothingness just waiting to be developed into something better, stock growers who looked at these same areas saw not empty space but rather crowded ecological communities that could make or break their business. As ranchers gazed across the postwar grasslands—whether in mountainous Montana, arid Arizona, or short-grassed Colorado—they saw vast possibilities but even more threats. Take, for example, a pair of photographs published in Wyoming's *Cow Country* in 1956 (figure 11). The photographs' accompanying captions read "Sagebrush control with burning" and "Mechanical removal of Sagebrush," which indicated a pasture where grass had been crowded out by encroaching sagebrush.[14]

Unlike the prickly pear (which, it is important to note, was not *ideal* cattle fodder but was palatable in small amounts), cattle cannot consume sagebrush, and when ranchers viewed landscapes full of the plant, they saw not fragrant, silvery-green bushes where rabbits might nibble, but rather competitors for grassland and rivals against their cows. *Cow Country* explained to inquiring ranchers that sagebrush could be eradicated in any number of ways, including bulldozing and burning. In the photos shown in figure 11, ranchers saw not sagebrush that had been "destroyed" (with

Figure 11. Sagebrush removal by burning (left) and sagebrush removal by machine. *Cow Country*, February 1956, 14. WSGA Papers, American Heritage Center, UW.

all of the negative connotations of such a verb), but rather a "noxious" shrub that had been "controlled" through the ingenious and hard ecological and industrial labor of the rancher. The absence of sagebrush, ranchers believed, allowed more grass forage to grow. More grass meant bigger cows. Bigger cows meant more money. More money meant more cows, and more cows meant more longevity for a culture they loved.

Sagebrush was not the only enemy plant under attack by grass-oriented ranchers. In the Southwest, all species of junipers (including alligator juniper, one-seed juniper, and Utah juniper) faced attempted eradication at the hands of ranchers. Ranchers in the postwar years (and even earlier, but with increased ferocity post–World War II) used available technological means to import hearty grasses and eradicate flowering plants as well as unwanted shrubs and trees, and they did so with the support of the federal and state government entities in charge of "protecting" the range. In 1952 W. M. Beveridge, the supervisor of the Prescott National Forest, celebrated the collaboration of ranchers and the U.S. Forest Service in ridding the watershed of shrubby trees. He explained that the eradication efforts were grounded in sound research, and his report to the cattle growers shows how important the partnership between ranchers and the federal government could be in refashioning an entire ecosystem to benefit cows.[15] Beveridge wrote, "It was indeed fortunate that a number of nearby ranchers had gained experience in practical methods [of eradicating Juniper] that enabled us to start off on a sound and efficient basis." In several instances ranchers eradicated the species on their public land allotment "at their own expense" during the off season, when their efforts would not sacrifice essential cow work. Beveridge and area ranchers believed that their mutual efforts resulted in the growth of more grass and an improved watershed. There was no mention of how the profound alterations to the habitat affected native, noncow life.[16]

That omission indicates where the ecological labor of ranchers may seem anything but ecologically friendly. If you have ever wandered in a mountain field full of larkspur, you know how beautiful it is and how much the pollinators—bees, butterflies, and hummingbirds especially—love it. You may have leaned in close to take a photograph of the vibrant and unique flower. Elk, deer, and other native fauna enjoy foraging the plant, and ranchers knew all this based on their own observations. But despite knowing the ecological benefits of plants such as larkspur, ranchers wanted it gone. Larkspur (*Delphinium* spp.) tastes delicious to cattle, and they will not hesitate to eat the beautiful purplish-blue flowers, but they are highly toxic for cows. Within the flowers and pods, at various times of the growing season, lurks a toxic cocktail of several alkaloids; while elk, deer, and other native fauna can tolerate the plant, cattle experience neuromuscular problems that can lead to respiratory paralysis, bloat, and death. For obvious reasons, ranchers focused on destroying the species that threatened their livelihood and in protecting (and even creating) an environment that would nurture their cattle. To do this, they enlisted the help of the USDA and the Forest Service.[17] Where enemies lurked—in the leaves and woody stems of sagebrush, in the berries of a juniper, or in the toxins of a wildflower—ranchers saw an urgent need for their ecological labor to protect their cattle, cultivate grass, and control the ecological economy.

Harry Day, the owner-operator of the Lazy B Ranch in southern Arizona, went to great lengths to ensure the adequate growth of grass on his ranch, even if it meant applying intense labor to defeat an enemy plant. In chapter 2 I wrote of his self-identification as a laborer engaged in eradicating invasive plants from his water draws, but it is useful to return to him to think more deeply about the ramifications of his struggle with the mighty cocklebur. His letter informing Abbie Keith of his late summer fight against *Xanthium* illustrates well how the industrial blurred with the natural on a postwar mountain West ranch and how biodiversity was irrelevant if it meant harm to cattle and grass.[18] He explained: "A number of years ago these cockleburs started invading our best flood water draws.

They kept increasing, year after year until finally we had great thickets of them where they shade out and crowd out all the grass and I fear that if something is not done to control them, they will finally "take over" all of our best flood water draws."[19]

Cockleburs were inedible for cattle, and, worse yet, they were crowding out good grass needed to ensure the profitable weight gain for cattle feeding on the range. Day was at a loss about the invasion, but he understood well the amount of labor he and his cowboys would have to expend to help the edible grasses recover so that his cattle could feed more productively. Day wrote that "to get rid of this pest the seeds must germinate each year and then be killed before they make another seed crop."[20] Staying on top of such a task would not be simple or easy to accomplish. In fact, Day explained, he "had been told that the seed of *Xanthium* would stay in the ground for at least three years," making them difficult to find and even harder to eradicate. He gained that information from agricultural extension agents who, in these postwar decades, regularly offered workshops on ecology and on new technological approaches to range management. Day's letter to Keith indicated his profound understanding of the intersections between ecology and economy on his ranch. He continued, "I acquired a power sprayer that works on the power-take-off of the Jeep and we have been spraying the thickets with 24D spray, with very good results. Apparently we got almost 100% kill. Last year I hired a plane to spray them but I think we got a larger percent kill with the Jeep spray, *but it involved much more work and we used a great deal more 24D, which is quite expensive*" (emphasis mine).[21]

Day's explanation of the ecological labor he undertook to keep the grass growing and his cattle healthy provides a vivid description of how humans occupied a distinct niche in the ecological economy as they fought against a profusion of "noxious weeds" in the hope of saving the organisms of grass and cattle. Day's battle to eradicate this invasive "pest" relied heavily on industrial products introduced into domestic use following their development and use by the U.S. military in both world wars. The herbicide of choice for postwar ranchers was 2,4-D. Agriculturalists' (including cattle ranchers) reliance on chemicals to control plants, insects, and even predatory animals increased exponentially following World War II.[22]

The Day example shows not only the amount of ecological labor devoted to making good grazing land but also the lack of control ranchers experienced on an everyday basis. We can also see how ambiguous was Day's use of herbicides if we read the above passages carefully. He benefited from the relatively new science of ecology by understanding how the plant reproduced, and he believed he benefited from the use of 2,4-D, but only through one form of application (via jeep) and not through another (via plane). Even after expending the ranch's cash resources on 2,4-D, Day ultimately had to resort to manual labor to complete the job. Thus, ranchers' relationship with science and technology in their attempts to control their rangeland often was fraught with misgivings because technological improvements were not always reliable, required dependence on resources outside the ranch, and ultimately increased the cost of doing business. To help ease their misgivings, ranchers wrote letters and attended gatherings where they used cow talk to share information and ask for advice.

It would be a mistake to assume that the use of chemicals supplanted the necessity of ecological labor on the part of Day and his hired hands. Day explained that after loading the poison into the jeep, spraying it on the plants, and waiting for the plants to die, he and his hired hands had to remove the weeds manually.[23] The manual labor may not have been desirable, but Day suggests he and his cowboys had to do whatever was necessary in order to enable edible grass to grow.[24] Day, like many ranchers, had to grapple with the control of noxious weeds on their private lands, but they also had to worry about weeds on public lands. In 1952 the MSGA passed a resolution asking Congress to appropriate funds for the control of noxious weeds on public lands. Again, ranchers' ecological labor, and the problems encountered in the exercise of it, served as a unifying cultural element for ranchers that morphed into formal political demands.[25]

Day's labor with the cockleburs says a good deal regarding his assumptions about the purpose of the nonhuman world. What is more important about this anecdote for my purposes is how Day's ecological labor created opportunities for cow talk. Day did not just learn about cockleburs and the new technoscience that could aid him in expunging the plant from his ranch, he also sought to communicate with other ranchers about his experience. A year later Day wrote to Keith again, hoping to share information with New Mexico and Arizona ranchers. This time he was interested in the cloud-seeding efforts being undertaken by the federal government in the late 1940s and early 1950s. Day explained that he had been keeping rain records throughout the period and was interested to see that he "had measured above average rainfall" for the two years (1951–52) when the cloud-seeding program occurred in his region. Since then, he had been following the scientific monitoring of rainfall in the Southwest through the work of a Dr. Workman at the New Mexico School of Mines and suggested to Keith that fellow southwestern ranchers might find Workman's data both "informative and interesting." He suggested she try to get Workman to speak at "one of the Ariz. Cattle Growers' meetings." Day believed the issue of rainfall to be essential to the ecological economy of southwestern ranching because green grass "cannot stay that way long without more moisture," and it was "hard for a cow to raise much of a calf on dry grass." "A cow needs green feed," Day continued, and "to raise a good calf there is nothing else that will quite take the place of it."[26]

Day sought to alter the ecology of his ranch to benefit his economy. Through his labor, he also hoped to contribute to the broader ranch culture. In his written discourse Day aimed to share information with other members of the ACGA about his efforts toward re-creating the ecology of his ranch, just as he hoped to enter into community with other ranchers in case he too might benefit from their ecological experiences.

Because *Xanthium* is invasive, its successful occupation of the water draws on the Lazy B indicates that these spaces may have been overgrazed, thus opening the way for *Xanthium* to triumph. Day never suggested to Keith that the presence of *Xanthium* indicated overgrazing, however. Despite his silence on the concept of overgrazing, the problem was well known among ranchers by the 1950s. The increased emphasis of federal government agencies on range conservation (which began in earnest during the New Deal) affected how ranchers thought about and approached range management, but ranchers continued to rely on their own practical experience with ecological labor to guide their ranching decisions.

In 1954, for example, Douglas Cumming of Nogales, Arizona, wrote to Abbie Keith to suggest that the best strategy for guarding against overgrazing was to grow "native cattle"—cattle that had been "born and raised on your own ranch"—because "the native cattle stay fatter, calve earlier and don't pile up down in the flat places, overgrazing there while letting the rough country go to waste." He explained that through the practical experience with the ecology on his ranch, he had decided that Brahman cattle were better than Herefords, at least in the dry southwest. He wrote, "The feed is gone on the lower end of our outfit right now [due to drought], but there are Brahmas on it in good shape. . . . I'm still not ready to go all out for Brahmas . . . but by golly they are good range cattle."[27] For Cumming and other ranchers, the first goal was to avoid overgrazing of range grasses, but when that failed the next goal was to find a way to maintain cattle's bodily health on poor range.

To do so, they needed not only to engage in labor but to also apply ecological knowledge to that labor. Combining scientific concepts (such as overgrazing) with their own experiences, ranchers like Cumming attempted to create a variety of labor strategies to conserve the grasses on the range so that they could be used more productively by cattle. These same ranchers in turn used opportunities of collective knowledge sharing to perfect their range management strategies, as they did in 1957 in the Roosevelt National Forest in Colorado.

There, under the watchful eyes of ranchers and government officials, the results of a five-year grazing experiment proved "the value of moderate grazing." The experiment, conducted on both private and public land, showed that cattle who grazed moderately on the range gained more usable weight (meaning the amount of beef produced on the body of the cow) than when they grazed lightly. The ranchers and officials did not experiment with heavy grazing because all participants feared that heavy grazing "would result in damage to the range and low cattle gains." An article describing the trial appeared in the October 1957 issue of *Cattle Guard* ("Five-Year Demonstration Proves Value of Moderate Grazing"). This is, of course, important in and of itself as it indicates the cooperation of ranchers and the federal government (with ranchers benefiting immensely from government largesse). Important, too, are the pictures that accompanied the article, which show ranchers traveling to the range to experience the results of the experiment. The *Cattle Guard* was sure to include pictures from the day at Art Sloan's ranch when ranchers gathered "eagerly" to see which was the most economical stocking rate for the range. As the ranchers gathered around figures of poundage and gazed at the fattened cows, they engaged in cow talk—fusing ecological concerns with economic ones and finding commonality with each other and government range special-ists in the process.[28]

Government-facilitated knowledge-sharing propelled cow talk among ranchers in the above example as surely as did the *Cattle Guard*'s article. Both helped to create a collaborative ecological world for cattle growers. Ranchers fashioned their own collective culture, but government agen-cies—especially agricultural specialists employed by land grant institu-tions, the Agricultural Extension Service, the Soil Conservation Service, and public lands agencies (such as the Forest Service and the BLM/Graz-ing Service)—also promoted rancher solidarity. Funding for each of these agencies increased in the 1940s, 1950s, and 1960s, and ranchers benefited immensely from the tax-supported government research and development. The emerging postwar culture of range ranchers, a group of private entre-preneurs, owed a significant amount of its existence to public institutions.[29]

Across the mountain West federal agents attended, and at times orga-nized, meetings of ranchers to discuss and witness developments in the ecological economy. In 1952 ranchers were treated to a full field day in the Bighorn Mountains of Wyoming. Those who attended the event witnessed the results of various experiments conducted by personnel from the Forest Service, Wyoming Natural Resource Board, and University of Wyoming agricultural experiment station on grazing, sagebrush control, and grass seeding. Agronomists and experts in animal husbandry shared with ranch-ers their conclusions regarding their conservation efforts on two national forest locales. The two locales had undergone soil treatments and range-management methods that included "sagebrush bulldozed off, bulldozed and lightly disced . . . grasses seeded 15 pounds to the acre with a mixture of [the legumes] broadleaf trefoil, alsike clover, and sevelra alfalfa." In addition, the "scientists planted Russian wildrye grass, intermediate wheat-grass, *Primar* slender wheatgrass, *Manchar bromegrass,* and timothy." (Note that only one of these species was native to the Wyoming range: slender wheatgrass.)[30] Range scientists explained to the gathered ranchers that research proved that those pastures grazed "moderately" showed both the least amount of damage to forage and the best weight growth of the cattle.

Learning about ecological strategies for range management was not the only purpose of the field day. Ranchers also took time out from their edu-cation to admire the results of their own ecological labor and cow work.

They gazed upon one another's cattle and proudly showed off their own economic and ecological products—namely purebred and commercial Hereford cattle. The field trip itself brought participating ranchers together, but the demonstration did not end with the setting sun. For those ranchers who could not make the demonstration, the pages of the ranchers' collective publication, *Cow Country*, memorialized and celebrated both the experiment and the group solidarity it promoted long after the event had ended. Of course, the photos and accompanying text proclaimed to the rancher audience that ecological labor, in the form of range management, reaped real economic benefits for ranchers, but the article did not just convey messages economic and ecological. The text and photography also told the audience that ranchers who joined together to learn about the management of ranch ecology benefited in ways that transcended the experiment.[31] Those who attended strengthened the home ranch and the community at large. The cultural dialog shared among ranchers as they learned from one another's scientifically based knowledge and experientially based beliefs also allowed them to share in an identity as modern ranchers connected to new knowledge and new technology by the expertise of government officials, even amidst continual posturing as historic laborers working in a time-honored industry.

Note that picture number four in figure 12 shows ecological labor in action. The rancher, on the left, is accompanied by a University of Wyoming official, and they are, according to the caption, "examining the remains of sagebrush destroyed by burning at the Covey-Bagley-Dayton ranch near Cokeville."[32] As the stories, photos, and captions represent, ranchers had monthly, and in some cases weekly, opportunities to pick up their stock growers' association publications or attend local meetings to engage in a discourse with other ranchers and government experts on the topics of range reseeding, grass conservation, and effective range management. Government officials regularly submitted articles with titles like "It Pays to Graze Correctly" and "Range Condition Classes," written by Soil Conservation Service agents, and "Crested Wheatgrass Grazing Values," written by employees of the Division of Range Research in the USFS, to stock grower publications throughout the mountain West.[33]

Ranchers themselves also wrote articles throughout the 1940s and 1950s, sharing their ideas for and material experiences with range management.

Figure 12. A grazing demonstration in Wyoming. "Mountain Meadow Grazing Results Told at Field Day," *Cow Country*, October 1952, 32. WSGA Papers, American Heritage Center, UW.

Wilma Turley wrote to the *Arizona Cattlelog* in 1949 that she and her husband Fred had "increased the forage" on their ranch in northern Arizona "nearly 100 per cent" during their twenty years of ownership. She explained that when they acquired the ranch, their "first consideration was to increase the forage on the range," and so "by rotation, deferred grazing, moderate grazing, re-seeding and soil conservation practices" they achieved their goal.[34] Turley's letter, not surprisingly, sounds eerily similar to the conclusions reached in Wyoming regarding the best way to manage ecology in order to benefit economically.

In addition to the print culture produced by their voluntary associations, ranchers also used their ecological labor surrounding grazing, grass, and range productivity strategies to create in-person networks through meetings sponsored by state and local livestock associations as well as government agencies and other organizations like the American Society of Range Management. At these meetings ranchers themselves often served as the experts. In their talks they explained how they employed their own experiences and the suggestions of range scientists to try to bring their pastures into better productivity. In 1953 Burton B. Brewster, of the Quarter Circle U Ranch in the southeastern Montana, gave one such presentation at the sixth annual meeting of the American Society of Range Management in Albuquerque. The title of his talk is important. He called his address "My Personal Experiences in Ranching for Profit and Conservation," and in it Brewster explained to the hundreds of ranchers gathered that he had learned of the benefits of crested wheatgrass firsthand and believed that the "conservation practice that has been very successful for our ranch and in most of Montana is the seeding of abandoned dry land field or barren flats to crested wheatgrass. . . . Our fields of crested wheatgrass have produced many tons of hay that we carry over for use in emergencies."[35] The *Montana Stockgrower* reprinted Brewster's speech so that those ranchers who could not attend the meeting could still benefit from his ideas. Brewster's speech represents an example of ranchers coming together across the region to share and learn of strategies for promoting the health of grass to further their goal of growing fat, profitable cows—even if it meant using imported species of grass in a monocultural method that would most certainly have hurt the biodiversity of the ranch. Experience could outweigh science, and the experts on the ground were the voices most prominently featured at ranchers' gatherings and in rancher publications.

Despite his omission of a discussion about species other than cows, Brewster's talk echoed a common admission among ranchers: the range had been mismanaged at some point in the past to such an extent that the grass has been harmed. In addition to this important critique of historic grazing practices, ranchers never ceased to maintain a sense of optimism in the range's ability to be "rehabilitated." Whether through human manipulation or through natural processes (especially the arrival of rain), the range seemed always to bounce back. In 1954, amid a formidable drought, Harry Day reported to Abbie Keith that "two months ago our range was in the worst condition it has ever been in. It was completely grazed off and we did not have one green blade of grass. Now it is in the best condition it has been in for many years. . . . It is amazing what a little rain will do to our Southwest ranges and our native grasses are also amazing in their ability to come back so quickly after several years of drought."[36]

The natural hardiness of certain grass species coupled with constant threat of drought or hard winters led many ranchers to embrace and experiment with non-native grass species. By 1950, thanks to increasing technology, riding out long droughts meant something new for ranchers like J. D. Craighead in Colorado. Structural and technological changes in the West and in ranching existed to help Craighead weather postwar climatic variations, but this technology was the kind that required Craighead to increase his dependence on the governmental technocracy that had arisen in agriculture in the late nineteenth and early twentieth centuries. Craighead grew much-needed feed crops (especially alfalfa) on 127 acres of irrigated land. This irrigation did not exist before the 1930s and was a direct result of increased investment in reclamation that had occurred all over the mountain West in the first three decades of the twentieth century. The Newlands Reclamation Act of 1902 signaled the age of water conservation in the West, but it was the increased spending of the federal government on reclamation projects during the New Deal that provided ranchers a wet safety net.[37] When drought hit in the postwar years, there often was stored water nearby that ranchers and farmers could use not only to water their cattle but also to grow feed crops. With the increase in available irrigation and the rise in soil conservation science, ranchers increasingly sought either to grow feed crops (like alfalfa) or to reseed the range.

By 1950 Craighead himself had begun to experiment with range reseeding and had planted crested wheatgrass on some of his land. He had also planted a ten-acre irrigated field in Kentucky 31 fescue. The latter crop made Craighead the first in Colorado to plant Kentucky fescue. His fellow ranchers understood that his decision to plant a species that had not yet been used on Colorado ranges represented something of a risk. This willingness to assume risk was something that all ranchers in the postwar West had to consider. Moreover, it represented one instance among many in which ranchers had to rely on the bureaucratic technocracy of American agriculture for expertise and advice. The use of new technology could, depending on how it was approached, get a rancher branded as either pioneering or reckless.

While farmers and ranchers accepted modernization during the postwar years more readily than farmers had accepted "book farming" in the mid to late nineteenth century, ranchers did not accept technology unquestionably, and only those ranchers who maintained an informed skepticism and adopted technology selectively could be assured of environmental success. These "pioneering" ranchers won celebration throughout ranch publications. Part of the label of pioneer signified that Craighead had survived and, at times, prospered in the cattle business. In this situation, largely because Kentucky fescue grew so successfully on the shortgrass prairie, Craighead's assumption of risk was respected and lauded because it signaled his experience-based understanding of the range environment.[38] The dominant ranch culture celebrated a rancher's willingness to assume ecological risk when and if the risk-taking rancher incorporated modernization with common sense (which really implied deep environmental expertise), knowledge (which was almost always grounded in practice and historical experience), frugality, and success (at least in the short term).

The trouble was that ranchers never knew when their choices would backfire. New grasses brought new pests that native grasses had not evolved to handle. Some grasses, such as buffelgrass, would eventually promote fire in a fire-adverse biome, something ranchers did not necessarily consider when they imported it in the 1930s and '40s from northern Africa.[39] Perhaps this constant potential for an ecological backfire is what led many ranchers to conceive of their labor in defensive, warlike terms.

Insects that threatened feed—in particular grasshoppers—represented for ranchers the best example of a battle that had to be fought against nature.[40] In the postwar years agricultural officials from various government agencies deluged ranchers with instructions and suggestions about how best to control the "unwelcome little green visitors" with precise bait mixtures made up of modern insecticides like chlordane, toxaphene, and others.[41] Not only did extension agents' detailed instructions overwhelm some individual ranchers, the poisons also were ineffective if used in isolation. If one rancher dutifully sprayed wet bait at precisely the right time in the grasshoppers' life cycle but her or his neighbor did not, then a severe outbreak could still occur. Thus, controlling insect infestations took considerable coordinated effort that often fell to the ranchers who were leaders in the community or owned the largest ranches. In 1949 Lyman Brewster was unable to attend to MSGA business because, as he explained to Ralph Miracle, "I have been delayed considerably in starting the roundup [the gathering of cattle, not the herbicide] because of the time I have had to spend in organizing the grasshopper poisoning campaign."[42] Convincing ranchers that coordinated control would benefit them all took considerable work. Letters, phone calls, and outreach had to wrangle a group of rather individualist folks away from the cow work they likely found more important, pressing, or fun. But the ecology of the range eventually forced ranchers toward the expectation that they would need to come together, not only through the local and state association groups but also through the assistance of top-down eradication programs sponsored by the federal government to win the battle against enemy species like the hearty grasshopper. And they would communicate about all those efforts via cow talk.

In nearly every cow-talk discussion about the ecology of the range, ranchers cultivated a language of enemies and allies in their quest to promote strong growth of grass. They often failed at conquering the competitors of forgeable grasses. Sagebrush grew, juniper invaded, grasshoppers ate, but the archives make it abundantly clear that ranchers' successes and failures were not really what mattered in sharing cow talk. What was most important for creating common discourse, and thus a collective sense of power, was demonstrating to each other the consistent ecological labor ranchers expended in trying to make grass grow. This labor within an industrializing ecology meant trying to conquer anything that impeded growth—of grass, of cows, of collective power—whether sagebrush or juniper or grasshoppers.

Recall the discussion in the introduction of Jane Bennett's concept of vibrant matter as an instigator of identity formation and political efforts. Both organic and inorganic nonhuman matter often ruled the lives of ranchers in the postwar West and propelled them into deeper interdependence—on one another and on the outsiders they feared so deeply. Insects and ranchers' attempt to manage them provide some of the most tangible examples of ranchers' collective experiences with vibrant matter leading them to lobby for government help. In the late 1940s and early 1950s, for example, at the urging of stock growers, the state of Wyoming appointed a five-person board to study and implement the state's grasshopper control program. Four of the five board members appointed were in the cattle business and well understood that Wyoming (and all range states) suffered yearly infestations of grasshoppers. They also knew that some years were worse than others. The trick to controlling the insects was to guess correctly what kind of year it would be, and 1950 promised to be a humdinger. Because conditions in 1950 seemed ripe for a terrible "invasion" of the insects, the cattle rancher representatives on the "hopper board," especially vice chairman J. Elmer Brock, wanted to take no chances and so asked for the maximum amount they thought they could get for "Operation Hopper"—$1.5 million. They ended up receiving $750,000 for the 1950 fiscal year and, despite the large sum, were certain that "the available funds were not sufficient to carry on an all-out program against the threatened hopper invasion" of the state.[43] Note the bellicose language ranchers used to explain their goal of ridding Wyoming of the yearly "invasion." Here a nonhuman agent threatened to upend the peaceful livelihood of all those dependent on grass. The agent forced ranchers to gather organizationally to defeat it. No lone rancher could win the battle, let alone the war. In speaking for the larger ranch community, the chosen representatives gathered, engaged in cow talk, and then acted politically to demand government help in controlling a renegade ecology so that they could maintain their industry's economic and cultural viability. The ecological economy of range ranching never was predictable. Prices rose and fell, grasshoppers came and went, and the two were directly related.

Ranchers understood the risks involved in growing cattle on the range, and they were understandably defensive in their desire to minimize those risks in whatever ways were feasible. To grapple with the risks they encountered every day, ranchers took specific ecological actions, including replanting range grasses, choosing specific breeds of cattle, relying on the hardiness of native grasses, bulldozing junipers and sagebrush, spraying bait on grasshoppers and poisoning their eggs, and demanding community engagement and government help in managing all aspects of this ecological labor. Without exception, the ranchers employed ecological strategies to increase their likelihood of success in the always unpredictable ecological economy of ranching. In all cases, the goal was to make the grass and cattle and the ranching way of life grow. Ranchers then shared their knowledge and practices with one another, thus creating a common identity and group solidarity grounded in material experiences, application of scientific understandings, nervous defensiveness, and historic confidence.

While ranchers took the opportunity afforded by range management seminars and material experiences in the day-to-day business of range management to unite as a cultural group, they did not agree on all aspects of the management of grass. For example, not all ranchers accepted wholeheartedly or unproblematically the ideology of range conservation. Just as there were tensions in the social world of ranch production, so too were there disagreements and divisions over the best approaches to scientific methods of ecological management. At times ranchers promoted blatant strategies without taking into consideration the larger ecological systems in which they worked. At other times ranchers believed conservation was crucial to their long-term survival. In February 1954 Abbie Keith wrote a column lauding the efforts of scientists in the fields of atmospheric and cloud physics to stimulate "additional precipitation" in dry regions. This manipulation of nature by humans did not disturb Keith in the least. She summoned Baconian sentiments when she claimed, "If it were sinful to improve upon nature, then we have been a very wicked civilization because from the earliest history of the human race, we have been fighting nature's laws, improving on her ways to make the world a better and easier place to live." Keith also used highly utilitarian language when she encouraged the scientists to do all they could to make the rain come. She rallied their efforts by exclaiming, "Nothing is impossible. . . . We have been given all of nature's elements to use [by God]—they are our clay, our brain is the tool to chisel them into beneficial use."[44] Keith exhibited little understanding of and little concern for the nuances of the arid bioregion that she hoped to change completely with cloud seeding. She demonstrated no concern for any negative consequences the scientists' efforts may have had on native flora and fauna of the Sonoran and Mojave deserts. Instead, Keith seemed to embrace modernization (even as extreme modernization as seeding desert clouds to force rain) uncritically.

Keith was, however, an unusual voice among the ranch writers; many others expressed healthy skepticism about range management and conservation issues. Eulalia Bourne, for example, grappled with complicated conservation issues every day as she went about her ecological labor. Bourne often discussed the land in her autobiography, *Woman in Levi's,* and she sometimes relied on stereotypical ideas about gender to make excuses for her "weakness for growing things." She explained that "through the makeup of a woman runs a soft streak that makes her a sucker for green leaves and bright posies."[45] This "weakness," however, clearly opened space for Bourne to promote ecologically responsible use of the land. For example, in a chapter entitled "The Wide Open Spaces Ain't," Bourne explains that "ranchers are of two minds about wildlife. . . . Most of us enjoy the sight . . . of such harmless creatures as deer, rabbits and songbirds. . . . As for the carnivores, large and small, that seem to thrive in our far-off country, the general rule is to kill on sight. And this presents a problem . . . [because] I have never, as far as I know, lost an animal to coyotes. . . . [Therefore,] I have told the trappers they cannot set traps on any land that I control."[46] Bourne understood that ranchers generally were united in their intellectual and material responses to wildlife, but she herself did not share the prevailing opinion of the value of herbivores and the harm of carnivores.

In August 1956 Lillian Riggs, an Arizona native, member of the Cowbelles, and frequent contributor to *Arizona Cattlelog,* wrote to discuss the increasing destruction of range land by the encroachment of so-called useless brush like Utah and alligator junipers. In the letter she urges her readers to take political action and demand sounder range management. In particular, Riggs wanted ranchers to lobby the Forest Service for even more support for controlling public lands ranges.[47] Illustrating her preference for more natural approaches to brush management, she explains, "Within the past four years or so, I have had opportunity to see what fires can do in the way of providing water for the streams, without damage to the forests." She underscores the importance of conservation management as she explains that "one thing we should always stress—not a single one of us wants to see any real timber destroyed."[48] Riggs was not a lone voice in the wilderness. Association periodicals and rancher correspondence contain pages upon pages of varied and diverse commentary on the cattle industry's conflicting need to utilize and manage the natural world while maintaining senses of place rooted in nature. Through the publication of these ecological discussions, ranchers shared knowledge and concern for the conservation of species whose presence on the range seemed precarious and whose presence they valued even as they denied their own complicity in destroying the ecology upon which those species depended.

In the spring of 1952, just at the end of quail hunting season, Arizona rancher Ernie Richards decided to write a story that was a defensive rebuttal to an article written in the February 1952 issue of *Arizona Wildlife Sportsman*. The article detailed the "vanishing grasslands" of Arizona. Apparently, James Cary, the sportsman penning the critique, thought that land fowl like quail seemed less prevalent. Richards took affront at the idea that ranching had anything to do with the diminishing ecosystems. He used anecdotal evidence to defend ranching's role in environmental protection, hinting that it was the increasing number of hunters on the range who were indiscriminately killing the birds. Richards explains that one rancher near Prescott "saw 1200 quail strung on wire which one bunch of hunters [presumably from Phoenix] had killed in one week end." Richards relied on the historic narrative so often deployed in rancher defensiveness to situate the whole problem squarely in the postwar urbanizing and industrializing West. He claimed: "We who knew the country before the days of smooth roads and fast cars know that all the quail didn't starve to death because of over-grazed ranges." He titled his piece "Arizona's Vanishing Cowboys."[49] In this one example, ranchers' increasing disdain for sportsmen and outsider incursions on range spaces meets their insistence that their ecological labor was not destructive but human population growth was. And that disdain was registered in cow talk broadcast to the wider ranching community.

As these stories show, beyond the central purpose of growing grass and cows, a variety of experiences and opinions shaped notions about how best to do that. Some thought conservation was increasingly overemphasized. Some thought it was essential for the perpetuation of the ranching way of life. Many ranchers disagreed with partnering with the federal government, but many more benefited from the government's expertise and subsidization. They argued and shared within the pages of their association publications about how best to handle the threats to grass and cows: junipers (bulldoze or burn?), sagebrush (bulldoze or ignore?), and larkspur (poison or avoid?). They debated about grass species best suited for their situations and questioned each other's decisions to practice certain kinds of grazing rotations. They hosted demonstrations, dinners, and meetings and wrote page upon page of letters to each other, to their association leaders, and to their government representatives. We can only imagine the hours spent on the phone (for those who had them) engaging in similar conversations.

Whether they were in agreement or whether they were in debate, ranchers talked with one another about their shared ecological and material worlds. And as they engaged in this cow talk, they were hard at work—protecting their homes and their ecoculture, which at any given moment might be attacked by enemies such as urban hunters, grasshoppers, or cockleburs. This hard work was grounded in economic and ecological priorities, and it provided ranchers with the opportunity to share more than information. It enabled them to overcome their diversity and unite in a shared cultural and political identity as "guardians of the grasslands."

Grass was surely the foundation of the business, and in much of the ranchers' cow talk grass appeared as savior and ally. Many things, from drought to grasshoppers, threatened this all-mighty resource. But grass was not the only thing required to grow healthy cows. Cattle themselves had to be nurtured and cared for if they were to achieve healthy lives from birth to slaughter. And those cows existed in a world populated with disease and bugs. The dangers of hunters accidentally mistaking a cow for a deer or the increasing competition for space on Forest Service lands and access to grass were almost nothing compared to the constant menace of the endless insects and microbes that invaded bovine bodies and promised to destroy not just the cow but the cattle community writ large. I turn to these small but mighty hazards and ranchers' attempts to control them scientifically and politically in chapter 4.

CHAPTER 4

Protecting the Herd

Cows' Bodies and the Body Politic

> After we have discovered the place and consequences of conflict
> in nature, we have still to discover its place and working in human
> need and thought. What is its office, its function, its possibility
> or use? In general, the answer is simple. Conflict is the gadfly of
> thought.
>
> —John Dewey, 1922

Bugs were everywhere. They were in beds, in fur, in intestines, in ears and
eyes and mouths. They lived in barns and saddle blankets. They lurked in
water troughs, feed buckets, and even on blades of grass. Ranching families were intimately acquainted with the insect world and disliked almost
everything about it. But perhaps they should not have rushed to judge-
ment. The small, often invisible, organisms bound ranchers together as
tightly as did bountiful grass or troubling sagebrush, and while there could
be disagreement about the best approaches to range management or to
the creation of new ecologies on the ranch, there was little disagreement
about the importance of saving cows from the most dangerous parts of the
ecosystem: diseases and pests.

The potential damage done by microbes and insects, which used cattle's bodies for their own survival, drove cattle growers together as perhaps nothing else could. During the immediate postwar decades, nearly
every rancher sought control of the tiny creatures and reached out to one
another to learn methods to ensure that control. While ranchers hoped for
total domination, they were often disappointed: time and again the bugs

won, and the control ranchers sought was repeatedly messy and incomplete. These partial successes and the persistence of the insect world to propagate itself required ranchers to constantly learn and adapt to the bugs as well as to the technologies invented to destroy them. To protect their herds from death and illness, ranchers had to engage both intellectually and physically, combining their understanding of pest biology with the technological tactics to exterminate them.

Recall Harry Day and his cockleburs. Day had explained to Abbie Keith that *Xanthium* was so obnoxious that it was "a pest" he classed "along with screw worms and pink eye."[1] Day's letter illustrates ranchers' obsessions regarding the promotion of health in their cattle, in this case range management as well as the avoidance of disease. In these years, therefore, it was not enough for ranchers to focus only on curated forage for their bovine charges. They also had to grasp the intricacies of modern pest control in order to grow the healthiest and fattest bovine bodies that post–World War II technoscience could produce. These efforts resulted in the creation of a body politic of ranchers that was the most powerful it had ever been.

Cattle's bodies are excellent hosts for a number of insect infestations and microbial infections—among the most serious in the United States during the time we are examining were blackleg, anthrax, brucellosis (or Bang's Disease), foot-and-mouth disease (FMD), leptospirosis, and bovine tuberculosis. Less serious infections numbered in the hundreds. Screwworms, pinkeye, cattle grubs, and scabies were among the more common. Ranchers' obsessions with these biological enemies peppered cow talk throughout the decades under study. Their frustration with laboring under the whims of this part of the ecological order was apparent in nearly everything they penned. Their sense of helplessness was compounded by the fact that the wrong pest infestation at the wrong time could spell economic ruin. Like the cockleburs on Day's ranch, insects, viruses, and bacteria refused to go away no matter how much effort ranchers put toward their eradication. The existence of bugs and microbes in and around their cattle's bodies, however, encompassed one of the most important aspects of ranchers' ecological labor and, like range management, helped herd ranchers ever more tightly into their associations where they generated a shared language of victimhood and hope.

One of the best examples of a pest that inspired such cow talk and result-ing cultural unity was the ever-present cattle grub. Cattle grubs are the lar-vae of the heel fly, which infect cattle when they deposit eggs on the body of a cow. The flies usually deposit the eggs near the heel of the cow; once hatched, the larvae migrate to the gullet, where they munch on the cow's feed and then move into the back of the cow, where they bore air holes in the hide and grow for six to eight weeks before exiting the cow to pupate. The larval and adult stages can damage cattle in a number of ways. Most importantly for ranchers is the loss of weight that results from the wild efforts of the animals trying to escape from the adult flies. (This is known as gadding.) The less a cow weighs at sale time, the less money the rancher makes off that animal. Ranchers fear further damage from cattle running into fences and other objects, causing property damage, injury, and some-times death. When the larvae bore their air holes on the animal's back, they produce running sores that can sometimes result in secondary infection. The holes in the skin also lower the value of the hide on the leather market.[2]

The grubs affected not only cattle's bodies but also the bottom line of the ranch business, and so the effort to eradicate insects like the grubs absorbed much of ranchers' material labor and cultural concern. Jane Ben-nett and other ecophilosophers have suggested that human agency is and has always been an assemblage of vital materials acting on one another (sometimes in concert and sometimes not). Ranchers act in powerful ways at the provocation of bugs and microbes. But bugs and ranchers were not lone members of the assemblage in the postwar decades, and ranchers sought to battle bugs and disease with help from others in the assemblage—county extension agents, pest-control technologies, techno-scientific experts, veterinarians and, of course, one another. In this chap-ter, I explore how the threat of dis-ease not only dominated ranchers' material experiences within the ecological economy; it also served to unite them via cow talk centered around a common cause of eradication.[3]

So, to return to cattle grubs—in 1951 the *Montana Stockgrower* published an article by J. P. Corkins, an assistant entomologist for the State of Montana. The article in effect lectured ranchers on the best way to spray for cattle grubs. To save their cattle, Corkins admonished ranchers to "go in and see your county agent. . . . He can undoubtedly give you some very good ideas. . . . While you are in to see your county agent, pick up a copy of the Circular No. 222 . . . [and] read this . . . very carefully before going ahead and if you follow the instructions to the letter, you can control cattle grubs." Claiming to base his expertise on "five years of practical experience in Montana," Corkins explained that it was "plainly possible" to control cattle grubs, but that Montana ranchers were using "ineffective" methods. While Corkins acknowledged that "effective spraying . . . for cattle grub control is a laborious task at best," he promised that if cattle ranchers applied his expert advice, success was likely.[4] That expert advice coming from a relative outsider may have made some ranchers bristle, as we witnessed in chapter 1. But when it came to bugs and disease, ranchers had to honor some outside expertise. Conquering their insect and microbial enemies was necessary for ranchers to remain economically solvent and culturally relevant, and they had to rely on technoscience to do it.

Despite its power to help ranchers conquer bugs, technoscience could not replace the day-to-day cow work required for keeping cattle pest- and disease-free. If anything, the application of technoscience involved even more diligent watch over cows' bodies; in the case of many infestations, like grubs, timing was everything. The key to ridding a cow of grubs was to treat the grubs at the moment when they were "about one inch long, one-third inch thick and a dark brownish-gray color."[5] Once the grubs were spotted, a rancher had to act quickly. By the 1950s experts like Corkins believed spraying grubs with pesticides was the best method of eradicating them. Unlike some synthetic pesticides, the accepted spray mixture for grubs was an organic compound derived from rotenone-bearing plants. Veterinarians advised ranchers to mix rotenone powder with water and common laundry detergent to achieve the most effective treatment.[6] After spraying the cattle, ranchers had to massage the backs of the cattle "with a dull garden hoe to make sure that all of the scabs [over the tops of the grubs] are removed."[7] The article explains in great detail the kind of sprayer the rancher needed to use, the spray mixture that was best, and the exact time of the year that spraying should occur (which depended on the biological cycle of grubs themselves). This strategy, like most disease prevention and eradication efforts, required extensive rancher contact with the many actants in the assemblage, including not only the grubs and the cattle but also the pesticides, the sprayers, and the veterinary experts.

Ranchers did not simply read articles like Corkins's and set about work on their ranches in isolation. Instead, they came together to share information about the relative successfulness of the strategies offered to them. In 1948, for example, John Greer invited ranchers from across Arizona to attend a spraying demonstration on his ranch.[8] After the demonstration, the ranchers engaged in formal ACGA business about how to contain a myriad of threats, including microbes and insects. The day at the Greer ranch afforded ranchers a chance to think about the material vitality of the bugs themselves while also allowing space for ranchers to engage in cow talk about solutions to those pesky pests.

It might seem strange to us that tiny larvae helped to create a shared cultural identity among, and unified political response from, a group of human beings as powerful as range ranchers, but that is just what the bugs did. In creating conditions that forced ranchers to gather physically and intellectually, the bugs became agents that prodded actions and reactions from ranchers within the assemblage of actors that grew around pest control. Bennett's thinking can help us even more here. She argues that "humanity and nonhumanity have always performed an intricate dance with one another."[9] In this case, ranchers' dance with the tiny bugs became a flashpoint for cow talk.

The Greer ranch gathering demonstrates that while ranchers read about solutions to their pest problems in their association publications, they also met in person to share in cow talk about the complexity of the ecological knowledge required to get pest control right. The threatening materiality of insects and disease in an ecology that already often seemed to be obstinate and uncooperative forced a variety of attempts at control—none of which were simple and all of which required an understanding of new and seemingly ever-changing technologies. Ranchers sought this understanding by engaging in cow talk.

Indeed, when it came to bugs, ranchers were experiencing something Linda Nash has called "inescapable ecologies." They simply could not escape the threats, and ranchers reacted by creating a "culture of knowledge."[10] The sharing of information about appropriate control of this part of ranch ecology then manifested into a vital community that made things happen. The ranch community solicited and published articles from experts, sponsored technological demonstrations, and lobbied for government support, all the while working daily to understand the life cycle of grubs, watch their cattle for signs of ecological stress, and utilize plants to offset the potential damage caused by the heel flies. In all these moments of ecological labor and cow work, ranchers used cow talk to articulate the intimate connections between the health of the cattle and the longevity and power (or powerlessness) of their community.

Indeed, the timelessness of combatting pests served to link ranchers not just with their neighbors down the road but with ranchers in other states and even from different eras. Bugs had tormented cattle in the mountain West from the moment bovines arrived in the region. Unlike their nineteenth-century predecessors, who had battled infestations without the use of chemical warfare, ranchers in the mid-twentieth century could hope to rid their cattle of unwanted microbial and insect bodies if they could just master the use of modern technologies of control. Although some mechanized technology made ranchers wary, the use of veterinary technologies, like rotenone, was lauded by almost everyone as the best way to save not just the cows' bodies but the ranchers' body politic as well. Both the microbes and the solutions to them served as vibrant matter that mobilized ranchers into a cultural community and inspired them to take political action. Some of the most effective action was ranchers' political advocacy for governmental help in controlling and preventing infestations.

Foot-and-mouth disease is perhaps one of the best examples of the politicization that resulted from microbial crises. FMD had been known in the U.S. borderlands for at least forty years by the time the 1946 outbreak in Mexico occurred. Word of the disease's emergence spread rapidly and caused most livestock growers in the United States great concern. The disease, while fatal in only 2 percent of cattle, is highly contagious and attacks the soft tissues in cows' mouths, hooves, teats, and udders. Infected cattle tend to stop eating and very often become lame and cannot move to food and water. The disease concerns cattle growers because of its effects on the healthy growth of their bovine charges. The microbes that infect the cattle move quickly and are not easily detectable until the animal becomes visibly ill.

The outbreak of FMD in Mexico in the mid 1940s sent waves of fear throughout the cattle community in the mountain West. At highest risk were those cattle in border states like Arizona, New Mexico, Texas, and

California. States as far north as South Dakota and Montana, however, also feared the outbreak because of the fluid movement of cattle in the international and intranational marketplace. The issue of FMD was more serious than that of cattle grubs, scabies, or any number of other, more minor, cow ailments, and the cattle community used the presence of this ecological malady to create unity through association. They also circled their wagons and lobbied intensively for assistance from the federal government.[11]

The disease, discovered in Mexican cattle sometime in the spring of 1946, came from several Brazilian bulls that ranchers in Mexico had bought and then shipped north.[12] By December 1946 the disease appeared in a herd about 450 miles south of the United States, which set off flurries of panic among the American cattle ranching community. Ranchers immediately began to act in their economic self-interest against this ecological threat. In February 1947, for example, the NMCGA sent out five thousand letters to nonmembers that sought to play on ranchers' fear of an outbreak north of the border (which had yet to occur) in an effort to goad them into joining the association. The letter suggested that the association needed to convince politicians and government representatives to take immediate actions to effectively control FMD.[13]

To convince the government to help control the spread of the disease, the associations needed to appear strong, reasoned NMCGA president George Godfrey, and they could only look powerful when large numbers of dues-paying ranchers belonged to the group. Godfrey explained in the letter, "We must fight this threat with every method and means at our disposal. . . . It is impossible to overemphasize the seriousness of this matter. . . . To be effectively heard, however, our organization must be strong and fully representative."[14]

Using the collective power of the associations, ranchers took formal political steps to urge the federal and state governments to take any action necessary to save their industry from the hazards of the disease. An angry Abbie Keith responded to an unfriendly editorial in the *Nogales Herald*, explaining that in certain situations, even "individualistic" cattle ranchers needed to rely on government regulations. She explained that "control of infectious and contagious diseases, both in humans and livestock, has always been a function of government."[15] Sharing this belief, ranchers gathered to lobby their elected representatives, participate on committees appointed to grapple with the threat, and pass organizational resolutions urging government protection.[16]

The formal political work bore fruit when the U.S. Congress passed Public Law 8, Sec. 568, in February 1947. The law gave the secretary of agriculture full discretion to cooperate with Mexico in "carrying out operations or measures to eradicate, suppress, or control, or to prevent or retard, foot-and-mouth disease in Mexico where he [the secretary of agriculture] deems such action necessary to protect the livestock and related industries of the United States."[17] This vague and broad language heartened livestock producers, who hoped Secretary Clinton Anderson would not only help to eradicate the disease in Mexico (through slaughter of diseased animals and the vaccination of uninfected herds), but that he would also approve measures to keep cattle from Mexico out of the United States. To achieve the latter goal, ranchers promoted a restriction on importations and a quarantine of cattle from Mexico (meaning no cattle would be allowed above a certain line arbitrarily agreed on by both the U.S. and Mexican governments). They also advocated building a fence along the entire 1,800-mile Mexico-U.S. border. Some of the goals were met. Using over $2 million worth of appropriations (about $26 million in 2022), the United States sent machinery, vaccinations, and a team of veterinarians to scour the Mexican countryside to educate Mexican ranchers about *aftosa* (as the disease was known in Mexico), to vaccinate uninfected herds, and to slaughter those Mexican animals found infected with the disease. The Department of Agriculture also appointed representatives to sit on a five-person commission to oversee control efforts in Mexico, and both nations agreed on a quarantine zone out of which they allowed no cattle to be traded or sold. (The zone was far south in the Mexican states of Tlaxcala, Vera Cruz, Puebla, and the Federal District.) The completion of the fence along the entire border, to the dismay of many ranchers, never happened.[18]

Ranchers' demand for the fence is a wonderfully illustrative example of their collective desire to sacrifice ecological balance for the safety of their own economic lifeways. They were worried about the havoc FMD's microbial power could wreak in their herds, and they believed that cattle from Mexico could be the source of that virus. They also knew, however, that domestic ungulates were not the only animals at risk of infection; wild animals, such as javelina, could also catch the virus. As one plea from the

California Cattlemen's Association explained, "No doubt by this time many of the wild animals of that country [Mexico] are infected. The natural and seasonal migration of animals minimizes the effectiveness of any quarantine. If, for instance, the javelinas (Peccaries) of northern Mexico become diseased, it will be physically impossible to prevent [FMD from] crossing into this country."[19] Closing the border on paper, according to many ranchers, would simply not be enough: nonhuman nature would pay no attention to a nonbarricaded, closed border. In this discussion, ranchers clearly understood that the political boundary between the two nations ignored ecological reality and argued that an impermeable barrier was needed to afford real protection. In this case, they cared little for their "individualism" and demanded assistance from the federal government, and they demonstrated little regard for adverse consequences for wild game that would result from shutting down native species' traditional migratory routes. The arbitrary, imagined border became acutely real in the lives of ranchers during this controversy, and when pushed to choose between the ecological well-being of the border bioregions and their domesticated, introduced species of cattle, the ranchers did not even pause, choosing the latter with near unanimity.[20]

The southwestern states were not alone in experiencing the threat of epidemic livestock disease. In the 1940s, '50s, and early '60s, brucellosis (or contagious abortion) concerned ranchers on the northern plains as much as the FMD outbreak alarmed ranchers in the Southwest. The brucellosis obsession existed most strongly in Montana, Colorado, and Wyoming because the bacteria tends to favor hosts in higher altitudes, but like FMD, brucellosis, pays no attention to state or even national boundaries and thus affected ranchers throughout the mountain region.

As we have discussed, ranchers attempted to convince themselves and others that theirs was a united industry, but in fact many paradoxes and divisions existed within the ranch community. Events in the ecological economy were no exception, and the effort to fight brucellosis unveils the kinds of tensions that could threaten to break the unity of the ranch community.

Ranchers rhetorically prided themselves on not wanting (or receiving) government aid, but when times got rough or they stood to benefit immensely from the power and expertise of the national government, ranchers did not shy away from demanding and accepting help. Unlike the FMD experience (which had generally been controversy-free within ranching circles), the government assistance in brucellosis eradication divided ranchers and served as a point of contention in range country. In 1957 a group of ranchers in the southeastern part of Montana broke from the MSGA and formed the Montana Cattlemen's Association (MCA) to protest the federal brucellosis eradication program. The fissure came from dissent regarding the MSGA's continued support of the state and federally subsidized brucellosis vaccination program, which had paid for vaccines of Strain 19 from taxpayer coffers. The members of the MCA, numbering nearly one thousand by 1960 (against nearly six thousand in the MSGA), disliked both the increased regulation that came with government involvement in the vaccination program as well as the idea that taxpayers were footing the bill for disease eradication on private ranches.[21] This is one of the few examples in the archival sources that anticipates the incipient turn to the political far right by some range ranchers. The MCA was willing and able to discern the contradictions in claiming a love for the free market and promoting individualism grounded in private property while also welcoming government supports for the industry. This interesting and important development suggests that a growing shift in the political culture of the group was on the horizon. But until that shift fully matured, ranchers continued to convince themselves that they were under threat from common enemies—especially those that lived in an uncontrollable natural world.

Despite the division that the issue of government-sponsored vaccination brought to the northern states in range country in the late 1950s, the existence of brucellosis as a threat to ranchers' cattle helped them herd together in their collective groups. Throughout the 1950s the stock growers' association periodicals consistently included articles updating ranchers on the new technological developments and the new policies regarding the eradication efforts.[22] Ranchers learned about brucellosis at their local association meetings, at regional beef schools, at meetings of national and international associations for range management, and at their stock growers' conventions. Montana state veterinarian J. W. Safford, for example, spoke on the topic of brucellosis before crowds of up to a thousand ranchers at the MSGA conventions of 1957, 1958, and 1959.[23]

Brucellosis, Safford explained, could result in the abortion of 75 percent of a rancher's calf crop for any given year in a herd infected with the bacteria. Even healthy cows who had a history of normal births could be carriers of the disease. The fight against brucellosis thus required ranchers to draw blood from their heifers and bulls and have it tested at an approved laboratory. If a cow in the herd tested positive for the disease, ranchers had to destroy the cow and quarantine the infected herd from which she came. They then had to clean up the area with disinfectants and hope that calf vaccinations would keep the disease from spreading.

In 1951 fifty-four of Montana's fifty-six counties agreed to participate in area testing in order to become modified-certified brucellosis free.[24] In the 1930s, before vaccinations came into wide use on individual ranches, infection rates hovered around 23 percent of all cattle in Montana. By 1951 herd infection was at about 4 percent, and seven years after the beginning of government-subsidized vaccinations, the incidence of the disease had decreased to less than 1 percent.[25]

That success came from ranchers' learning, sharing, and understanding information about a newly complicated approach to pest management. Grasping the scientific data documenting the natural behavior of the Brucella bacteria, as well as the science behind quarantine and vaccination, was essential if ranchers were going to win their battle against the disease and save their livelihoods and their cattle's lives. That education took time and required access to information: thus, the technoscience of pest management became a critical component of cow talk in these years. Whether it was FMD or brucellosis, ranchers rallied around one another to protect the herd. They shared ideas about how and when to watch their cattle for signs of stress, shared best practices for disease-eradicating cow work, and supplied one another with the veterinary-based ecological knowledge necessary for keeping their cattle healthy.

By the postwar decades almost all of those best practices contained elements of scientific management that were grounded in research that few ranchers could afford to conduct on their own. Of course, access to the information had to start somewhere, and ranchers increasingly turned toward their associations to facilitate their access to the latest research. In these postwar decades, each of the associations increased their commitment of member dues to support research, outreach, and education. This formal association support was often unanimously agreed upon, and it ensured that cattle operations from the smallest to the largest would benefit from the finest research and data collection. In 1950, for example, ranchers at the MSGA's annual convention unanimously passed Resolution Number Four, which supported the "control of diseases of Livestock and animal disease research in general."[26]

None of this was cheap. The monitoring and treatment were, if not subsidized by the government, downright expensive. Even worse than the economic expense of eradication and control efforts, however, was the expense ranchers could incur if they lost control over the bacteria within their herds. When that happened, they had to slaughter the herd and endure costly animal losses. To protect their ranches' economy and ecology, then, ranchers had to control brucellosis and other bovine diseases. As a result, ranchers committed to a kind of mutual aid in their associations to financially support disease eradication and prevention. This could mean devoting membership dues to sponsor continuing education opportunities in the field. It could mean organizing regional vaccination events. It could mean lobbying the federal government for subsidized support. Making any or all of those commitments to joint eradication and prevention efforts made up yet another component of cow talk in these years, and owners of operations that varied in size benefited from the collaborative knowledge-sharing and cow work that resulted from a collective vow to fight the invisible threats that seemed to lurk everywhere in range country.

Through their correspondence and gatherings, ranchers supported their own education about pest management, but they knew that informal learning would not be enough to combat the worst of the outbreaks. In fighting pests and disease, ranchers embraced modernity as surely as they questioned it in other areas of their lives. Ranchers consistently tried to access ecological knowledge about new medicines and management strategies, but they knew they needed support, so they increasingly demanded more of their associations and more of one another. Disease and the threat of disease, therefore, often brought cattle ranchers together into association—united around a common enemy and a shared threat—and provided another cause for cow talk.

Wildlife control also occupied a central place in ranchers' ecological economy and served as yet another reason for cow talk during the 1940s and 1950s. Wildlife control, like disease avoidance, was ever-elusive for

ranchers and required much storytelling and experience sharing. Chapter
1 gives examples of ranchers claiming to be advocates for some wildlife
(providing ample forage for herbivores in particular), but if wildlife threatened the health of their herds, ranchers were quick to defend their cows.

Wildlife competes with cattle in many ways, which is why from the late
nineteenth century through the postwar decades, a virtual war of extermination was waged against natural predators who threatened domesticated
animals. Since the nineteenth century, livestock producers in the U.S. West
collaborated with state and federal governments to eradicate wolves, bears,
mountain lions, and, most prominently, coyotes. Other animals threatened
cattle as well. Rodents, whose numbers reached into the millions, faced
extermination because they could eat enormous amounts of grass. The
control of big game animals also seemed gravely important to ranchers in
their quest to fatten their herds. Deer, elk, and antelope especially provided
formidable competition for cattle on the range. Rodents and herbivorous
ungulates fought cattle for the sparse grass and thus endangered both cattle's lives and ranchers' livelihoods.[27]

Throughout the postwar decades, ranchers exerted their labor in the
complex ecological world of predator-prey relations and often found that
power over nonhuman nature eluded them. This was yet one more area in
which ranch culture could turn defensive. In August 1949 Elliott Barker, the
New Mexico State game warden, wrote to George Ellis on the Bell Ranch
to inquire whether their use of 1080 poison had "operated successfully"
in "eliminating" coyotes.[28] Ellis responded that yes, indeed, 1080 "is without a doubt the most effective thing we have ever had for this purpose."[29]
But there was a hitch. Barker also prompted Ellis to address whether there
"was any damage done by the killing of other mammals, such as, valuable
fur bearers or of birds, particularly of the scaled quail." Ellis's response is
illuminating:

> In regard to the quail I have never seen any sign of damage to them. I
> did see quite a few dead buzzards and crows. We had only a fair hatch
> of quail here but I think this is due almost entirely to almost daily
> rains, many of them very hard, during the hatching season. I see a
> good many single pairs of quail with no young . . . but I also see many
> coveys of very young quail which must be late hatches. . . . The most

remarkable effect of the coyote control has been on the antelope. They have by far the best crop of young I have ever seen here. I would say 50% better than last year. Incidentally we had no bob tailed calves when we branded this year—the first time this ever happened.[30]

For Ellis, the experiment with 1080 was more than justified, first, because it had nearly "eradicated" the coyote and thus saved the Bell Ranch's cattle (tails and all). Second, Ellis's cooperation with the state game warden in placing the poison all over the Bell Ranch had enabled a more "desirable" species to proliferate. Third, Ellis believed the poison had not harmed other wildlife. Just as ranchers began to see a decrease in such species as the coyote, however, the numbers of rodents or ungulate herbivores skyrocketed. Ellis ended his letter to Barker by offering another observation: "We do have more rabbits already. Whether there is a connection or not I do not know." Jack rabbits in New Mexico had been an ongoing problem for agriculturalists since at least the 1920s, and their numbers continued to mushroom, due in large part to the suppression of predator species. Ellis shows an acute observation of the ecology of his ranch when he notes the increase in the rabbit population, but he also seems unwilling to connect the obvious dots. Many, if not most, ranchers shared Ellis's attuned understanding of the broader ecology of their ranches, but their decisions rarely privileged nonbovine creatures because such decisions might undermine the health and welfare of their cattle.

The eradication of coyote populations had similar effects in Arizona and Montana. Arizona rancher Jo Jeffers was quite aware of the precariousness of range and wildlife management. In her 1964 autobiography, she suggested that "the demolishing of coyotes by government poisoners often leads to an overabundance of rabbits that are far more destructive to the range than the coyotes. Still, coyotes must be controlled or they would overrun the country, killing small calves and lambs when the rabbit supply diminishes."[31] Most (though certainly not all) ranchers would have agreed with Jeffers's assessment of the conflicting outcomes of coyote eradication programs. At a state Fish and Game Commission meeting in 1954, Art Nelson, a central Montana rancher, explained that "antelope and deer are very much on the increase" and that there were "6 1/2 times more antelope in . . . 1953 than there were in 1949" (the year that 1080 came into widespread use on western ranges).[32] As Ellis, Jeffers, Nelson, and other ranchers knew and could testify, predators could not be separated from other wildlife because they all were connected. If all the coyotes and mountain lions were killed, the populations of jack rabbits and mice, of deer, antelope, and other big game increased—sometimes exponentially.

The labor expended to try to exert control over wildlife, therefore, rarely was successful. Rabbits took advantage of the absence of their predators and proliferated as only rabbits can. Antelope and deer refused to keep their numbers to a level that, in the minds of ranchers, would not interfere with cattle's use of grass and other forage. Ellis explained with some annoyance that although most of the year had been coyote-free at the Bell, he had "recently" seen "two tracks and one coyote. Meaning, I think, that a few are drifting back in." Coyotes continued to move into spaces newly cleared of their species despite the best efforts of ranchers to control them.[33]

Coyote's persistence is an example of what Diogo de Carvalho Cabral calls a human-nonhuman "negotiation." In his study of ant-human interactions on coffee plantations in nineteenth-century Brazil, Cabral argues that the nonhuman actors forced negotiations of power and action with their human neighbors.[34] When historians read texts written by humans who have interacted with the nonhuman, it is easy for us to see only a subject-object relationship. But in the case of coffee farmers in Brazil battling ants or of ranchers in the mountain West lamenting coyotes' persistence, there was indeed intense negotiation. Coyotes pushed ranchers to form committees on coyote control in their associations. Coyotes forced ranchers to meet with the state fish and game commissions and to form local groups to discuss and lobby around the need to keep wildlife at what they considered optimum numbers. Ranchers' collective activities around predator and wildlife control included creating legislation featuring bounty programs, lobbying for the use of new predator-removal technologies (such as 1080) by the state and local land management agencies, and working with the game commissions to change hunting permit systems.[35] Most of this political activism grew from deep-seated fear of losing one's cattle to a powerful assemblage of nonhuman ecological actors. Coyotes, rabbits, and even the heel fly had their own agency that forced ranchers to admit their vulnerability and to act defensively. In decades in which the world seemed to be shifting in threatening ways, efforts to gain the upper hand in any negotiation with wildlife seemed freighted with added symbolic significance for ranchers and made that human-nonhuman negotiation a central part of cow talk. Even with all that talk and ranchers' sometimes herculean efforts, the wildlife just kept "drifting back in."

Although no amount of political maneuvering or technological adaptation could maintain control of the nonhuman elements of the ranch, the struggle to control or at least endure the ecological economy had the effect of making ranchers feel as though they all were engaged in a common quest against shared enemies. Their labor with and on behalf of their cows in an unruly environment united ranchers in a way nothing else did and offered nearly endless opportunities for cow talk. They understood that their way of life was grounded in an ecological economy that they knew to be tenuous and potentially uncontrollable. This shared understanding provided the raw material around which they fabricated cultural meaning that they then used to fashion an ever more formal political arsenal as a special interest group.

To conclude, I turn to another example of cow talk. Throughout the immediate postwar decades, the MSGA routinely featured idealized images of ranchers' ecological labor on the covers of its association publication.[36] These images often presented the uncontrollable nonhuman actors present in range country as invisible or at least well managed. The cover for the June 1956 issue shows the symbolic power of ecological economy to promote rancher collectivity (figure 13).

The center of the cover contains a picture of three ranchers engaged in the labor of branding a calf in the middle of a lush grass pasture.[37] The grass looks healthy and robust. Healthy, presumably disease-free Hereford cattle stand grazing in the picturesque background. "Undesirable" animals, from antelope to coyotes, are conspicuously absent. The image serves as a useful example of ecological labor because it shows the intimacy that ranchers experienced in dominating both the nonhuman environment and their cattle. Kneeling in grass, touching the cow's body, and communicating with each other (as is obvious by the upturned face of one of the ranchers) represent the aspects of ecological labor that I have examined in this chapter. Control of microbial diseases, insect infestations, and cattle's bodies was not easy work during the decades studied here, but that control

Figure 13. The June 1956 cover of the *Montana Stockgrower*. MHS Research Center Archives, Helena.

was understood by ranchers to be essential for maintaining the health and well-being of the herds of cattle and the community of ranchers.

The group work shown in the image coupled with the decision of the MSGA to frame the image with ranchers' brands from across the state served a unifying purpose. The brands and the ranchers engaged in branding suggest that ranchers were not individuals engaged in a lone, industrialized enterprise. Rather, the image, like so many of the visual examples of cow talk created by ranchers in the mid-twentieth-century West, emphasizes the collective, ecological labor required when producing bovine bodies.

The concept of ranching as an ecological, as much as an economic, undertaking is important because it highlights how the vibrant matter of the nonhuman environment directed ranchers' fears, understandings, and expectations. It reveals how ranchers could be united in conversation about the power of the nonhuman to force particular actions in and understandings about the uncontrollable ecological world of the range. Looking at cattle ranchers in the immediate postwar decades not only helps illuminate the ways in which labor can be informed by and created through nonhuman nature, it helps us also to understand how critical both can be to identity construction, the creation of cultural unity, and the assertion of formal political power.

In the ecological economy, which we focused on here and in chapter 3, the market lurked on the periphery of our discussion. Those ranchers who could afford to deploy 1080 or 2,4-D in their quest to control the ecology of their home ranches engaged directly with a larger, rather impersonal industrial marketplace. Ranchers also daily connected to a capitalist market when they ultimately sold the products of their cow work and their ecological labor. In the postwar decades the market for cattle underwent cycles of contraction and expansion, but the general trend was expansionary as cattle prices rose to new highs every few years. Despite this expansion, the market and market relations still could serve to pit rancher against rancher in an economic Darwinian struggle. The market was not simply a divisive element in ranchers' lives, however. As they did through their experiences with modernization, cow work, and ecological labor, ranchers utilized aspects of the market economy to create a sense of identity that led to a surprising cohesion. It is these market relations and the affinity they ultimately engendered to which I turn in chapter 5.

CHAPTER 5

Beef Fudge

The Market as a Unifying Practice in Ranch Culture

These days it's hard to distinguish between a boastful rugged individualist and a plain damn fool.

—S. E. "Eck" Brown, president of the United Livestock
Producers' Association, 1953

As the previous chapters show, the ecological economy surrounding range ranching in the postwar years brought ranchers together culturally through their labor. To produce cows for the market, ranchers interacted with and sought control of the nonhuman world on their ranches and then shared information via cow talk about the success or failure of their control. The last two chapters reveal that the successful production of a cow depended on a rancher's knowledge of her or his range as well as the bodily health of each animal. Selling and profiting from the production of cattle, however, required not only successful growth of the cow but also decent market conditions and consumer demand for beef. Any survey of range ranching in the postwar decades must include some discussion of the powerful presence of the market in ranchers' lives and ideologies.

In 1959, the year of the MSGA's Diamond Jubilee, the *Montana Stockgrower* published a cartoon (figure 14) that suggests how market conditions constantly preyed on ranchers' imaginations and took up cultural space within the ranching community. That year ranchers had received fabulous prices for their cattle and gleefully rejoiced in their good fortune.[1] The text accompanying the cartoon depicts ranchers excitedly reporting "good grass," "surplus feed," and "good prices." In the midst of their glee, the

Figure 14. This cartoon shows ranchers' impressions of the unpredictability of the market. "Do We Have to Do This Again?" Artist unknown. "Words of Warning," *Montana Stockgrower,* July 1959, 11. MHS Research Center Archives, Helena.

ranchers appear to be driving ever more cattle toward a cliff. The chasm at the bottom of the cliff contains the bones of cattle who had died in 1916–20, the 1930s, and 1952. A reader cannot help but sense that the ranchers are about to run the animals right over the edge. The one cowboy to the left, who sits precariously perched on his mount near the edge of the abyss, seems to suggest that the ranchers themselves might follow their bovine charges into the ravine.[2] By 1959 ranchers had learned that the postwar market, like markets in other times, was dependent on countless uncontrollable factors—many of them ecological. The image shows ranchers engaged in a market that was, quite literally, taking them for a ride.

The text that accompanies the image, however, offers ranchers solutions for what they could do about finicky market conditions. First, they could counter market volatility with cow work by breeding cows in balance with available grazing on their range (through scientifically based ecological labor, of course). Next, they could guard against market unpredictability by not overcommitting to fancy technological purchases. Most importantly, however, the advice explained, ranchers could gather together and recognize that "others in the business . . . face the same future as you." "When trouble comes," the column presaged, "you will all need help and there is strength in numbers."[3] The image and its attendant copy reveal not only the skepticism with which ranchers greeted the machinations of the free enterprise system but also the strategies they used to overcome their worry about an unruly economy.

The image in figure 14 also depicts ranchers employed in a particular moment of production—that moment when they took their cattle to market. For ranchers, the marketing and consumption of beef were woven as intricately into the overall production of cows as were feeding, watering, and vaccinating their herds. Many scholars have separated the spheres of consumption and production, but some authors, such as Dana Frank and Steven Lubar, have suggested that historical actors did not always consider the two spheres to be opposed.[4] Thanks to the efforts of ranchwomen during these decades, the two spheres were joined via the project of beef promotion. This endeavor to increase demand for beef relied on cow talk, and no one did it better than the Cowbelles, ranchwomen who joined the new women's auxiliaries of their local cattle growers' associations. These auxiliaries played an increasingly important and relatively new role in marketing their ranches' products and attempting to ease ranchers' fears of a wild marketplace. Ranchwomen's new role included conducting publicity campaigns in their local communities that promoted both beef and the rural culture of ranching.

In 1958, for example, the Montana Cowbelles entered floats in parades across the state to convince their fellow Montanans to buy more beef. The public messages represented in the floats indicate all of the ways in which ranchers, under the guidance of the Cowbelle organization, sought to overcome the tension inherent in market relations through cow talk that was deeply gendered (figure 15).

The float, peopled by actual ranchers from the surrounding community, carries a cow being fed by a stock grower and a family sitting down to a dinner of beef. The float shows the production-consumption continuum and gendered roles that the consuming public would presumably recognize as familiar. As the float explains: stock growers raise beef; Cowbelles promote beef (and serve it to their families at dinner); and consumers enjoy beef. At the head of it all, of course, is a cow standing at the very front of the float. The banner suggests to the parade attendees that the

Figure 15. 1958 Montana Cowbelles parade float. Montana Cowbelles, Inc., MC 192, MHS Research Center Archives, Helena.

sale of beef benefits not only those in the cattle industry but the broader local community as well.

Just as they did not separate cow work and their domestic labor on the ranch, ranchwomen also did not compartmentalize the ranch-to-market labor. For them, all aspects of ranch life were seamlessly linked. (Even the float shows each element of the beef industry flowing right into the next with no physical or ideological separation.) The float also demonstrates one of ways the Cowbelles used cultural rituals (the parade) to assert their presence in issues of economic import. In laboring to create demand for their beef products, ranchwomen fashioned a space for ranchers to rally around the market issue of consumption while also creating increased opportunity for their own unique cow talk about their roles in ranch culture.

We might assume that the market and its capitalist interactions would serve to alienate ranchers from each other and divide ranchers in fundamental ways. As this chapter will show, however, ranchers—in part thanks to the Cowbelles' efforts—never allowed the market to divide them permanently. Instead, through their associations, ranchers simply folded discussions about the market into their wide-ranging cultural discourse of cow talk. That is not to say that ranchers never experienced alienation from each other over market relations. Cattle theft weighed on the minds of most ranchers in range country, and the archives contain disturbing stories of violence and intrigue regarding theft. In addition, ranchers did not all agree ideologically on issues of macroeconomic policy.

Despite these areas of potential alienation, however, ranchers buttressed their identities as laborers with a capitalist mentality and put their faith in consumption and one another. In ways that may seem contradictory, ranchers seemed to believe that they were united in their competition. The efforts of the Cowbelles to promote consumption of their ranches' products employed a romantic idea of the endless capacity of capitalism and cattle to grow. This productive, feminized labor of promotion, while never empowering ranchers to overcome the volatility of the market, did help to create a sense that the only thing ranchers needed to succeed in market competition was increased cow talk and a never-ending demand for beef.

In the postwar years ranchers had three choices when marketing their cattle. First, they could choose to avoid hauling their cattle long-distance by selling directly to buyers in local markets: they could sell their livestock on local ranches to buyers who came directly to the sale. Secondly, ranchers could sell their products at public auctions, usually located in a regional town, to buyers such as local ranchers, feeders, and sometimes representatives of the packing industry. Thirdly, ranchers could choose to ship their cattle to terminal markets, which were central sites, often in metropolitan areas and near transportation hubs (like Chicago), that served as assembly and trading places for agricultural commodities. In the 1950s and 1960s, approximately 43 percent of ranchers in the mountain West sold at either terminal markets or public auctions.[5] If they chose any of these methods, ranchers had to get their cattle to the markets, which for many meant paying high prices for transportation. During those two decades the cost of getting a cow to market ranged between $2.15 and $5.56 per head. The farther a rancher lived from a marketplace, the more expensive the process could be. Competition for trucks and railcars often pitted ranchers against one another as well as against the companies who owned the trucking or railroad services.[6]

The gritty world of transportation was just one area where ranchers interacted with a harsh and impersonal market that could have severed the bonds the ranch community shared through their fear of outsiders, their cow work, and their ecological labor. But a discourse around the experience of the market (as opposed to the market itself) became a peculiar offshoot of cow talk and was taken up largely by ranchwomen. In promoting beef consumption as the best way to ensure beef production, ranchwomen helped to bridge any alienating competitive chasm that may have existed for ranchers. Before I turn toward market cow talk, however, I will look at the aspects of the market that created tension in ranchers' lives.

There are scores of ways in which ranchers competed with one another over scarce commodities in a capitalist marketplace. Reams of paper have been used to chronicle western agriculturalists' struggle to gain access to limited water and grass, but perhaps the best example of a market tension specific to ranching is cattle theft.[7] Across range country during the postwar years, wandering cows and thieving neighbors caused a great deal of stress. Each rancher kept a proverbial eye out for thieves, and cattle growers' association personnel devoted a great deal of labor toward preventing and prosecuting theft. Each association, for example, had a standing brand and theft committee and offered bounties for any cow thief caught in the act.[8] In addition, the market reports in association publications could also contain reports on current livestock theft investigations. The numbers are impressive. For example, in 1964 the Montana Livestock Commission inspected 26,000 cattle in the month of May and had eighty-five investigations of theft. Of those eighty-five investigations, inspectors recovered thirty-eight animals for their rightful owners and convicted eight persons.[9]

The high incidence of theft investigations (eighty-five in a typical month) indicates that in the context of high livestock prices in the postwar years, cows were a hot commodity. As a result, ranchers feared constantly for the safety of their herds. The highways that brought increased access both to markets and to neighboring ranches also enabled thieves to load several head in a truck and make a fast getaway. Ranchers shared stories with one another of grand larceny that existed thanks to modern methods of rustling.[10] From 1945 to 1965 the issue was so prominent, in fact, that individual ranchers chose to purchase signs warning trespassers that ranchers stood united against theft. In the late 1950s the NMCGA made signs for their membership to post on their ranches. They warned away trespassers and would-be rustlers and offered rewards for their capture. The rewards, coupled with institutional support of the organization in monitoring theft investigations, could ease ranchers' minds somewhat.[11] Membership in associations, at least nominally, protected member ranches from theft.

When thefts did occur, the thieves were often outsiders who traveled from nearby urban centers to steal cows and either butcher them immediately or sell them at market, but outsiders did not always constitute the thieving element in the mountain West.[12] The scarceness of fences in some areas of range country meant ranchers' cows could wander away from home and get mixed up with other ranchers' herds. Brands, as designations of ownership, coupled with ranchers' local knowledge of their neighbors' operations, usually helped to clear up the confusion generated by such roaming beeves, but now and then a dishonest rancher would simply alter the original brand (or brand an unbranded calf) and incorporate the animal into her or his herd. The new "owner" could then sell the animal as their own and capitalize in the era of high prices. When the wandering or stolen animals were sold at market, a third party, sometimes unwittingly, assumed possession of an animal that had not been sold legitimately. The ambiguity of ownership such circumstances generated could and often did create animosity among ranchers engaged in the murky world of cattle marketing.

Tracing the mysteries of herd ownership fell to the state livestock commissions. Generally, the commissions hired investigators, worked with local law enforcement, and relied on their inspectors at local, state, and regional markets to keep track of the buying, selling, and ownership of cows. Like all human systems, this one was imperfect. Much of the system relied on the informal networking of local livestock commission inspectors, which in turn required not only cooperation with local law enforcement agencies but also meant inspectors had to listen to local gossip to reunite cows with owners and prosecute rustlers where appropriate.

Montana brand inspector Leo Overfelt's weekly log entry, dated April 26, 1958, gives insight into the convoluted day-to-day search-and-rescue efforts required to keep cattle moving legitimately through the process of production and marketing in range country. His narration of one case in particular helps illustrate the methods ranchers used to rob one another.[13] The record indicates that Florence Hofland purchased from John Hatch the four animals in question. When asked by Overfelt to produce bills of sale (the proof of legitimate purchase in any cattle transaction), Hofland was able to show that she had bought the calves from Hatch, who had bought them from William Show Jr. And there was the rub. Apparently, Show had not come into possession of the calves legally—in two weeks' time, he would admit to stealing the calves during his criminal trial. Because much of Show's illicit activity had involved ranchers near the Fort Peck Indian Reservation, among cattle growers who were either Nakona (Assiniboines), Dakota (Sioux), or Anglo ranchers who leased reservation lands, Show stood trial in tribal court and received the maximum sentence: ninety days in jail and $180 fine, plus court costs.

Ultimately, over the course of a week, Overfelt discovered unclear ownership at six of the twelve ranches he visited. As Overfelt tracked the Show case, he came across close to a dozen other cows in ranchers' herds throughout the Cut Bank area that were "estrays"—cows that had a brand *not* of the ranch on which they were found. The moral of the story for our purposes is that the quest for profit within the cattle industry could and did lead ranchers to steal from one another. Theirs was not a perfectly harmonious community.[14]

Another area of the market that brought ranchers into tension with one another was the debate over the proper level of state involvement in a post–New Deal economy. The dialogue centered around the extent of government involvement in the macroeconomics of the livestock industry after World War II illustrates how the specter of the market could cause contention in range country, but it also exists as a kind of extended cow talk.

Although during the hard years of the Great Depression many ranchers longed for government assistance, they also dreaded the regulation that might accompany such aid. Despite official opposition to government intrusion in the industry, many cattle growers requested federal help even as they hoped that help would come without regulatory hindrance on their businesses. They lobbied for higher tariffs on beef, fats, and hides; lower freight rates (meaning increased regulation for railroads and other interstate shipping systems); low interest rates for feed, land, and cattle loans; and increased regulation of the marketing and packing of beef.[15]

On some levels, ranchers received the kinds of support for which they hoped. In 1933, for example, the Federal Emergency Relief Administration began buying beef from ranchers to feed some fifteen million people and imposed few regulatory restrictions on cattle producers' activities. The inclusion of cattle in the Jones-Connelly Act in April 1934 and the cattle purchasing programs begun under the Drought Relief Service in June of that year did not require producers to enter into relief programs, but if ranchers chose to sell their beef to the government, they were required to enter into agreements on production limits. Low-interest loans also appeared for ranchers and farmers. Such institutions as the Commodity Credit Corporation and local and state production credit associations issued these loans, and local farmers and ranchers often sat on the loan boards.[16] In combination, these support services meant that in six months' time, from June to December 1934, the federal government had bought (and largely killed) eight million head of cattle and provided $525 million in aid to ranchers.

By 1939 range ranching as an industry had survived, thanks in large part to the federal government assistance it had received. By 1943 the average price per hundredweight for cattle in the mountain West was $11.86, almost double what it had been in 1939.[17] Soaring prices led President Roosevelt and Congress to step in to regulate the economy through price controls. The moment that the Office of Price Administration implemented price ceilings on beef, cattle ranchers began to howl, thus beginning a debate within the ranching community about price controls that continues to this day.[18]

The debate became especially heated in the early 1950s during a time of profound stress for cattle producers. By 1950 the United States' participation in the Korean War had begun to cause concern in economic circles about the possibility of soaring prices that, experience had shown, often followed war. The fear was justified, at least where cattle prices were concerned. In 1951 prices for cattle had soared to an all-time high of $29.69 per hundredweight; by April the Office of Price Stabilization had decided to put a price ceiling on meat. The legislation enabling these ceilings expired in 1953 and, according to economists and government officials at the time, had been successful as prices began to decline.[19]

The decline in prices in 1953 and again in 1954, however, may or may not have been a direct result of economic policies at the federal level. By 1952 cattle ranchers across the mountain West were experiencing a drought the likes of which had not occurred since the driest years of the dirty 1930s.

Between 1953 and 1956, each state in the mountain West experienced one of the driest periods on record. Maps created by the National Climatic Data Center reveal the statistics for 1953, 1954, and 1956 (the height of the drought). The NCDC has replaced the stationary maps it published in early decades with animated maps that are worth perusing. They show how the drought in these years in the mountain West states included in this study worsened significantly throughout the middle 1950s.[20]

By 1956 Arizona, Montana, Wyoming, Colorado, and New Mexico each had experienced one of the thirty-seventh driest years on record. (The record begins in 1895 and so includes the great droughts of the 1930s.) For Arizona and New Mexico the year 1956 was the driest on record, and for Colorado and Wyoming that year ranked in the top eleven driest years. For many cattle ranchers, then, the early 1950s counted as an emergency era—a time when government aid was needed sorely by many, desired by some, and feared by almost all.

Just as the federal government began to address inflationary trends with price controls in a post–Korean War economy, cattle ranchers began to dump their products on the market because they could not afford to keep them. Prices reflected these phenomena. In New Mexico prices plummeted from $27.70 per hundredweight in 1951 to $14.30 in 1953. The prices would not rebound until 1958, once the worst of the drought had passed.[21] Ranchers had increased the numbers in their herds during the war years and continued to expand their operations during the good years (1940–50 and 1952–56). One rancher remembered that the period of good times of the late 1940s through 1951 was a time when "we [ranchers] took on obligations that [were] hard to pay off in bad times."[22] Such sentiments indicate the short-term nature of many ranchers' economic thinking and behavior. During the late 1940s ranchers had taken out loans to increase the mechanization of their operations. This ready credit in turn enabled ranchers to increase their herds and helped them to keep up with increased demand on the part of consumers who had more disposable income with which to buy beef.[23] When the hard times hit again in the early 1950s, many ranchers were left holding the bag. In debt and out of feed, they flooded the market with beef.

This flooding meant that, more than ever, ranchers were in competition with one another. They had to out-compete their rival ranchers in quality and quantity of their herds, but they also often struggled with one another for off-ranch jobs in the small towns that surrounded ranching lands. As cattle prices fell, prices on other goods and services remained steady, and ranchers, like most agriculturalists in the 1950s and 1960s, were caught in a cost-price squeeze. To pay the mortgage on the ranch and to make their loan payments, many ranchers (especially women ranchers, because of the perceived flexibility of their labor) had to take jobs "in town."[24] In the early 1950s, ranchers' economic decisions came to mean not the difference between large profits and small but between solvency and bankruptcy.

This meant ranchers had to compete with one another. And compete they did. But they also did something else. In addition to grappling with the new hard times on an individual basis, ranchers also began to discuss among themselves whether the drought years necessitated federal emergency government assistance. Turning inward, toward the community of ranchers, they engaged in discussions about the best course of action. Government assistance, in the form of price supports and the federal purchase of cattle, had been whispered about among ranchers in their associations and at their communal gatherings since at least the years of the first New Deal. So across the West in the drought years of the 1950s, ranchers engaged in conversations about the dangers and benefits of government support, and these exchanges, while revealing schisms in opinion among ranchers, reveal one more topic of cow talk that could result in commonality—if not in agreement—among ranchers.[25]

Association leaders, elected from cattle growers who tended to run larger operations, often exposed their audiences to vehement antigovernment ideology. In 1952, for example, Lloyd Taggart, the president of the WSGA, explained to the five hundred attendees of the WSGA annual convention that "our people are being lulled into a false sense of security when they are made to believe that something is gained by government aid. . . . Washington does not become a partner in any of our financial undertakings without demanding certain controls and we soon find ourselves dictated to by political appointees who know as little about our business and problems as we do about the intricacies of world diplomacy."[26] Taggert clearly hoped to play on the enduring trope in ranch culture that "they" (outsiders, government officials, easterners) always should be suspected of trying to hoodwink the insider community of ranchers. Echoing the claim of access to local knowledge that ranchers used in their dealings with the state in matters of wildlife and modernization, Taggert was sure that he espoused the beliefs of "most stockmen," but many in attendance (and many who were not) did not agree with the idea that all government help was inherently harmful.

In 1953 both the MSGA and the Colorado Cattlemen's Association (CCA) sponsored price-support polls of their members to ascertain how ordinary ranchers felt about the price-control issue and government handouts. The polls revealed that while most respondents did not favor price supports on cattle, they did favor some government support. By January 1954, at least 554 ranchers had answered the MSGA poll. Of the respondents, 461 opposed price supports, but 381 favored government purchase of beef to "stabilize the cattle market." The question of whether ranchers "favored no help of any kind" was divided almost evenly. In Colorado the numbers were much the same.[27] The decision of the MSGA, the CCA, and other state associations to launch such polls, and the willingness of the members to answer the polls, indicates that the issue of government support weighed heavily on the minds of cattle ranchers and that they were willing and eager to enter into a collective conversation about the issue. The results of the polls illustrate that ranchers could be deeply divided about the issue while also sharing common ideas about the need to help ranchers out of the droughty situation in which they found themselves.[28]

The proponents of government aid were a self-conscious lot. Lest they be accused of being overly communistic, most of the authors chose to assert their independence and their rugged individualism before they proceeded to explain why aid did not usurp one's sovereignty. In Arizona, Doug Cumming wrote a letter to the ACGA "in favor of government aid" and explained, "Sure ranchers are an independent breed and perfectly capable of standing on their own hind legs. They don't *have* to have government aid. For over twenty years, though, they have been paying Uncle Sugar checks to help pay for price supports for everything except cattle. Maybe the cattle industry should be independent of the rest of the American economy; but it darned sure isn't, and the rest of the American economy has more screwy props under it than a Salvadore Dali painting."[29]

Cumming was a small rancher whose own herd rarely numbered above two hundred head, but he did not blame large ranchers for growing and selling too many bovines; rather, he castigated the federal government for

offering other industries price supports. Cumming's letter, while illustrating the position of a small owner-operator, also shows how ranchers used
cow talk in their musings about economic policy to avoid blaming one
another in public. In referring to ranchers collectively as a "breed," Cumming was able to suggest his own fondness for and respect of ranchers as
a cultural group, even as he took a position he knew would be unpopular
with many of his "breed." Ranchers like Cumming who desired government help probably experienced the hard times more acutely than others.
They certainly were the more economically savvy of the group, because
they recognized themselves as occupying the unenviable position of being
caught in a cost-price squeeze.

The issue was not solely class-based, however. One of the most prominent
ranchers in New Mexico, Albert K. Mitchell, supported emergency cattle
buying by the federal government to aid the "deplorable" situation in which
ranchers found themselves in 1953. Some (including Abbie Keith) greeted
Mitchell's backing and support of the NMCGA's emergency price supports
(through the creation of an artificial demand by the government) with skepticism, but Mitchell and the NMCGA stood strong, arguing that they viewed
"the current situation as an emergency which has been created by sixteen
years of New Deal political planning for agriculture combined with a nationwide drought situation."[30] The cause of the emergency, according to Mitchell
and the NMCGA, lay not in ranchers' unwillingness to cull their herds but in
the bad planning of the federal government and rotten weather.

Ranchers' material experiences and subsequent cultural conversations
about the drought bore political and economic fruit in 1956 when the
federal government and various state governments created a temporary
relief package for drought-stricken cattle folk. In both New Mexico and
Arizona, the states where the drought was most onerous, the cattle associations worked vigorously to convince the congressional delegations that
they needed legislation to help relieve the "distressed conditions." In the
early years of the southwestern drought (1952–53), thanks to the lobbying
efforts of the associations, cattle ranchers received cheap feed, extended
(and inexpensive) government credit, and reduced freight rates on cattle
and feed. Ranchers could apply for relief through the USDA and receive
the certificate for aid on hay purchase.[31]

Small ranchers found the above program very helpful. Irven Taylor and Alvin Tso, who both ran small operations, wrote to Abbie Keith to explain how critical it was that they obtain feed during a year when they had experienced a winter, spring, and summer without any appreciable moisture. Tso, a Navajo rancher in northern Arizona, ran only twenty-five head and explained to Keith that "we (I and several other Navajo boys) are running cattle in the Arizona Strip. . . . The ranges are poor and dry and like every other member says we are wondering how we're going to pull through the long winter. . . . We do appreciate the work of the people who are making the drouth relief programs possible."[32] Clearly, Tso and Taylor would have agreed with those ranchers in the mountain West who favored some government assistance—even if they would not have necessarily supported full price supports.

Mrs. Jo Flieger, from Winkelman, Arizona, also agreed with the drought assistance and in October 1956 wrote to her good friend Abbie Keith to express her position in "firm support" of price supports on all livestock. Flieger believed that "70 per cent of cattle producers want the Price Support," and she suspected that even those "Rugged Individuals so styled" would "sure accept [price supports] in full acclaim" if they came forth. Flieger urged her fellow ranchers to "wake up! We are living in an age of Organization and this old idea of 'Rugged Individualism' is gone like the buffalo from the plains."[33]

Those ranchers who opposed price supports (and all sorts of other federal government controls, including ownership of grazing lands) used Cold War rhetoric often and to more effect than the language used by proponents of government support. In trying to convince their fellow ranchers that government aid was dangerous, opponents of price supports appealed to patriotism, Americanism, and anti-Communism. Opponents tended to argue that the drought of the 1950s did not constitute a real emergency and that temporary help from the federal government had a nasty habit of becoming institutionalized and permanent. Ranchers against price supports hoped that in suggesting that permanent government aid would undermine American democratic, economic freedom, they could convince all ranchers that ranching, American style, meant independence from both support and control by a centralized government.

The fear of Communism and socialism (ranchers usually conflated the two) was so strong that it often overpowered the fear of a vacillating market. In March 1950 the NMCGA even went so far as to issue a special resolution that urged its members to "hold to freedom" and to resist a government that continued to insist on substituting "an artificial economy" for the economy on which America had been founded. That original economy had flowered in freedom, according to the NMCGA, but in 1950 it was at risk of becoming a "completely socialized state."[34]

Three years later the NMCGA would support a government buyout of cattle to relieve the emergency drought situation. Even at the same 1950 convention that saw the special resolution, the NMCGA resolved to continue to ask the U.S. government to assist the central government of Mexico in its efforts to suppress the outbreak of FMD. Like other mountain West associations, the NMCGA also supported more stringent import tariffs (on beef and hides) and legislation that would limit the amount of beef imports allowed on the domestic market. Three years earlier, in 1947, ranchers across the West had celebrated gleefully the death of a proposed treaty that would have allowed Argentine beef to be sold in the United States.[35] At the same time, ranchers argued for less restraint in export laws and hoped the federal government would assist them in opening global markets for beef. Ranchers also accepted untold millions of dollars in research and development efforts from the USDA and Department of the Interior. Ranchers' independence built on the existence of a market free of government intervention was a myth, but it was a deeply compelling myth that they continually recycled in their cow talk to bolster their belief that government intrusion meant sacrificing not just one's personal economic freedom but the health of America itself.

The debates over government intervention and price supports in the early 1950s illustrate a schism among ranchers. Nevertheless, ranchers downplayed the ideological tension generated through their arguments by utilizing and emphasizing what they had in common even as they debated. In all of the correspondence and publications that I reviewed, ranchers insisted on their commonalities by stressing that all grassroot ranchers experienced private indebtedness, high prices of feed, the effects of drought, the joy of green grass, and the thrill of selling one's cattle for decent prices. Ranchers casually ended their letters to one another with run-of-the-mill cow talk—reports of the weather, discussions of current cattle prices, or updates on the state of the range in their locale.[36] These may seem like trivial points, but these casual references to a way of life grounded in an ecoculture aided ranchers in maintaining connections with one another even as they heatedly debated ideas about the functioning of the market. Ranchers agreed to disagree because they were all, essentially, on the same side—they were Americans, westerners, businesspeople, and, most importantly, ranchers. What is most interesting in ranchers' discourse about the functioning of the market, then, is not so much their diverse ideological positions but rather their consistent use of cow talk— the language they used to keep that diversity in check.

Jim Smith used analogies that were idiomatic of ranching to make his point to the Greenlee County Cattle Growers Association, during the wearisome month of August 1953, just as Arizona ranchers were losing hope that monsoonal moisture would arrive. Smith explained that riding the uncontrolled law of supply and demand (he made no mention as to the law's nationality) was "like riding a wild bronco, without saddle bridle or surcingle." Continuing the horse analogy used by so many ranchers, Smith wondered why ranchers would ever "let these powerful forces go unbridled in boom and bust cycles to the periodic destruction of those who should be their masters." "Supply and demand," Smith argued, "might be a good horse, but don't let him take us to destruction."[37] Smith directly linked supply and demand to a ranch animal—the horse—as he also exerted the idea of control over nature, so prevalent in ranch culture.

The market in theory was a somewhat divisive concept among the ranching community, but the market in practice provided another opportunity for ranchers to soothe division and materially celebrate their pride in cow work and their identities as environmental laborers. As ranchers attended country sales on local or regional ranches, they participated in spectacles that could render the market divide less visible. In the autumn of 1947 Con Warren held one of these sales in the Deer Lodge Valley of Montana. Con must have awakened full of excitement, for he was about to conduct his first purebred sale. He had been anticipating his first sale on the ranch for years. After three years at the University of Virginia, Con decided that, despite a flair for writing, he wanted to return to the Deer Lodge Valley and work for his grandfather's business.[38] For two years, Con worked as a hand on the ranch; in 1932 he began an eight-year stint as the manager of the operation. In 1940 he applied for a $100,000 loan and bought the ranch outright. As manager of the Kohrs ranch, Con had begun raising a herd of registered Hereford cattle, and it was the offspring of this herd that he intended to sell at the 1947 auction.

To publicize the sale he mailed hundreds (if not thousands) of postcards to prospective buyers all over the country. He and his wife Nell answered countless inquiries from prospective buyers. He placed advertisements in stock growers' association publications like the *Western Livestock Journal* and the *Montana Stockgrower*. He and his hired hands worked diligently with the cattle to get them at their physical best for the sale, and when it was all said and done, Con and the Conrad Kohrs Ranch Company had profited $68,000 from the sale of his cattle.[39]

The kind of sale Con hosted on that autumn day in 1947 was quite common throughout cattle country during the postwar years. In livestock towns across the mountain West and on purebred ranches in every state, men, women, and often children attended. The sale offered an opportunity for cattle folk to come together to celebrate their ecological labor and their cow work that had culminated directly in a product for market. These kinds of auctions should not be mistaken for the sales that sold steers for slaughter. Pure-bred bull sales sold bulls to ranchers who would breed them to their cows and heifers, ultimately creating new life. This is not a minor point. The kinds of sales like the one Con staged in 1947 celebrated the beauty, strength, and endurance of a particular genetic line of cattle. Ultimately, those genetics might result in offspring sold to slaughter, but this genetic market had a different emphasis than a sale for slaughter would have had. Con and his workers spent hours beautifying the cattle for a ritualistic display. They oiled hooves, brushed tails, and conditioned the bulls' fur all in the anticipation of selling bulls and impressing other members of the cattle community. Hosting and attending such an event played a crucial role in ranchers' cultural celebrations. The sales, after all, were the culmination of cow work and demonstrated the competency of ranchers as *ranchers* in the social world of production.

Con Warren's cattle sale could seem, on the surface, deceptively simple. It was a capitalist market transaction—a producer selling a product to a consumer. But the sale was much more than that. The sale provided a space

Figure 16. Wyoming ranchers at the Chicago Livestock Exposition sales. WSGA Papers, Box 190, Folder 14, American Heritage Center, UW.

where the bodies of cattle and ranchers mingled in an economic dance that venerated a culture of cattle raising. In inviting others who were in the business to gaze upon the products of the unseen labor that went into embodying cows, Con asserted an identity as both laborer and owner. As ranchers from all over the mountain West attended the sale, they, as consumers of the product, engaged with one another and with Con in discussions about prices, the quality of Warren cattle, and the vigor of the industry overall. These discussions united the market participants in a culture of commodification and were yet another form of cow talk.[40]

At many of these sale gatherings, a sense of economic kinship permeated the geographic space of the sale because, at least visually, the sale space was a democratic arena. Anyone could attend regardless of their intention to buy. In theory, all who attended could and would discuss the commodity being paraded before them. Take, for example, photographs of two different sales (figures 16 and 17).

Figure 17. A smaller livestock sale in Wyoming. WSGA Papers, Box 190, Folder 14, American Heritage Center, UW.

At the Livestock Exposition in Chicago and at a local Wyoming sale, not all could afford to buy the calves, bulls, or cows, but all could afford to look. Note how the cow is at the center of both photos and how the bleachers are not separated in any socioeconomic way at the Wyoming sale. In the photo from the Chicago exposition, a woman is being congratulated for her cow, suggesting, at least visually, that market spaces could include women fully. In some ways, then, social, gendered, and classed distinctions disappeared in the space of the sale, suggesting that socioeconomic and gendered divisions could be ameliorated through the very act of gazing upon the cattle. The democratic space of the sales was echoed in print in the association publications after the fact. Through this intentional rendering of the market as cooperative and communal, ranchers interpreted a competitive enterprise that might have polarized their political coalition as a positive, unifying experience.

In addition to physically attending and celebrating cattle sales, ranchers also publicly recognized their economic unity through announcements in association publications and letters to one another. All association publications contained market columns announcing sales, prices, and other events and data of interest to ranchers. In 1956, as Keith responded to Alvin Tso, the

Navajo rancher on the Arizona Strip, she urged him to send in news from his part of the state and explained that other ranchers would be interested to know if he sold his "winter calves or yearlings."[41] This sharing of information about the marketing of cows allowed ranchers to keep tabs not only on one another's progress but also on the health of the industry more generally.[42]

The marketing of commodities helped ranchers not only to create capital and maintain their economic solvency; it also reinforced a broader culture rooted in an ethos of production. The cattle being sold during the postwar years were at the very center of ranchers' identities because the production of bovine products enabled not only the economic but also the cultural existence of ranchers. While the sales provided an opportunity for ranchers to compete with one another in a market-driven capitalist enterprise, they also provided an occasion during which ranchers shared a collective identity of production and a collective culture of ranching, both of which would have been reassuring in hard times. Sales helped ranchers surmount, through reassuring spectacle, what might otherwise have been a profoundly alienating capitalist experience.

Ranchers also created commonality in the marketplace by engaging in the cow talk of beef promotion. Beef promotion unified ranchers because it advanced the one market topic on which all ranchers could agree. Ranchers used consumption of beef and the increase of demand for beef far more than any other market topic to create camaraderie within the livestock community. Both K. L. Switzer and Albert K. Mitchell, two ranchers on opposite sides of the price-support fence, agreed that ranches should be able "to eat their way out" of the poor price situation.[43]

Ranchwomen largely assumed control of this beef promotion. Their activities occurred generally within the organizational infrastructure of the Cowbelles, the women's auxiliaries of the various cattle growers' associations. The first chapter of the Cowbelles organized in 1939 in Douglas, Arizona, to create social opportunities for the ranchers in Cochise County. In addition to engaging in social activities, however, the Cowbelles (both state and local chapters) in all five states took up the mantle of beef promotion and industry outreach.

I say "took up the mantle" because concerted efforts to promote beef and meat had existed formally since 1922. Agriculturalists and legislators formed the National Livestock and Meat Board in 1922 to promote beef, lamb, and pork. The existence of the board came about legally through federal legislation that established a voluntary checkoff to fund the board. Cattle ranchers, for example, voluntarily agreed to pay five cents per carload of cattle.[44] (A carload equaled approximately twenty-five head, which meant the cost was about .02 cents per head.) So beef promotion was not new in the United States in the postwar decades, but ranchwomen's assuming responsibility for it at the local and state levels was new.

Cowbelle chapters began popping up in all of the mountain West states during the postwar years. Despite the organization's founding in Arizona on a local level, Wyoming became the first state to create a statewide Cowbelle organization in 1940. The Colorado Cowbelles organized in Alamosa, Colorado, in 1941, while the Montana women came online in 1952. That same year the organization became nationwide when the American National Cowbelles was established. Last but not least, the New Mexico Cowbelles organized in 1957.

Cowbelles' beef promotion did not just sell beef; it also soothed the strains the market put on rancher unity and provided a space for a group of rural women to come together in the spirit and labor of cow talk. By the early 1950s, as Cowbelle Joyce Mercer explained, the Cowbelles intended "to speak up for women on the ranches."[45] The best way to do this, the Cowbelles believed, was to insert themselves into public discourse about supply and demand. Ranchwomen's labor identities were already unique in that they blended the reproductive with the productive, as I indicated in chapter 2. As the Cowbelles organized around the issue of beef promotion, they reconceptualized the relationship between production and consumption in similar ways.

In their efforts to bring their economic products before a consuming public, the Cowbelles used gender-specific messaging. They understood that most people consumed beef but that their advertising needed to target men and women differently. In the case of the postwar hegemonic expectations for middle-class American housewives, the message needed to convince women to care selflessly for their families through consumptive buying. In the case of the typical, masculine American man, ranchwomen believed that their advertising needed to explain the benefits of ingesting protein-laden food. Just as it colored the social world of production on ranches, then, gender also snuck into the cow talk surrounding the activities related to increasing beef consumption. Cowbelles' promotion was not a radically feminist activity, but it was radically clever. The promotion exploited ideas about the dominant proprietary roles of the two genders to sell T-bones and unite ranchers yet again in commonality. The Cowbelles also bridged the divide between the public and private—between their own private lives as ranchers and the broader, nonranching public and also between the insider ranch community and the increasingly hostile outsider society. In promoting beef, the Cowbelle organization came to represent a venue through which cattlewomen could help cattle folk across the West bolster their collective identity as ranchers by strengthening the business of beef.

Simultaneously, and perhaps even more intriguingly, these promotion activities allowed the women themselves to embrace their unique identities as rural women. Cowbelle beef promotions included cultural productions that provide insight not only into their public communications about the products of their ranches but also into their own assumptions about their roles as rural women in this historically specific moment. Even though they broke gender stereotypes in their day-to-day lives on the ranches, they were well situated to speak to female consumers whose lives rested on the patriarchal, gendered assumptions of the postwar decades. As Cowbelles promoted beef, they toed a fine line between being "real women" and "real *ranchwomen*."

The 1955 campaign "Lil' Dudette," created by the Arizona Cowbelles, serves as a perfect example of how Cowbelles straddled gendered expectations for who they were as women. In that year, Arizonans would have seen an ample-bosomed, blonde caricature named Lil' Dudette in images across the state (figures 18 and 19). This Marilyn Monroe–like figure would have welcomed them at the Arizona State Fair, spoken to them from the pages of magazines and newspapers, hailed them from clothing labels, and greeted them at the meat counters in their local grocery stores. And it was in that year that Lil' Dudette became the mascot for the Arizona Cowbelles.

Lil' Dudette came to the ranchwomen's group courtesy of Reg Manning, "Arizona's renowned caricaturist." Manning had created Dudette for the Prescott Sportswear Manufacturing Company, which used her on the label of their "very popular western shorts." From there, Lil' Dudette was "loaned" to the Arizona Cowbelles for use in their beef promotion campaigns.

MEET "LIL' DUDETTE" – our newest and most important Cowbelle member

Mr. Reg Manning, Arizona's renowned and favorite caricaturist who created this charming little Miss, is happy to have her join the Cowbelles. She also comes to us with the blessings of the Prescott Sportswear Manufacturing Company which uses her on the label of its very popular western shorts. In addition, we are indebted to the State Fair Commission who claim Lil' Dudette, by adoption. Many of you will remember her as the symbol and hostess of the Arizona State Fair this past year.

We have heard a great deal, currently, about Brotherly Love but to be on the receiving end of this Brotherly Love is most gratifying. I am sure cattle people join with me in expressing our gratitude and appreciation to Mr. Reg Manning and these fine gentlemen for their cooperation in allowing Lil' Dudette to venture out in the BEEF industry.

From time to time you will hear from and about Lil' Dudette. We know you will admire and love her as she brings you the Word on BEEF!

We heartily agree with Mrs. Tom Field, Vice President of the American National Cowbelles when she says:

"BEEF IS LIFE. It is fuel for love, joy, work, action and living.

Beef is one of America's most important foods."

Perhaps Lil' Dudette can help as we keep telling the world "*how proud me of the part we are able to play in making our country a greater America, proud of our contribution to the physical, mental and moral well-being, of each man, woman and child in these United States — proud of the great importance of improving and furthering the beef supply — the lifeline of every civilized nation in the world.*"

In the weeks and months to follow — Now you listen! and remember
LIL' DUDETTE – EATS BEEF – YOU BET
and so must you!

—Johnie Fain

MARCH, 1955   Thirty-five

Figure 18. An article on Lil' Dudette in the March 1955 issue of the *Arizona Cattlelog*. ACGA Manuscript Collection, AHS, Tempe.

The Cowbelles utilized Lil' Dudette to promote the product that enabled their day-to-day economic viability—namely beef cattle—and her slogan, "Lil' Dudette eats BEEF . . . You Bet!," sent a seemingly simple message.[46] Yet the Cowbelles' use of Lil' Dudette, with her blonde hair, cowboy-like accoutrements, and sexy short shorts, was anything but simple.

Indeed, the use of Dudette beautifully illustrates the Cowbelles' cultural savvy as well as their struggle to redefine expectations of womanhood. They knew well that Lil' Dudette capitalized on the sexualized power of white womanhood to sell products, and they turned that power toward selling beef. When it came to interacting with the public at large, the Cowbelles were happy to subsume their producer identity under the mantle of stereotypical female roles. Lil' Dudette was a culturally specific symbol whose primary fulfillment and identity came not from productive activities in the workplace but rather from purchasing and consuming goods (i.e., hamburgers). We

Figure 19. Lil' Dudette consuming a hamburger on the March 1955 cover of the *Arizona Cattlelog*. ACGA Manuscript Collection, AHS, Tempe.

never see Lil' Dudette growing a cow, only consuming one. Furthermore, Dudette consumes while wearing sexually revealing short shorts that would have been inhibiting for real ranchwomen. In using Dudette, the Cowbelles expected to capitalize on 1950s expectations for ideal womanhood, and they did so by playing on societal hegemonic notions of male heterosexuality and women's binary beliefs about themselves. Cowbelles believed that as an advertising spokeswoman, Dudette's ample bosom, thin waist, tight clothing, and bare, shapely legs, would be consumed by men (who would find her erotically attractive) and women (who would long to look just like her). Having "bought" Dudette, they would also buy beef.

Dudette and the other advertising campaigns were thus formulated for a very specific audience that ranchwomen believed they needed to reach most—namely the middle-class housewife. It might seem that this decision to stereotype women as consumers by centering only the average woman's purchase and preparation of beef for the men in their lives would mean for-getting a discussion of ranchwomen's own role in the production of beef. However, understanding that Lil' Dudette did not represent adequately the complexity of their cultural way of life, the Arizona Cowbelles decided to offset the idealized and somewhat ridiculous image of Lil' Dudette with someone real.

In November 1955 they chose Connie Cook to fill that role. Like Lil' Dudette, Connie Cook was an Anglo woman who was "charming," "slender," and had "natural taffy-colored hair." Unlike Dudette, though, Cook was more than an overly sexualized image. Alongside her husband, she ran the large Cook Ranch in southeastern Arizona. She was also an accomplished horsewoman, an active Cowbelle member, and committed participant in the ranching industry. (In 1955 she was the secretary of the Cochise-Graham Cattle Growers Association.) Cook was feminine and domestic, but she also rode a horse like few others, supported a multigenerational Arizona ranch-ing family, and often flew the family's plane to survey the range on her ranch (figure 20). Connie Cook was Lil' Dudette but a whole lot more.[47]

As their choice of Cook to play the real Dudette illustrates, members of the Cowbelles were uncomfortable with the idea of being stereotyped into an objectified cartoon. The gal with the short shorts who was only consum-ing (and not producing) beef simply was not an adequate representative of real ranchwomen and their lived experiences. In Montana, a popular Cowbelle poem read thus:

"Happiness Is Doing Our Thing"
Calling the vet.
Doing the bookwork
Writing the letters
Being the extra hired man
Cooking for branding crews
Rushing to town for repairs
Warming milk for baby calves
Participating in community affairs
Learning to operate complicated machinery
Spending hours in the saddle checking cattle
. . . And cooking, cooking, COOKING!!!⁴⁸ (Emphases mine)

Bill and Connie each have their pilot license. They say a flight over the Cook Spread is the quickest way to learn the water and fence situation.

Figure 20. Connie Cook, the "real" Lil' Dudette, and her airplane. Elizabeth Johnson, "Four Generations of Cooks: In the Cattle Business at Willcox since 1893," *Arizona Cattlelog*, November 1955, 16. ACGA Manuscript Collection, AHS, Tempe.

The Montana Cowbelles saw that producing labor in the home (cooking), engaging in outdoor ranch work wherever necessary (being the extra hired *man*), learning technical skills, and participating in community affairs culminated in their identities as happy, albeit probably exhausted, ranchwomen doing "their thing." When Cowbelles took on beef promotion they saw it not as a frivolous female activity apart from the ranch. They saw it as an extension of their roles as women on the ranch, and it helped extend their professional producer identities beyond those apparent in the above poem. Nel Cooper, during her infamous Arizona membership roundups, was known to ask incredulously, "Golly gals, don't you know Cowbelles isn't just another woman's club. It's a serious business organization. . . . [Through membership, you'll have] the privilege of being allied with the grandest herd [note the cow talk] of women you could find the world over."[49] Using cow talk, Cooper urged the women to recognize their roles as ranch businesswomen who interfaced with the beef-consuming, nonranch public. This identity as serious businesspeople became more and more essential to the Cowbelle organization as the 1950s progressed and the group began to understand the need to improve public relations between the cattle industry and the public at large.

The Cowbelles' public campaigns blended both the social and the serious in fascinating ways. In the remote Plateau Valley in western Colorado, eight women gathered and dreamed up the "Beef for Father's Day" campaign that by 1960 would be a nationwide phenomenon with over ten thousand women in thirty states concocting schemes for inspiring wives and mothers to cook beef for the fathers in their lives. Capitalizing on a social holiday and driving home their professionalized marketing message allowed Cowbelles to maintain their positionality as wives and mothers while also communicating as businesswomen. Other creative ideas flourished over the years: sponsoring and organizing local picnics, sending beef to President Dwight Eisenhower, awarding beef to the first new father on Father's Day, and having governors and mayors formally proclaim beef as the "traditional" Father's Day dish.[50] The Beef for Father's Day and Lil' Dudette campaigns both publicly embodied the gendered characteristics of women to which ranchwomen felt sure other women would relate. While the Arizona Cowbelles used Cook for their own sake, they used Dudette to communicate, in the decades of Marilyn Monroe and June Cleaver, to the broader community of middle-class women.

Through very specific identity creation and public performance, the Cowbelles were able to weave the mutually contradictory tasks of promoting the economic product of their ranches, maintaining their cultural identities as beef producers, and reifying the hegemonic gendered notions of nonranching women as sexualized consumers.[51] In the gendered world of range ranching, only ranchwomen could venture beyond the ranch gate to the nearest supermarket or into the local townswomen's kitchens to engage in cow talk with nonranchers. As ranchwomen took over the task of communicating with the average housewife, they occupied a liminal space between the gendered domains of production and consumption as only they could, and in so doing they became the salve that healed any cuts that market tensions might inflict on the ranch community.

Just as they held the ranch together via multiple identities and multiple work roles (baking cakes and fixing water pumps), so they held the community together as they sought to tame the wild bucking of market capitalism. The decision to complicate a marketing campaign mascot with a real ranchwoman represents perfectly how ranchwomen sought to expand the narrow definitions of postwar womanhood for themselves, even as they seemed to accept those narrow definitions for other women. And all the while, the Cowbelles seamlessly blended the feminized sphere of consumption with the masculinized sphere of production.

By the mid-1960s Lil' Dudette had apparently retired, because the Arizona Cowbelles were searching for a new mascot. Mrs. Jack Brooks, Arizona Cowbelle president in 1966, wrote to the Wyoming Cowbelles to inquire about Wyoming's latest spokescow, Barbie Q.[52] The Wyoming Cowbelles had created Barbie Q in 1960 to carry out much of the same kinds of marketing that Lil' Dudette had done in the 1950s. While she wrote about ranch life and the cow business more generally within *Cow Country*, it should come as no surprise that Barbie Q's specialty was giving recipes for cooking beef just right. The Wyoming Cowbelles intended Barbie Q to share recipes both within the ranch community and, like Dudette, with the larger consuming public.[53]

With her sidekick Pati-O, Barbie Q engaged in gossipy conversation in the pages of *Cow Country* for three years. The brainchild of ranchwoman and Cowbelle Rubie K. Dover, Barbie Q was a Hereford cow that walked upright on two legs, wore a petite necklace, had long, mascaraed eyelashes, and carried a barbecue fork in one hoof. Her friend Pati-O was an Angus heifer who served as Barbie Q's best friend and confidant. The two cows would meet for a monthly "over-the-fence" rendezvous where they would have a cow talk (quite literally) about everything from recipes to modernized technologies to breeds to cattle conventions—all the while using the gendered vernacular that was so common in cow culture. In September 1961, as she "enjoyed a mid-morning snack of rain washed blue-stem still glistening in the draw," Barbie Q told Pati-O of a study that she had heard about from the Kuriyama Food Research Institute. Dr. Kuriyama had discovered that food choices affected people's lifestyles and dispositions. Pati-O listened to the list, which included affectionate carrot eaters, emotional banana eaters, and refined tea drinkers, and suggested: "We might add beef to that list. Men who favor beef are good-natured, forceful and lucky since beef contains all the essentials necessary for health and energy. With the numerous cuts of beef and ways to prepare it, women who cook with beef approach the status of story book wives."[54] Cowbelles, like Barbie Q, believed wholeheartedly that promoting beef helped people not only become healthier physically but also enabled men and women to perform assigned cultural ideals of masculinity and femininity. Beef promotion not only helped the cattle industry: according to Pati-O it also helped society more broadly.

All Cowbelle beef promotion activities focused on getting the word out about the importance of eating beef and the vital contributions the ranching industry made to the mountain West states. The numerous recipe books they created for purchase exemplify one of the recurring and most successful of the Cowbelle activities. The books generally were inexpensive and were meant not so much as a fundraising opportunity for the Cowbelles but as a public relations ploy to get housewives to buy (and cook) beef. The recipes were those that ranchwomen supposedly served in their own homes and that their cowboys and cowgirls enjoyed most. The list of recipes is endless, but some of the dishes included beef fudge, date-beef squares (cookies), meatloaf, and beef stroganoff. According to the Cowbelles, a woman should make beef fudge just like regular fudge with a little browned hamburger thrown in. Everyone needed chocolate and beef in their diets, so the combination of the two seemed a brilliant idea to many Cowbelles. (The combination is actually rather appalling; I have tried it.) In marketing beef as an ingredient for fudge and other dishes, the Cowbelles took the cows' bodies that they were instrumental in creating and gave them to America's housewives as edible commodities in the form of popular, familiar dishes.

These public activities aimed at affecting the market stemmed from ranchwomen's desire to promote consumption from the vantage point of the producer. Their own identities as indispensable laborers who had important stakes in the business set them on the course for working publicly for the industry. And work they did. Consider these figures for Arizona. In every year from 1956 to 1962, the group selected a Father of the Year for the state and presented the winner with a beef prize; in 1956 alone, the Laveen Cowbelles pasted 138,000 "Beef for Father's Day" stickers on envelopes mailed by banks and businesses, and the Yavapai local group placed 7,500 stickers in their county; in 1959 the local chapters produced more than eight television and radio programs reminding mothers to cook beef for Father's Day. By 1967 Colorado Cowbelles had created and distributed 3 million place mats, nearly 3 million napkins, 100,000 coasters,

15,000 recipe cookbooks, and 12,000 Weight Watchers menus (telling folks to eat steak for breakfast). Other states reported the same level of activity.[55] They wrote voluminously about their activities. They corresponded with one another, attended meetings, served on committees, and contributed columns to each of the stock growers' association periodicals. They also were visible physically as they attended local and state fairs, rodeos, sales, and conventions. In short, Cowbelles and ranchwomen were visible in the 1950s and 1960s in ways ranchwomen never had been in the past. The above stories and evidence show how incredibly savvy Cowbelles were in their marketing campaigns for the promotion of beef to the consuming, nonranching public. In promoting beef consumption, the Cowbelles were also very careful to project an image of ranchers unified around the hope of an ever-increasing market for beef. If ideological market relations could divide the community of ranchers, the Cowbelles' uniquely female-centered efforts in that market could relieve the tension and assert a positive image of the livestock industry just where it needed it most.

In conclusion, as competitive actors in a capitalist marketplace, ranchers fundamentally contended against one another for pieces of the economic pie. This competition could and did create tension within ranch communities; we saw one manifestation of this through the issue of theft. Additionally, ranchers did not agree on how a post–World War II and post–New Deal economy should work. In the mid-1950s, as a severe drought hit the entire mountain West, ranchers had the cause and opportunity to come together in their collective groups to discuss the need for and appropriateness of government assistance. On this issue, ranchers were divided profoundly. Large ranchers needed price supports less than small ranchers. Still, during the hay bailout of 1956 (and on multiple other occasions), all ranchers benefited from some form of government benevolence. Even though ranchers disagreed about the benefits of government largesse, ranch folk of all classes continued to privilege their identities as rugged, knowledgeable ecological workers and savvy businesspeople. Ranchers asserted those identities in their cow talk about their ranching business, and this cow talk tied them together in solidarity despite their divisions.

Amid market anxiety and the resultant friction among the ranching community, the solution of marketing and promoting beef consumption surfaced. More Americans eating more beef, ranchers believed, would alleviate at least some of their troubles. Ranchwomen pursued the promotion of beef consumption most enthusiastically and exploited the liminal gendered space between their positions as producers and their "feminized" roles as consumers to assume the responsibility of beef promotion. They happily promulgated the business by producing consumer marketing that utilized their unique labor identities to create powerful cow talk that soothed the alienation of a relentlessly capricious market. The zeal they brought to their promotional efforts—efforts with which no rancher could disagree—served to strengthen the community of ranchers. In being visible in the public marketplace in a variety of ways, ranchwomen again sacrificed their own labor and time for the benefit of the culture of ranching. In addition to being productive laborers on their private ranches, the Cowbelles also produced public labor through their activities promoting beef consumption. This work was aimed to ensure the continuation not only of ranchers' economic livelihoods but also their cultural identities. And while they were at it, Cowbelles were careful to redefine postwar womanhood—at least for themselves.

In the end, all ranchers hoped that Americans would "eat more beef," and Cowbelles' efforts to make this hope a reality helped pull ranchers across the divide of capitalist competition and assisted in drawing them more tightly into their associations. Cowbelles' important cultural work and endless cow talk did not end at the grocery store: they were also critically important in the project of gathering ranchers' memories. I explore the role of collective memory in cow talk in chapter 6.

Branding the Past
Collective Memory as a Cohesive Agent

> You're dealing with an industry where people have to believe in what they're doing to get it done, and that's just as true of ranching as it is in getting history down properly.
>
> —Ralph Miracle, 1972

> Everything seems to indicate that the past is not preserved but is reconstructed on the basis of the present.
>
> —Maurice Halbwachs, 1925

By the 1940s ranchers could sense the precariousness of their position and power in the once sparsely populated range spaces of the mountain West, and they suspected that the trespassers, government agencies, recreationists, tourists, and new urban residents were likely to misunderstand the ranching community. But ranchers also seemed to be uneasy about their own understandings of themselves in these decades. Who were they, after all? They relied on range scientists to help them during the Great Depression. They were consistently dependent on a fickle marketplace. During the drought of the 1950s, they increasingly used irrigation infrastructure to shore up their operations. By the 1960s they benefited from roads taking them and their cows to market, and throughout these decades, they expanded their reliance on technoscience to aid them in cow work. So ranchers, too, seemed to be changing with the times. Perhaps that is why there exists in the archives pages and pages of memory-making. The memories were recorded in multiple forms, including association histories, pioneer histories, written autobiographies, artifact collections, and oral histories.[1] Ranchers created some of these records for widespread public distribution; others appeared in the pages of association publications intended only for the eyes of the membership. Still others were donated by ranchers, their families, and the cattle growers' associations to archives and artifact collections in repositories across the nation to ensure the permanence of their version of the historical record. According to minutes from the WSGA's historical committee, which had been formed officially in 1941, histories of the industry and the association needed to: "1) be sympathetic and complimentary of our industry, 2) reflect a true . . . picture of our industry, 3) improve the general image of the cowman" and remind ranchers of their proud heritage. As ranchers bemoaned the encroachment of outsiders into range spaces, grew their cows in new ways, and debated the wisdom of adopting new technoscience to assist them with their unruly ecologies and cow work, they also devoted considerable time and effort to memorializing their industry and creating a heroic past as a way to fortify faith in themselves. These memories were integral to cow talk and an important vehicle for the political unification of the ranch community.

The memories created in the postwar years promoted a historical consciousness steeped in a proud sense of self; yet within them are also hints of an identity in flux. Historian David Wrobel has argued that pioneer reminiscences of the Old West were a "testimony to their sense of declining status rather than to their established power," and this was partly true for cattle ranchers in the postwar years.[2] The memories of mid-twentieth-century ranchers, however, were not only a display of a sense of declining status but also a demonstration of their self-importance. It is obvious in reading the histories and memoirs they created that they believed themselves to be a powerful collective presence in the New West of the twentieth century, even as they sensed that their power might be dwindling. To curb the latter phenomenon, they sought to remember their collective power and to memorialize a particular version of their history as permanent and ongoing. To this end, ranchers drew connections among their mid-twentieth-century industry and that of their cattle baron predecessors of the nineteenth century, and they celebrated their former power and prestige in order to stake a claim to legitimacy in the newly alienating modern era.

In association histories, individual ranch histories, and family memories, nonhuman nature exists as *the* critical link between modern cattle folk and their cattle baron predecessors. Spring and fall roundups, droughts, heavy rains and snows, insect plagues, and the changing quality of grass on the range occupied central roles in the dramatization of ranching's past and present. Even as postwar ranchers attempted to control an unruly nonhuman nature, it was the presence of that nature that allowed their culture to claim a timelessness that defined them as a people.

This literary device of nature as constant is illustrated well by a reminiscence that Lucille Anderson wrote in 1948 of her life on the Crescent Ranch. She wrote to the ACGA's *Arizona Cattlelog* and explained to the ranch readers that she and her husband had sold the ranch and were very sorry to leave the "way of life" of ranching. In remembering the importance of nonhuman nature to ranch life she wrote: "I had several bouts with Mother Nature. I thought her unnecessarily rough in showing me the plain, unvarnished facts of ranch life." But, she assured her readers, "the remembering is not painful but rather fun . . . early morning, branding fire . . . high river, drought, grassy hills, buying bulls, watching clouds, night sounds, crawling things, weaning calves, fence repair, saddlin' up." Lest neighbor ranchers worry about the sale of the ranch to strangers, Anderson assured them that while "people say to us, 'it won't be the same without the Andersons . . . the old landmark gone' . . . [I say] nothing stays the same and as for the old landmark—it won't budge an inch."[3] Anderson and others writing their memories in these postwar decades insisted that modernity might have arrived, but ranchers' persistence, grounded in the land itself, would never "budge an inch."

By the mid-twentieth century, range cattle ranchers in Arizona, Montana, New Mexico, Colorado, and Wyoming increasingly took pride in their refusal to budge. As ranchers responded to myriad changes and challenges facing the industry, they attempted both literally and figuratively to remember their industry. Believing that "true" history would not only help their public image but also draw them together even more tightly in collective affinity, associations encouraged ranchers to historicize their identities and to join their associations. Thus, memory-making became one of the most important tools for Cold War ranchers who wanted to construct a cultural edifice in which they could house their claims to legitimacy even as they feared their power slipping away.

Ranchers' memorializing was textbook settler colonialism. This phrase describes a process whereby non-Indigenous peoples invade a locale and plan to stay. That staying includes constructing partial histories that exclude Native claims to land and spaces, building structures that protect the newcomers, and using language that seeks to replace Indigenous peoples with unchallenged supreme power over property and resources.[4] Importantly, settler colonial histories include as much amnesia as remembrance. Where ranchers are concerned, this partial remembering centered on the "fact" that their toiling as graziers was timeless, that violent conflicts with members in their group rarely occurred and were quickly (and judiciously) resolved, and that their hard work had rescued western range spaces from the wild, unproductive use of Indigenous hunters and from misguided ranching practices of the past. Of course, violent conflicts with Indigenous peoples rarely make the pages of the ranchers' memories, and, as chapter 1 documents, conflicts with other outsiders were never the ranchers' fault. Even in private reminiscences, hard work, sound management of grass, and careful relationships with cattle and other ranchers won inclusion. Theorist Rob Nixon has called this process the "imaginative work of expulsion."[5] And ranchers perfected it in the years under consideration here. It was ranchers' incomplete rendering of the past that allowed them to reconfigure their industry's collective history in a conscious political act meant to reveal to outside, threatening entities (past and present) a sovereign culture united in perpetual heritage and lasting pride.

Most of the mythic stories were collected by the privileged group of owner-operators. The memories emphasize values of entitlement and bravery. Chapter 1 shows this group creating a discourse of threat to and harm for their way of life (located in their fears of the modernizing West) to create a cultural belief in their own victimization, so it might come as a surprise that there was so much attention devoted to historicizing their agency. But these actions were two sides of the same coin. If they were being attacked in the present, it made good sense to remind themselves of their past fortitude and to remind others of the same. Ranchers sought both to record their individual and collective memories for their own consumption and for use in communicating their power to a public audience. In recalling the past, this group of anxious agriculturalists sought to influence the present as well as the future.

In this chapter I will explore how ranchers capitalized on print, aural, and spatial mediums to create, disseminate, and consume their collective history. These memory products—whether they were autobiographies, oral histories, or association chronicles—focused almost always on the dominant aspects of the daily lives of range cattle ranchers, and the most dominant of these was the nonhuman ecologies of their ranches and their relationship with those ecologies. The ranch ecologies sometimes appear as friend and ally, but very often nonhuman enemies provide a common foe that ranchers must subdue through their skilled work and their neighborly kindness. The second most dominant theme in the collective histories is an ever-present nostalgia for cow work as it existed before the technoscientific mechanization of the postwar era.

In privileging earth, cows, and labor, the memory productions curate a form of cow talk that glosses over social tensions among classes, genders, and races—choosing instead to emphasize a past replete with social harmony and environmental triumph. In these memories the range cattle business was not founded on colonial violence and conflict among the varied human claimants of the West's grazing lands (whether Indigenous peoples, other Anglo ranchers, homesteaders, or Mexican and Basque sheepherders), and women's roles in the culture were never problematically subordinate. Rather, in the memorializing stories, range ranching arrived on the heels of providence, women and people of color remained rightfully ancillary to the main plot of the story, and Anglo male visionaries engaged in virtuous, but difficult, entrepreneurship.

The most obvious manifestations of the settler colonial approach to ranch history came from the official associations. In the decades studied here, there is an obvious uptick in historicization as the associations, and their members busily set about recording the histories of the industry and of the individual members who constituted it. Remember, the history committee of the WSGA was established in 1941 and proceeded to organize and pay for at least three histories of the association and Wyoming ranching over the course of twenty-five years. Other states engaged in similar publishing efforts. The flurry of record making was particularly noticeable for its focus on the importance of the range itself, and of grass in particular.

The WSGA's second official history, written in 1954, begins with an evocation of the persistent timelessness of the range—especially grass and cattle. Maurice Frink, hired by the WSGA to write *Cow Country Cavalcade: Eighty Years of the Wyoming Stock Growers Association,* begins the story with a romantic depiction of the landscape in which Wyoming ranchers conducted their business.[6] Wyoming "was a land of lifting hills, of fragrant sagebrush flats and white peaks shining in the sun, a land of little rivers flowing through great plains of grass—*grass whose life-giving power lived on even under the snows of winter*—a wild, free land" (emphasis mine).[7] Even as years passed and cattle and sheep used and overused the sagebrush flats of short-grass country or the desert lands of the Southwest, ranchers and their memorialists consistently asserted the staying power of forage.

Drought, overgrazing, the incursions of outsiders, fences, mechanization—none of it could overshadow the enduring essence of the grasslands. Frink explains: "The trail herds are gone, the cattle wars are over, the open range is no more, but it's still cow country—and though even the cows are different, it's a land of peace and promise. It will be that as long as the rains come and the grass grows."[8] This particular aspect of collective memory carried powerful justification for ranchers: because the land could rejuvenate itself, there was no need for regulations on land use. Indeed, ranchers would use this recollection of mother nature's resilience to argue against regulatory oversight of their grazing regimens for much of the twentieth century, and they based that argument on the firm belief that their historic use of the land taught them all they needed to know.

In the late 1940s this use of memory manifested in a mini–sagebrush rebellion in which ranchers demanded spatial autonomy from all federal land management agencies. In these years, the WSGA and NMCGA both urged the return of federal grazing lands to the state governments. This early version of the Sagebrush Rebellion was a direct reaction to the increasing control of government agencies over public lands grazing, and ranchers relied on their collective memories to make their case that the reduction of allotted grazing lands should cease, especially on Forest Service lands.[9] The two-front attack on federal control was an economically motivated political move to gain benefits in the present, but in justifying their positions, ranchers and association officers used the past.

For example, in defending ranchers' stance on the grazing question, NMCGA president George Godfrey argued, "Anyone who states that the Federal Domain is in worse condition than it was 20 years ago under open range conditions does not know what he is talking about."[10] In the article (published circa 1947), Godfrey admitted that overgrazing had happened and could occur again, but he believed firmly that through "sound management" (i.e., diligent labor on the part of the rancher) and the heartiness of the land, the range had improved and could continue to do so. Positioning himself and other ranchers as the true experts, based on their history of land use, Godfrey asserted that "the grazing lands of the West were being put to profitable use before the establishment of the National Forests or other federal land management bureaus."[11] That was to say, in short, ranchers did not need new experts to help them understand the land that they had long nurtured and prodded into production. Echoing Godfrey, Oda Mason, president of the WSGA, urged Forest Service officials to cease their unfair and "unjustified" management of the forest resources: "The mountains, rivers and snow and grass in our vicinity are Acts of God and will go on forever as they always have."[12] Mason's statement not so subtly implies that regulation of such enduring, infinite, and divine resources was not just unnecessary but futile.

Under the leadership of men like Godfrey and Mason, the collective associations of ranchers wrote their congressional representatives urging them to introduce and pass legislation returning federal lands to state (and eventually private) ownership; they passed resolutions advising a reconsideration of "drastic reductions in the forest permits"; and they prodded Congress to investigate the grave policies being implemented by the Forest Service. The legislation never happened, but the investigation did. (In 1946 Congressman Frank Barrett held hearings throughout the western states to uncover bureaucratic abuses of livestock growers.) The pressure led the Forest Service to create advisory boards, patterned after the Grazing Service's advisory boards, to hear rancher complaints and to facilitate better communication among Forest Service officials, ranchers, and the broader public. This policy outcome partially satisfied the ranchers, and the controversy faded, only to raise its head thirty years later.

What is significant about the controversy is how ranchers used a discourse of expertise grounded in memories of historic, effective, and righteous land use to effect very real policy shifts within the federal government.[13] Nathan Sayre's work on the inconsistency and arbitrariness of grazing policy that was based on early twentieth-century preliminary and incomplete range science would ring true for many of the ranchers, who did not believe that a one-size-fits-all approach could ever work in managing the range. [14] In ranchers' opinions, only a single rancher investigating his or her own ranchlands over a significant amount of time, with memories of management that succeeded and failed, could know what the land was capable of.

Twenty years after releasing Frink's 1954 book, the WSGA commissioned yet another official association history that employed nonhuman nature in much the same way as had Frink, Godfrey, and Mason. Highlighting the righteousness of using Wyoming's principle natural resource (at least in the minds of ranchers)—grass for grazing—seemed to John Rolfe Burroughs, the author of this newest history, the best way to accomplish the task the WSGA set before him. Burroughs thus began his story, published by the WSGA in 1973, with the Wyoming landscape and used the grass of the Great Plains as the central nonhuman character in the great historical drama of early cattle ranching. As a frontispiece, Burroughs inserted a quote from Carl Sandburg: "I Am the Grass; Let Me Work."[15] The decision of Burroughs and the historical committee of the WSGA to give grass a privileged position in their identity-narrative reinforced the belief in the primacy of the land and the importance of grass in the lives of *all* ranchers. By using grass and land as the foundational actors in the history, the author and the association immediately created the potential for ranchers to feel camaraderie with one another because they all relied on a similar ecoculture, regardless of their relative status in the industry.

The initial chapter of *Guardian of the Grasslands* also intimates that ranchers' nostalgia for the way ranching had been done in the cattle baron era of the open-range days (1860–1900) existed uneasily with their belief that conservation and stewardship were crucial for the continued health of the industry. They often acknowledged the abuse and overuse of the range in the open-range days and asserted their more modern understanding of the limitations of the range. They reasoned that the experiences of their nineteenth-century predecessors combined with their increasing knowledge in the present gave them unique qualifications as stewards of that range.[16]

This claim to guardianship over the natural resources of the range became especially pronounced in the 1940s, and the idea that ranchers are conservators of grass and range continues through the present day in much rancher discourse. Burroughs incorporated the conservationist ethic in his first chapter by quoting WSGA president Lloyd Taggert. Taggert, in his annual address at the WSGA convention, explained that "it is apparent that we must find methods of getting the greatest possible good out of limited ranges. . . . We should watch with keenest interest the development of various grasses and the possibility of using them on some of the poorer ranges."[17]

Taggert's ability to recognize that some ranges were poorer than others stemmed from his own historical position. By the 1950s ranchers were well informed about range carrying capacities and the potential for overuse. As chapter 3 described, ranchers generally learned this information from federal and state government officials who had long been engaged in soil and range management and conservation (which began in the1910s and picked up much momentum in the 1930s due to the prolonged droughts of that decade). Much of the need for conservation grew out of the long history of range overuse beginning in the days of the cattle barons.[18] In the thirty years after the end of the Civil War, ranchers drove millions of head of cattle from Texas to Kansas railheads and in the process trampled native grassland ecosystems and completely altered the microenvironments over which the herds passed. But rather than focus on those missteps, twentieth-century ranch histories focused on the lessons learned by a community eager to do right by the grass and their cows. Range conservation efforts came out of the science of ecology and out of a commitment to grassland science by such researchers as Frederic Clements and Arthur Tansley in the 1910s and 1920s; by the mid-1950s three decades of research on range capacity was accessible to ranchers through the USDA's land-grant institutions. After 1914 the USDA's Extension Service also helped ranchers to think about range conservation. Taggert and others knew that one way to maintain localized control over their access to grazing lands was to argue that they, and they alone, could apply lessons learned from the barons, the scientists, and their own experiences with their ranches.

Despite the nod toward the idea that moderation and conservation were needed to keep grazing lands at their most productive (i.e., healthy) status, ranching histories like the one written by Burroughs are filled with nostalgic yearning for the "good old days." To conclude the first chapter, he quotes from the autobiography of an "old-time" cowboy, Otho Dunham, who recalled a time when "the wild hay was heavy and tall, usually over the stirrups. The wild red top looked like grain waving in the breeze. Wild flowers grew everywhere every color in the rainbow and with the cattle grazing, and mountains all around, it made a picture man never forgets."[19] Memories of the capacity of the range to grow "heavy and tall" with wild hay higher than an equestrian's stirrups served as proof for ranchers of the benevolence and constancy of the land. While there existed an obvious need for ranchers to guard the range, the range itself was an able and resilient provider. In these memories, ranchers privileged the days when the grass was tall and the risk of running out of it was short.

Ranch histories also made sure to emphasize the message that despite any mistakes or harsh conditions brought on by climate and precipitation variations, grasses biologically require grazing. Thus, ranchers never discuss conservation without discussing proper use of grasslands—which was, in their opinion, smart grazing. The range, according to the mentality in ranchers' reminiscences, was always at its best when it was being used by graziers. In *Guardian of the Grasslands*, for example, Burroughs explains that "for hundreds of years the grass worked for the buffalo, the Indian being the ultimate beneficiaries ... [and then] the cattlemen and the cattle took over."[20] In rancher memories, human cultures and grazing cultures changed, but the grass endured. In *40 Years' Gatherin's*, Spike Van Cleve explains to his readers that "grass is our crop, and we convert it to beef or mutton, just as for thousands of years it was converted into wild meat for the Indians."[21] Van Cleve's point, like that of so many ranch-life memorialists, is that despite some ranchers' overuse of the range, the land and the grass seemed always to recover when graziers put cows to pasture and managed their domesticated ungulates properly.

While grass appears almost always as an ally in memory sources, ranchers present other aspects of nature as not nearly as benevolent. In these stories, it is through a veneration of ranchers' traditionally skilled work and knowledge that they were able to overcome the trials they encountered historically and persistently as they guarded the grasslands. Rancher Wallis Huidekoper notes in the "The Story of the Range," published in the January 1951 issue of the *Montana Stockgrower*, that "Mother Nature at odd times carries a wallop." This "wallop" served to unite ranchers through cow talk about memories of triumph in tough times. Cyclic natural events, blizzards, droughts, insect plagues and the like, functioned as reminders to ranchers that as self-sufficient as they might have been, they also found times when they had to set aside their individualism and band together in association in order to survive.

The blizzard of 1886 was one such quintessential natural challenge that took up symbolic space in the northern states' ranch histories. One of the worst blizzards to hit the Great Plains in historical memory (including in Indigenous accounts), it decimated the open-range cattle industry.[22] Ranchers lost anywhere from 60 to 100 percent of their herds, and no one, it seemed, was spared.[23] In ranchers' memorial cow talk, that winter serves as a crucial flashpoint. It not only represents one of those tragic moments that every good story needs, it also represents a moment when ranchers came together to help one another. Thus, the stories about the winter of 1886–87 also always carried with them moralizing overtones. Only the best cattlemen, those smart enough not to overstock the range and savvy enough to reduce their herd sizes, recovered enough to continue in the business. Whenever a rough winter arrived in Wyoming, Colorado, and Montana, ranchers summoned the cultural memories about 1886 to compare their fates (and their fortitude) to that of their predecessors.

In 1949 Great Plains ranchers experienced another blizzard that they believed to be as bad as the big one of 1886. Because the blizzard of 1949 was still fresh in the minds of Wyomingites, it received its own chapter in Frink's 1952 history. The title of the chapter, "Another Winter They Won't Forget" is telling. Because of the cultural dominance of the 1886 blizzard in the oral cultures of ranchers throughout the West, Frink did not need to explain *which* winter they would not forget. Everyone knew. Frink ended the chapter by saying, "For the people of Wyoming cow country, 1949 was truly a winter they won't forget and don't like to remember." Even though the people of Wyoming cow country may have wanted to forget the blizzards, they purposely remembered them and, in so doing, created community through cow talk about a shared experience against a common foe.

The 1949 storm was remembered by ranchers as an event they survived (rather than one that put most of them out of business) largely through fortitude and pluck. Assistance from family, neighbors, and fellow ranchers figures into the stories as the primary mechanism for success. Assistance from state and federal agencies is acknowledged in the memories, but it is not celebrated to the extent that individual and locally organized strength and resilience are. Frink explained that the WSGA "became the focal point of the rescue work." Russell Thorp, executive secretary of the WSGA, and Fred Warren, a Wyoming rancher, convinced Gov. A. G. Crane to create a State Emergency Relief Board to coordinate such efforts as Operation Haylift (a relief effort that dropped thousands of tons of hay on the ranges of Wyoming for the starving and stranded cattle). According to Frink's account, only heroic actions occurred. There are few accounts of mistakes, accidents, or ineptitude in his rendition, and throughout the chapter, despite the outside assistance ranchers received, Frink depicts them as responsible individuals in charge of digging themselves out of the drifts. For example, he explains that "the ranchers who received supplies paid for these themselves. Public agencies broke the roads open and even, in some instances, provided the means of transportation and delivery of food, medicines and livestock feed, but the actual supplies were bought and paid for by persons receiving them."[24] Here is a perfect example of mythical recounting of ranchers' self-sufficiency in the face of trouble. The story is told in such a way that any rancher reading it would be proud to be a member of such a tough and determined work culture that had little need for outside help or oversight. The challenges presented by weather, like droughts and blizzards, joined landscape and grass as important cultural bonds in ranchers' memorializing cow talk because they could be similarly celebrated.

Thus, work and nonhuman nature came together in the memories to unite ranchers over time and space. The shared, theoretically timeless, aim of growing cows connected nineteenth-century ranchers with ranchers in the post–World War II era from Wyoming to Arizona. Work with cows was all that really mattered in the cattle business, and the memories and histories made that cow work, which was in reality becoming increasingly modernized, seem remarkably traditional.

Richard Goff, in his history of the Colorado Cattlemen's Association, captured this sentiment when he explains to the CCA membership:

Even today, the cow-calf operator follows pretty much the same basic patterns of herd management as his forebears [referring to Biblical, Spanish, and "cattle king" herdsmen]. . . . It is interesting to look back over the past century and study the types of men that were attracted to the early cattle business. . . . They came from a variety of backgrounds. Some failed and some prospered. But the successful ones invariably had, or quickly developed, a deep understanding of bovine nature and the peculiar economics of the industry . . . , but in looking back over the past century, it is surprising how small the basic changes [in growing cows] actually are.[25]

According to Goff, the goal of ranch labor, to grow healthy and fat cattle, had not changed substantially in the eighty years separating the open-range cattle barons and the mid-twentieth-century ranchers. Using this reasoning, ranchers in the postwar years marshaled an argument from (bovine) nature. In naturalizing their existence, ranchers were able to argue that theirs was an identity closely linked to the heroic cattlemen of the bygone era: they conducted essentially the same kinds of labor within the same kinds of nature. Success required only an understanding of and control over cows and the land.[26] Ranchwoman Betty Accomazzo wrote that ranchers in their eighties could still do "physical work that would make many a young man cry" and suggested the perpetuity of cow work when she explained: "Some . . . [still] . . . sigh with relief when the last animal is loaded . . . after the roundup and his mate calls the last cowhand to her dinner table for grub. It's her way of thanking the neighbors for a job well done until the next roundup."[27]

For Accomazzo, as for most ranch memorialists, men and women shared in continual (and gendered) ranch labor that assuredly would continue just as it always had. To ensure their permanence, ranchers sought roots in a long past by bridging the chasm between the modern and the traditional industry. They accomplished both of those aims by creating a narrative of work that had remained unchanging in all the ways that mattered.

The connection between the past and present did not exist only in association propaganda, however. Individual ranchers also celebrated their connections to historic ranching by contributing to joint publications meant to publicize ranching's longevity (and thus its righteous place in the U.S.

West). In 1953 the Yavapai Cowbelles decided that they would gather oral pioneer ranch histories for a radio show broadcast in Prescott, Arizona. The ultimate result of this labor was a two-volume memory production published by the Cowbelles in 1955. The stories contained within *Echoes of the Past* are full of illustrative examples of the historic longing captured in many ranch remembrances. In a chapter entitled "Sense and Sentiment of Cowmen," Learah Cooper Morgan, the editor of the collection, writes about the sentimentality of cowmen for one another and for their animals. Morgan explains, "The admirers of historic cattlemen and cowboys like to feel that they were men of both sense and sentiment ... and so they were. I myself have ridden the range enough to realize full well that when cattlemen and cowboys—and cowgals—hit the brushy trails for fourteen or sixteen or even longer hours in times of seasonal work or during an emergency, it is the command of the heart rather than of the head which gives them the strength to go that last mile."[28]

Morgan emphasizes a memory of cowmen and cowboys as hard-nosed, rational businessmen who were also driven by their hearts, but she is sure to include the presence of "cowgals" who engage in the masculine labor of riding the range. In rancher memory productions, women figure somewhat prominently. But as we saw in depictions of cow work, women's full range of responsibilities in ranching's past is rarely depicted. While these women are certainly shown to be helpmates, their most obvious role in the Anglo ranchers' collective past are as "cowgals"[29]

Women are mostly cowgals even in memories authored solely by ranchwomen themselves. In telling the story of Nell Ritter, Morgan describes a woman who, after her husband's death, had to "assume full responsibility for the conduct of *her* ranch. With the *help* of her son Curtis, twenty-three, and a hired ranch hand, she took to the saddle in earnest, *as she had often done* during short periods of seasonal work during her husband's lifetime" (emphases mine).[30] It is telling that in this reminiscence, like so many about "old-time" ranchwomen, the woman assumes leadership. She is most decidedly not the helpmate of men but rather is being helped by them. Additionally, her assumption of responsibility on the ranch was not an exceptional event. She had "often" done so. Morgan explains, "It was in her favor that ... she had the confidence of a good horsewoman and a woman competent with firearms. She shot equally well with guns ranging through the 30-30 rifle, the shot gun and the 22. And, although her target was usually a predatory coyote . . . or a rattlesnake . . . making his threatening challenge . . . upon one of the flower-bordered walks of her ranch yard, she felt competent to defend her home and her business interests."[31]

The depiction of women who combined "flower-bordered" walkways and firearm prowess, who cooked for the ranch hands and joined them on the roundups, appears throughout Anglo rancher memory productions in the postwar years. Memory productions such as these placed Anglo women at the center of ranchers' identity-narrative, and thus they served to connect further those who had deep investment in ranching culture in the postwar years. If ranchwomen were to do the hard labor of marketing beef fudge to a newly urban and suburban consuming public, they deserved to feel fully connected to the business of ranching, present and past.

Family longevity, as told by ranchwomen, was a common theme in the reminiscences. In the late 1940s and early 1950s, the *Arizona Cattlelog* gathered stories about intergenerational ranches from its readership. To answer the call, Mrs. Harry Hooker wrote to the *Cattlelog* in 1949 about the Sierra Bonita Ranch, thirty miles north of Willcox, Arizona, in the upper Sulphur Springs valley. She explained that "as far as we know, this is the oldest ranch in the State that has been continuously operated and handed down through the family to the fifth generation."[32] Her article details not only how Harry Hooker (the original Anglo owner of the ranch) conducted his cattle business but explains the changes that had occurred since 1935, when the ranch management was taken over by Harry's grandson, Harry the second.

Like most of the memory productions of range cattle ranchers in the mid-twentieth century, this article focuses on the difference between the industry in the nineteenth and twentieth centuries. By the mid-twentieth century the Hooker ranch was but a fraction of its former size because in Harry Hooker's days "all the land was open range," and a person could control an "immense amount of range if he owned the water thereon." Through this strategy, Hooker had "acquired and used several thousand acres of land and ran 20 to 30 thousand head."[33] By the time Mrs. Hooker was writing in 1949, the ranch had only two thousand head. Still, Hooker insisted that the mid-twentieth-century spread was connected to the historic ranch through landscape and labor.

After celebrating the grand business and labor success of cattle baron Harry Hooker the first, Mrs. Hooker turns toward celebrating the present, yet selective, modernization that Harry the second brought to the ranch. In addition to new tanks for grain storage, five deep-well turbines pumped water for an "expensive . . . [but] absolutely dependable" water supply. Protein mixed with regular feed assured cattle (purebred Herefords, naturally) would fatten reliably and quickly. She argues that the growing of healthy and fat cattle for the market, while being undertaken in some new, modern ways, was also quite similar to the way Harry the first had ranched; after all, the ranch occupied some of the same land and still relied on the range for raising calves and for farming feed. Despite changes and modernization, human use of the land for a particular kind of labor, namely raising cows, united nineteenth-century and twentieth-century ranching.

Thus, ranchers were not above capitalizing on America's love affair with the open range and cowboy culture to shore up their own status in the mid-twentieth century. To capture that particular memory and make it their own, ranchers proudly donated hundreds of thousands of artifacts to museum collections across the mountain West. The collection and display of a physical representation of modern-day ranchers' connection to ranching's nineteenth-century past was never so obvious as it was in the creation of Grant-Kohrs National Historic Site (GKNHS) in Deer Lodge, Montana. The sale of the Grant-Kohrs/Warren Ranch to the National Park Service (NPS) in 1972 culminated a long process wherein the history of the cattle baron era intentionally eclipsed the less romantic industry of the mid-twentieth century. Rather than incorporating all one hundred years of ranching history that existed on the location, the majority of the interpretation of the spatial memory site concerns the cattle baron Conrad Kohrs (and his partner Johney Bilenberg), the grandfather and great uncle of the Warren family who chose to sell the ranch to the NPS.

Like Mrs. Hooker and many other ranchers in Montana, Arizona, Colorado, New Mexico, and Wyoming, Con Warren, the grandson of Conrad Kohrs, was intimately linked with the cattle baron era because his family and his land connected directly with that glorified period. Warren was at least dimly aware of this history, but it was his wife, Nell, who really understood how useful the Kohrs-Warren Ranch could be in the history of the

cattle industry. She was proud of the work that she, Con, and their two children conducted on a ranch that encompassed a hundred years of nearly
continuous cattle operations.

In 1960 the National Survey of Historic Sites and Buildings informed
the Warrens that their ranch was eligible for Registered National Historic
Landmark status. As the years went on, Nell became ever more convinced
that ranchers would benefit immensely from the preservation of the Grant-
Kohrs/Warren Ranch because that would offer the public at large a place to
go to appreciate the glory of the industry. Nell believed that convincing the
public that ranching was a righteous and worthwhile use of the range was
urgent by the 1960s, and so, late in that decade, she pressured Con to begin
talks about the possibility of selling the ranch to the NPS with the hope that
it could be transformed into an interpretive historic site. The negotiations
to do so were long and arduous, but finally, in 1972, the deal went through
when Congress enabled the NPS to purchase and create the GKNHS.[34]

Nell had hoped for an inclusive depiction of ranching from the 1870s
through the mid-twentieth century. She and Con had, as so many ranchers
did, saved and sequestered away ranch artifacts from each era, and they
considered the objects treasures that connected them with their heroic
ancestors. Nell insisted that the Warrens donate the ranch's vast artifact
collection, most of which hailed from the earlier eras of ranching, and the
NPS was able to refurbish completely the nineteenth-century ranch house
and display many of the tools used in the early days of cattle ranching in
the Deer Lodge Valley. Partly because Nell and the Warren family had valued the material memory of nineteenth-century ranching, she was able to
make available a material record for the NPS. Much to her dismay, however, the days of the mid-twentieth-century Warren ranch are mentioned
rarely if at all at the GKNHS. Nell and Con had wanted the monument to
communicate an image of the persistence of ranching to the visiting public, but the NPS administrators, believing that the American public would
more likely gravitate toward the romanticized years of the cattle baron and
the open range, decided to cut the century of continuous ranching history
in half and focus the interpretation of the site on the "glory days" of the
Grant-Kohrs era.

The site offers brief mentions of Con Warren and his work with purebred
cattle and horses. The site mentions his veterinarian prowess and hints at

his labor on the ranch, but for the most part the spatial memory site that is GKNHS has forgotten the Warren era.[35] This forgetting is significant, because it was the historical consciousness of Con and Nell that inspired them to keep the nineteenth-century artifacts that made the NPS interpretation possible. The Warrens' experiences with the NPS, a federal agency with little local connection to Montana ranching, mirrored the experiences ranchers had with outsiders in general. Those outsiders, whether tourists or government agencies, just did not seem to understand the modern industry, no matter how hard ranchers tried to explain it to them.

The Warrens' preservation of nineteenth-century equipment was not anomalous and is representative of ranchers' practice of conserving relics that took them along nostalgic paths of remembrance. These ranchers had been preserving historic artifacts for years as a visceral connection to their imagined past. The Warrens, like ranchers all over the West, held onto the material history of their ancestors as an intentional cultural practice.

Recall the old chuckwagon on the Bell Ranch that gave way to modernization. Mattie Ellis recognized that a modernized and mechanized chuckwagon symbolized the passing of an era. To capture and preserve the historicity of the old wagon, Mattie snapped a picture of the Bell Ranch chuckwagon in 1956. She captioned the image, which showed several ranch hands getting the wagon ready to hit the range, thus: "Loading the old Bell chuck wagon at Headquarters for the summer branding work in 1956. This was one of the last trips out for the old wagon, since this item of range equipment was motorized the following year."[36]

Mattie, who helped to pack the wagon for its forays onto the range, did not just wax nostalgic about it. Indeed, like Nell Warren, Mattie ensured that generations hence would be able to see what a real, historic wagon looked like; in 1957 she had it "refurbished and presented to the Museum of New Mexico, where it has since been on display."[37]

Russell Thorp, the longtime executive secretary of the WSGA, encouraged this memorializing custom of preserving material culture as early as 1945. On his visits to members' ranches, he would find endless amounts of material memorabilia piled in the attics, basements, and barns of ranchers, and he encouraged them to donate it to museums and even to the association itself. Nearly thirty years before Con and Nell Warren sold their ranch to the NPS and donated their historic artifacts, Thorp was busily ensuring the modern memorialization of ranch life. This collecting of material memory was another form of cow talk, one that united ranchers in both a shared past and a historic present.

At the dedication ceremony, Thorp explained that the boxes he was dedicating to the state contained historic range relics such as old branding irons, handmade saddles, spurs, bridles, chuckwagon equipment, Dutch ovens, and other "ranch paraphernalia." In his speech, Thorp was careful to point out that these items were not trash but rather were living memories that told the story of cow culture. That story was one of "glamour and romance, of tragedy and heartbreak, of hard work and splendid accomplishment."[38] In some cases, ranchers kept old tools to recycle and use on the ranch, but the moment they dedicated the relics to the WSGA, the relics became icons of a time ranchers hoped to venerate and replicate (at least partially).[39]

The objects that Thorpe, the Warrens, and other ranchers donated to public institutional agencies (the State of Wyoming and the National Park Service) served to freeze time for some who gazed upon them. Historian Susan Crane explains that the "fixing of memory" through the storage of artifacts "constitutes an apparent permanence of the recollected."[40] In many ways her theory holds true for ranch culture in the West. Through the collection and display of tools from the early days of cattle ranching, time could be captured and stopped, thus slowing the modern shifts that seemed to be intruding on the industry. In addition to freezing time, the display of such artifacts in ranching country also symbolized cultural continuity grounded in work customs and created a sense of belonging among the ranchers. The material presence of an old branding iron, for example, recalled the cyclic process of branding that ranchers had been undertaking since the earliest days of range cattle ranching and continued to do in the mid-twentieth century. An old branding iron, used since the nineteenth century on its home ranch, was not just a rusting piece of metal. Rather, the iron represented for ranchers a materialized memory of cyclic and ongoing cow work.

The donation of old branding irons was linked to an iconography of amnesia. Ranchers willingly overlooked and dismissed long histories of range exploitation and land theft when they used brands uncritically in their personal correspondence and in association official publications. The reality of land that had been stolen from Indigenous communities by the federal government and sold at low prices to wealthy cattle barons was rendered invisible by the signs of ownership captured in metal and burned flesh. Obscured as well were claims to and overuse of commons (lands not officially claimed as private property) by Anglo ranchers from all sizes of operations. In addition to overlooking racial conflict on the open range, brand iconography also silenced the echoes of violent cattle rustling by renegade Anglo cowboys.[41] By using symbols that could be read in multiple ways, ranch propagandists allowed community and individualism to exist side by side unproblematically. These two ideas, much like modernity and tradition, existed alongside one another in the collective cow talk of range cattle ranching thanks to the capture and display of historical artefacts like branding irons. Langdon Winner has argued that artefacts have politics, and branding irons are no different.[42] Although they were the personal property of individual ranchers who publicly proclaimed rights of ownership once the brands were registered with the brand inspection agencies in each state, they were used by ranchers politically to communicate commonality and promote unity. Whereas the irons of the cattle baron era were used to ward off potential rustlers and raids, by the postwar years ranchers began to use brands (and the history they symbolized) to represent a cohesive group culture to ward off outsiders and the threats of modernity.

The Cowbelles were particularly adept at exploiting brands in tributes and propaganda to create an iconography of industry cohesion. Throughout the postwar decades it became standard cultural practice for Cowbelle chapters from each of the five states to produce brand materials as a kind of amalgamating symbolism. When the T-Bone Cowbelles, from Carbon, Stillwater, and Sweet Counties in Montana, published their brand book in 1962, they explained that brands were much more than marks on a cow's body. "In a country such as ours with its ranches in the valleys, grazing in the foothills and the high green summer feed in the mountains, brands have a special significance. To some, their iron has brought wealth and distinction, other have found happiness with modest outfits. . . . To others their brand is like a heritage they hold dear."[43] The organization and wide distribution of brand books served to erase the complex, difficult, and often violent heritage that characterized ranching history by allowing ranchers to remember the past as they wanted. And when ranchers gazed on brands, they generally remembered stories of their collective greatness.

Additionally, brands and their graphic depiction in brand books symbol-ized labor in a particular work culture and represented memories of a non-human nature that both accepted and resisted efforts to be controlled. The T-Bone Cowbelles explained, "To the old-timer thumbing through a brand book, it brings memories that represent a story each in itself. Some are stories of success, some of failure and hopes that failed to come through. It may have meant a big time with the next brand owner ... stories of drought, hail, insect pests, winter hazards or something else to test the strength of man's endurance."[44] Ranchers controlled an individual cow by burning the brand into the hide, but they did so amid an unruly ecology that threatened to keep their hopes from being realized. Each brand signi-fied all of that and served memories to ranchers via cow talk in and about the brand books.

The Cowbelles explained that they believed brands signified "a land and a life we all like," and it was their "hope" that their expression in the brand books might bring ranchers "pleasant memories and useful service."[45] The organization and wide distribution of brand books served to erase the complex, difficult, and often violent heritage that characterized ranching history by allowing ranchers to remember the past as they wanted. And when ranchers remembered, they generally repeated stories of their col-lective greatness.[46]

The brand books allowed that erasure mainly by listing together ranch-ers of all classes (including ranchers who ran spreads of all sizes and cattle folk who no longer owned cattle but who kept their brands registered), of both genders, and of all races. The authors organized the books accord-ing to symbols in the brand rather than by owners' last names, the size of the ranch, or some other arbitrary designation. The result is that brands become a language unto themselves. The brand is itself the story, and ranchers knew just how to read a brand and knew to look (as in the book shown in figure 21) for a heart brand in the heart section.[47] Of course, brands enacted economic protection by keeping individual rancher's cows from misadventure, but perhaps just as importantly, brand books guarded the ranch community culturally by providing a visual testimony of the ideal of equal social relationships among ranchers. Brand books were simultane-ously inclusive and exclusive—defining those who belonged as those who could read the cultural language of this aspect of cow talk and those who

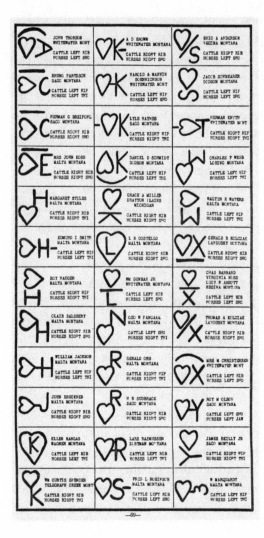

Figure 21. Phillips County Livestock Association, *Brand Book Phillips County, State of Montana*, 1957, in PAM, 1959. MHS Research Center, Archives, Helena.

could not as outsiders and interlopers. The books, in subtle ways, protected the memories of ranchers from intrusion by those outside the ranching community who did not share the work, the land, or the heritage.

On the bottom of the cover of the *Montana Stockgrower*, one can see an "M" branding iron lying over a fire. This choice of including hide and iron as the masthead and footer of the publication's cover further shows the importance of the language of the brand in ranch culture, and it cleverly

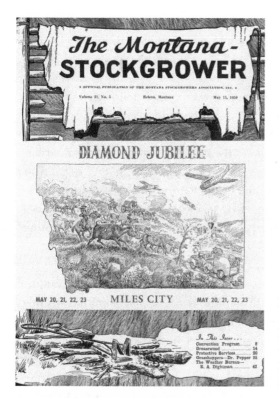

Figure 22. Cover of the *Montana Stockgrower*, May 15, 1959, advertising the Diamond Jubilee. MHS Research Center Archives, Helena.

connotes the one thing most important to ranchers in their quest for identity in the modern age: namely, unfettered possession of cows and all that is required to grow healthy ones. This possession required ranchers to privilege a singular historic narrative.

The best manifestation of such a selective narrative presented itself at the MSGA's Diamond Jubilee celebration in 1959. The four-day celebration not only included amnesiac remembrances of historical social relations, it also encompassed the memories of work and land that were so central in all of the ranchers' collective memories. Consider the image in figure 22, which appeared on the cover of the *Montana Stockgrower* announcing the Jubilee.

The image spatially blends the old and the new just as the postwar memory productions did more generally. Take, for example, the truck in the lower right-hand corner of the image. The truck, surrounded by airplanes and cowboys on horseback, is speeding toward Miles City, the location of the convention. With a horse in the bed, animal power is conjoined with mechanical transportation—the horse, while outmoded, still needs to be present to signify the connection of the old ranching tools with the new. To the left, cowboys engage in an old-fashioned cattle drive—driving their bovine charges toward the convention over conspicuously rich grasslands. Cattle and cowboys dominate the image because, even in 1959, the collective culture of range cattle ranchers depended on labor with cattle just as it had in 1884. In the distance shines the host city, and its urbanity is striking when contrasted with the rurality of the ranchers' environment of grass and cattle. By blending the old and new through the use of space, the artist shows both the past of ranching history as well as its present. And this was precisely the goal of convention planners as they organized the 1959 MSGA annual convention.

This was to be no ordinary convention. The MSGA intended the Diamond Jubilee to be not just a meeting of ranchers but also a cultural memory production in itself. In addition to the usual committee meetings on current issues with the federal government, the problems of cattle disease, markets, and taxes, and general cow business, the convention also sponsored an hour-and-a-half-long "historical parade," an "old-fashioned" roundup, and historical pageants. Even the town of Miles City decorated its storefronts and businesses in late nineteenth-century garb. Organizers of the jubilee, like the artist who drew the cartoon on the cover of the *Stockgrower*, utilized space to create a political geography of memory. The spatial reenactments of the past, on modern MSGA members' bodies, in the fairgrounds, and on the faces of the modern urban buildings, served to commemorate publicly the cultural power of ranching history.[48] In addition, by gathering in such great numbers (there were over three thousand people in attendance), the MSGA members reinforced the notion that they still maintained a powerful presence in the present day.

Ranching's past was not undifferentiated and uncomplicated, but ranchers' memories make it appear as such in order to fortify their appearance of unity in a world that threatened to render them invisible and irrelevant. As ranchers created the memory of their industry's history, they blended a laudation of the early beginnings with a tentative embrace of modernization. They connected their current ranch labors with the labors of their predecessor heroes on an enduring landscape of grass and cattle, and they attempted to ignore the ever-present tensions of race, class, and gender by prioritizing cow work over any social discord. In doing so, they created an identity that was not just past but present as well. This identity and appearance of unity allowed ranchers to posture publicly in a way that shored up their political demands to be left alone, supported, and celebrated (all at once). They claimed time-honored expertise before Congress, demonstrated their righteous presence on the range in their public histories, and celebrated their dominance in a variety of public rituals and memory gathering at every opportunity. Ultimately, remembering and forgetting provided a cultural platform on which ranchers could rest their claims for continued power and permanence.

Memories of the heyday of early ranching may have helped to constitute ranchers' collective identity, but deep down they were very aware that they were living in a world quite different from the one they celebrated. While some things remained constant (grass, cows, and hard work), too many things were changing in ways that caused ranchers to fear for their longevity. New technology, new gender relations, and new relations with outsiders (such as tourists and the federal government) meant that ranchers could not depend solely on a common heritage. They also had to build cultural cohesion in the present, and they did so through sharing stories and engaging in cow talk about the experiences of triumph and failure in their everyday lives. Increasingly, they shared these stories through formal means created by the associations. In the next chapter I turn to the cow talk formalized by the state cattle growers' associations.

CHAPTER 7

The Salt Lick

Intentionally Gathering the Cattle Community

> This is a fast and in many ways a changed world we live in today. Adaptation and cooperation have become an essential part. The day of the lone wolf . . . has gone with the free open range. We've had to learn to live with barbed wire and red tape and to work with our friends and neighbors in self protection.
>
> —Ralph Miracle, 1955

As each of the preceding chapters has shown, ranchers leaned on cow talk to engage in the larger project of creating a singular ranch culture that promoted a sense of group (and political) unity. Ranchers communicated with one another through a culturally created system of representations and language that was accessible only to ranchers as a way to create insularity and group affinity. In their cow talk, ranchers argued about price supports, bemoaned modernization, celebrated their collective history, and talked a lot about their work with cows.

While this system of images and words centered on cattle, it was more than simply a way to talk about cows. Ranchers' cow talk was also a way for them to continually reassure themselves that rancher solidarity was real. It was rooted in tangible, concrete contexts and everyday, material experiences that ranchers shared. As international studies scholar Benedict Anderson has explained, the success of newspaper print culture in creating nationalist identities relied, at least partially, on print culture's ability to convince its readers that despite the fact they often did not know one another, they could be assured that they all had something in common because they all engaged in "steady . . . simultaneous activity."[1] For ranchers, that simultaneous activity included everything and anything involved in growing a healthy cow. Cow talk served as the vehicle to chronicle this steady and simultaneous activity. And whether it was printed on ranch stationary, shared at conventions and sales, communicated through humor, symbolized via brand images, or mentioned in letters and other correspondence, cow talk allowed ranchers to understand themselves and represent one another to outside, presumably hostile, entities.

In 1965 Montana rancher Bill Grieve submitted to the *Montana Stockgrower* a perfect example of cow talk. He wrote:

The Cattleman's Job

When we started raising cows, we hired out to be tough;
The history of the business told us parts of it were rough.
The rules are pretty much the same as since the West was won—
'Just gather up your guts and do the things that must be done.'
When an early blizzard hits you with your stock on summer range,
Just saddle up and gather them, don't wait for it to change;
For while a change is certain, there are two ways it can go,
And the betting odds are heavy that there'll be a lot more snow.
We've read and heard a lot about the storms we had last fall,
Of ranchers having so much stock they couldn't care for them all.
While the critics were condemning, (and keeping nice and warm),
Real ranchers tended to their stock, out in the bitter storm.
I'd like to ask a question of those who always find fault,
Who claim the cowman is getting rich, and isn't worth his salt;
I wonder if you'd take the risks on a horse in drifted snow,
And spend your days in bone-chilling cold of twenty to forty below?
Or when the banker tells you that financially you can't survive,
Would you keep on buying cake and hay to keep your cattle alive?
There are exceptions in everything, some in our way of life,
Some ranchers are rich in other fields, some married a wealthy wife.
But I will tell you this my friends, most have earned their way,
When things got tough and others quit, their motto was to stay.
So if a man has a lot of cows, I can't think that's bad,
For the way he likely got them—he took care of a few he had.[2]

Grieve's ode to "most" ranchers captures in one creative swoop every element of cow talk. The ultimate goal of a cattleman's job was to increase the numbers of cows he (and the poem does assume the masculine) had. Cattle foreground most of the poem, but Grieve's verse also incorporates all of the elements of ranch culture discussed in this book so far—modernization, memory, markets, and ecological labor. Grieve relies on collective memory of individuals doing what needed done to "win" the West. It is clear in this poem that the ranchers for whom Grieve writes are connected with those old timers in some manner but assuredly are not the same men. When Grieve refers to the marketing troubles ranchers faced regularly, he makes sure to explain that despite hard times, a cowman worth his salt still would sacrifice in order to buy cake (meaning cottonseed cake) for the cows. Grieve addresses, too, ranchers' ecological labor when he focuses on their wherewithal in the face of the cruel elements of nature. His reference to "our way of life" completes his tribute to the labor culture of "real" ranchers who are ready and willing to take risks in order to maintain their identities and their lives as ranchers, in spite of imminent monetary bankruptcy (and in spite of the rare incursion of women in the industry in the guise of "wealthy wives"). Perhaps most importantly, Grieve assures his rancher audience that their success is always based in diligent labor and savvy management within seasonal rhythms—after all, Grieve's hero is a man with lots of cows who got them not through government intervention or universal luck but rather through personal risk and committed caretaking.

Like the ranch community more broadly, Grieve's poem is not tension-free. But his glossing over the possible tension makes his literary creation representative of cow talk more generally. What he does not mention is almost as important as what he does. When Grieve discusses the "winning of the West," he does not mention those dispossessed by the imperialist acts of Anglo America. Grieve also seems nonplussed by the appearance of ranchwomen as solely "wealthy wives." A Navajo rancher like Alvin Tso or a female owner-operator like Eulalia Bourne might have bristled at both of these exclusionary aspects of the poem. But they very well may have been willing to ignore them, because it is obvious that the tension with which Grieve's poem most concerns itself is the tension that existed between the ranching community and outside critics. Someone, somewhere, is finding fault with ranchers, and it is to this criticism that Grieve appears to be responding. The poem would have resonated within the ranching community far differently than it might have in a New West city like Phoenix or Denver. For the urban resident, the poem could have smacked of zealous self-promotion, while ranchers could have walked away from such a depiction of themselves with some measure of pride. Indeed, that is what cow talk was in many ways. It was a system of rituals, images, and words that allowed ranchers to identify proudly with an occupationally specific set of values, vocabulary, and traditions. In an era when ranchers felt profoundly threatened, cow talk assured them of their place in the mountain West. Cow talk indicated to ranchers that despite some tension within their community, they shared generally in a similarity of purpose and experience and were united in defense of their time-honored way of life against menacing outsiders.

Thus far we have seen the aspects of ranch life that created the context for cow talk to exist and then focused on examples of ranchers using that context to create opportunities for cow talk. This chapter investigates the specific mechanisms that allowed for formal gatherings of ranchers around cow talk. In particular, the cattle growers' associations of this era worked tirelessly to afford ranchers the opportunities to gather in solidarity. Of course, cow talk is most readily accessed in print, and indeed the association publications and the personal correspondence among ranchers, often facilitated by the association staff, contain numerous manifestations of the language. Specifically, cow talk occurs in monthly columns throughout the association publications. These columns debated the ins and outs of the cattle business as well as capturing poetry, personal stories, and photographs from ranchers themselves. It is difficult to uncover how the audience received the cow talk presented in association publications, but it is possible to prove that ranchers across the West wrapped their personal communication with one another in the comfort of cow talk and thus absorbed, both privately and publicly, the distinct language. The use of cow talk reified ranchers' sense that they shared a unique way of life worth preserving. This chapter will focus on more examples of the association culture that acted as a salt lick for the ranching community. In cow work, the salt lick provides important minerals for cattle growth; ranchers would put the block-shaped licks out for cattle to utilize when they needed to. Like a salt lick in a pasture, the associations provided space and resources to nourish ranchers' sense of identity and community. This professionalized curation of cow talk was essential to the creation of an appearance of unity in one of the more powerful postwar special interest groups in the U.S. West as they turned toward increasingly strident and even sometimes violent defense of their industry and their lives.

Previous chapters detail how cow talk was shared among individual ranchers, but it was also, and maybe more importantly, cultivated and curated by the state associations with the enthusiastic support of member ranchers. When ranchers came together in their state cattle associations in unprecedented numbers in the postwar years, countless ranchers wrote to their publications to express their gratitude for and belief in the organization. James Hogg from Meeteetse, Wyoming, was thrilled with the work the WSGA did on behalf of cattle ranchers in 1956, and in sending in his dues he urged the association to "keep up the good work." Agnes Bishop retired from the ranching business that same year but maintained her membership in the ACGA because she learned "many years ago that ranch life is very much a partnership business" and she was, therefore, happy to keep her membership in the cattlemen's association as there was much "to do" for the industry. Like Hogg and Bishop, many of the ranchers articulated a sense that times were changing, especially on issues of modernization and the ecological economy.[3] These ranchers suggested the need to rally around common issues if they were to persevere in the new age. Economic, ecological, and political concerns inspired this organizing, and ranchers became increasingly interested in shaping public policy at the state and even national levels during these years.

   A group of agriculturalists desirous of having formal political influence was not new in rural America in the post–World War II years. Indeed, cattle associations' postwar efforts resembled the advocacy of agrarian special interest groups that began to emerge most strongly during the Gilded Age and Progressive Era. These new groups, according to sociologist Elizabeth Clemens and other scholars, sought to fill the void left by the late nineteenth-century decomposition of the two-party system. The nonpartisan, special interest advocacy of groups such as the Farmers' Union and the American Farm Bureau Federation sought to secure "bureaucratic beachheads and policy initiatives" and turned away, somewhat, from seeking to alter electoral outcomes.[4] In the postwar years the cattle growers' associations took on many of the same advocacy characteristics. Certainly, the association personnel continued to devote some of the groups' energies to electing representatives sensitive to cattle interests, but as we have seen throughout this book, they also sought to protect the cattle industry through public engagement and policy manipulation.

The discourse ranchers used to describe their own organizing centered, perhaps contradictorily, on their desire to maintain their individuality. Here they share much in common with blue-collar union members: neither ranchers nor union members seemed to see irony in joining a group to remain autonomous.[5] Ranchers appear to have believed that having an organ to speak for their collective needs was becoming an essential component of maintaining their traditional, individualistic way of life in the complicated postwar world.[6]

Those ranchers who joined the associations in these years did not hail from one class, as they had in the early years of the associations. In Montana, for example, most members came from the middling class of ranchers. They neither ran huge numbers of cattle nor controlled vast amounts of acreage. In Arizona, a combination of midsize and small-size ranches comprised the bulk of the ACGA memberships in these years. New Mexico reported similar membership patterns. In 1947, for example, the NMCGA delineated their membership based on the number of head each member ranch owned. According to the numbers, 6 percent of NMCGA members owned 500 head or more, 8 percent owned 250–500 head, 8 percent owned 150–250 head, 27 percent owned 75–150 head, and well over a third (35 percent) of members owned 75 head or fewer.[7] These statistics reveal that the wealthiest group of ranchers did not make up the bulk of association membership. Abbie Keith received letters from all classes of ranchers who suggested that they belonged to the ACGA for a variety of reasons. Some middling ranchers took advantage of their membership by asking Keith to send word if she heard of any pasture available for "four hundred" head. Letters such as these existed alongside letters from ranchers who ran twenty head, had no real reason for writing, but who simply enjoyed learning of other ranchers' experiences.[8] The associations, therefore, seem to be less like unions (where most members were of the working class) or the solidly middle-class and white-collar groups that formed in the 1950s, because the membership base of the associations appears to have had few classed demarcations. Most importantly, the associations seem to have had something to offer all classes of ranchers.[9]

In addition to recognizing tangible benefits from association membership, ranchers' decisions to join also stemmed, at least partially, from the systematic attempts of paid professional association staff to increase numbers. The executive secretaries of the state associations tended to be salaried employees paid by members' dues to keep the organization on track. The secretaries organized the annual conventions of each association, kept track of the association membership lists and finances, communicated with state and federal elected representatives, tracked legislative activities, published the associations' newsletters and magazines, and monitored the activities of the various standing committees.

In general, the executive secretaries of the 1940s, 1950s, and 1960s had some connection to the cattle industry. Whether it was a childhood spent on a cattle ranch, a summer job tending cows, or a longtime affiliation with the industry, associations hired few executive secretaries from the outside.[10] Their personal connections to the industry aided their efforts to convince ranchers that they could understand their concerns. These connections also could explain why the secretaries of each association discussed here had remarkably long tenures during the immediate postwar years. Eddie Phillips spent thirty-four years as MSGA secretary (1929–54) and was succeeded by Ralph Miracle, who headed the MSGA from 1954–69.[11] Abbie Keith came to the ACGA in the 1940s and remained with the organization until the late 1960s. Horace H. Hening headed the NMCGA for most of the time covered in this study (1940–60). In Colorado, David Rice Jr. joined the CCA in 1949 and remained executive secretary until well past 1965. Russell Thorp presided over the day-to-day operations of the WSGA for nineteen years (1930–49), and he was replaced by Robert Hanesworth, who ran the organization for fourteen years (1949–63). Thus, in the twenty years under consideration in this study, at most two transfers of power occurred in each of the five states covered. This stability of leadership most certainly helped the associations create continuity of purpose and procedure and could, at least partially, explain the successful membership drives that each state association undertook in the postwar years.

The association personnel's membership sales pitches almost always included pleas for ranchers to recognize the modern age in which they lived. As chronicled in the epigraph above, Ralph Miracle, executive secretary of the MSGA, tried to convince members and nonmembers in 1955 that "the day of the lone wolf . . . has gone with the free open range. We've had to learn to live with barbed wire and red tape and to work with our friends and neighbors in self protection."[12] The newness of the day meant not only that ranchers' daily operations had changed, but also that their approach to collectivity had to change as well.

In Wyoming the modernizing of the organization took visible form in the WSGA's publication *Cow Country*. In September 1950, under the leadership of editor Robert Hanesworth and assistant editor Myrna Agee, the WSGA changed the format of their association's publication to make it look more modern. They did so with some trepidation: WSGA members had been receiving their association's news in mimeographed form for over twenty years. Hanesworth and Agee hoped to make the publications slick and professional while also maintaining the folksy feel of the older publication. When the new edition of *Cow Country* went out in 1950, Hanesworth included a letter to the membership explaining: "It will be difficult, indeed, to take the place of the publication as you have known it, but every effort will be made to make it the same *personal* and interesting publication that it was." To accomplish their plans to make the publication one of the best in the industry, Hanesworth explained that they needed "the cooperation of each and every member" and that part of that cooperation could come when ranchers contributed "pictures, news items, comments and criticisms and suggestions" to the staff.[13] As one can see from the covers shown in figure 19, the new format did indeed indicate a visual break from the earlier, more amateurish bulletin.

The bulletin's handwritten titles and hand-drawn mast contrast sharply with the use of photography and the typeset mast of the new official magazine cover. In 1950 the WSGA seemed to come of age. Part of this modern look could have resulted from new revenue that came from increasing member dues.[14] Such an expanding operating budget gave the associations better access to publishing technology. Despite the modernizing of the publications, however, the images association personnel used on the covers tended to be blatantly antimodern—focusing almost exclusively

Figure 23. Examples of modernizing association periodical covers: the hand-drawn, mimeographed *Cow Country* from August 10, 1949 (left) and the slicker *Cow Country* issue from October 15, 1950. WSGA Papers, American Heritage Center, UW.

on traditional elements of ranch culture, including pictures of cowboys riding horses in wide-open spaces and pictures of cattle grazing. (Almost all of the covers of the association periodicals replicated the one in figure 23.) Association personnel undertook a focused and consistent effort to make the postwar associations appear up-to-date and contemporary while at the same time renouncing modernization through the iconography of cow talk.

Other state associations also polished their image through their publications (beginning in the late 1930s and complete by the early 1950s) by increasing their use of photography and, in some cases, revamping the entire layout of the publication. The *Montana Stockgrower* had the most consistency from the 1920s to the 1960s. From 1929 the publication had the same layout, but it began increasingly to use photography in the late 1940s. The *Arizona Cattlelog* began in 1945 and took over the less formal, less consistent newsletter that had been sent to members since the 1920s— although the newsletter continued to supplement the magazine through-out the postwar decades. Like the *Cattlelog*, the CCA's publication, the *Cattle Guard*, had a postwar birth, beginning publication in 1955.

The *New Mexico Stockman* has perhaps the longest and most complicated history of the five publications. As early as 1916, the NMCGA recognized the need for an organ through which members could stay apprised of news of interest to cattle growers. For three years, the association sporadically mailed a "monthly" newsletter. Finally, in 1919, Horace Hening Sr., secre-tary of the Central Printing Company of Albuquerque, suggested to the NMCGA executive board that they merge with his company's *New Mexico Ruralist*. Because Hening devoted his *Ruralist* to all rural New Mexico, it reserved only about four columns for cattle news. The NMCGA tolerated this arrangement for about three years until, in 1922, the members and board officers decided they needed their own publication. This publica-tion became a quarterly bulletin, and the NMCGA mailed it to over one thousand interested parties for fifteen years. In 1937 the NMCGA and the New Mexico Woolgrowers' Association joined forces to publish the *New Mexico Stockman Magazine*. Although the editors intended to include news about and for the sheep industry, by the late 1940s most articles centered on cattle.[15]

Despite this long and complicated history, by the postwar years the edi-tors of the *New Mexico Stockman* began to exercise a discourse of fear of the modern to convince ranchers that they needed the NMCGA. In 1952 an advertisement for the latest membership drive in New Mexico read: "Do your state officials, or your sanitary boards look out for the interests of your industry in Washington, in Congress and before the departments? You know they do not. They have other duties to perform. But your Associ-ations . . . keep able men constantly on the alert to protect *your* interests . . . *Very often* in the recent past, their activities have saved you . . . THERE HAS NEVER BEEN A TIME WHEN THIS WATCHFULNESS OVER THE WELFARE OF THE LIVE-STOCK INDUSTRY WAS MORE NEEDED THAN NOW" (emphases in original).[16]

According to association personnel, the newness of the age meant New Mexico ranchers needed organized help to remain on the ranch. These same kinds of messages appeared in Montana. Ralph Miracle, a consummate salesperson, dreamed up multiple membership recruitment campaigns throughout the postwar years. One drew directly on the idea of the modern. The ad showed a caveman walking barefoot with his club; the text reads, "Do you have a neighbor who still carries on the fight for survival in the old way—ALONE?? The Modern Way is Through the MSGA." The ad not so subtly capitalizes on ranchers' fear of being left behind.[17] Ranchers often wrapped references to their experiences with modernization in a discourse of fear and victimization, but they could also evoke "the modern" as pressure to keep up. Not all experiences with modernization were negative, as chapters 1, 3, and 4 show, and both the idea and the process could be mobilized to goad ranchers into joining together.

Even though much membership recruitment came from association personnel, ranchers who belonged to the associations also propelled membership drives. In particular, association officers and committee members, who were almost always ranchers themselves, labored tirelessly to convince the membership, the bulk of whom operated their own midsized ranches, that they did not have the time to keep up on the increasingly complicated world of agricultural policy, and because ranching was entering a "new" age, ranchers would benefit from organization. As early as 1945 ACGA president Fred Fritz was telling members that "today, organization has become more vital than ever before. . . . Organization, when properly applied, is an instrument to promote sound and constructive policies . . . [and these] are the fundamentals of true representative government."[18] The rank-and-file membership, according to Fritz, would do well to trust the representatives in the associations to provide protection. Julian Terrett, past president of the MSGA, put it bluntly in a 1953 membership recruitment letter. He explained that ranchers could not afford to *not* to belong to the MSGA, mostly because the organization had "a President, Executive Committee, and Advisory Committee all of whom stand ready on a moment's notice to take any action necessary to protect the interests of cattlemen."[19]

Bob Schafer, membership chairman of the CCA and a rancher from east-central Colorado, went on a statewide membership recruitment campaign in 1955. The CCA particularly was proud of the fact that Schafer's efforts were voluntary and "all at his own expense." Leaving the ranch in the hands of his wife and two sons for several months, Schafer traveled 12,000 miles and recruited eight hundred new members for the CCA. Part of Schafer's chore was to reinvigorate a rather impotent organization. (The CCA had almost ceased to exist due to lack of support in the late 1930s.) To do so, he attempted to persuade cattle ranchers that the industry was experiencing hard times and could only be protected through a strong representative organization. He recruited both large and small ranchers and had to assure many that the new incarnation of the CCA would not be dominated by large cattle barons (as it had been in the late nineteenth century). According to the *Cattle Guard*, of the hundreds of ranchers with whom Schafer talked, he failed to convince only about two dozen to join the new and improved CCA.[20]

Schafer's membership drive is particularly noteworthy because of its cow talk components. Not only did Schafer use cow talk to convince ranchers they should join the relatively impotent CCA, the association's executive secretary David Rice decided to devote two long articles to Schafer's efforts, a decision that extended cow talk within the ranching community well after Schafer returned to his ranch. Schafer sent a "steady stream of reports" to the CCA telling of the conversations in which he had engaged during his journey. He discovered local situations where ranchers needed help in straightening out a grazing problem or smoothing over a brand inspection misunderstanding—which involved some aspect of cow work. Rice's articles regarding Schafer's journey further reified the elements of cow talk present in Schafer's promotional efforts. Importantly, according to the articles, Schafer "bucked" snowstorms, cold mountain winter weather, and "miles of strange roads." At times, just as every good rancher could understand, the endless effort left Schafer feeling "dragged out." Through it all Schafer remained "patient" and "quiet," convincing ranchers that association members' unselfish labor would make the entire industry stronger. In referring to never-ending strenuous labor in rough conditions, Rice used tropes familiar in and valued by ranch culture. Cow talk, then, not only helped Schafer convince all but "two dozen" ranchers to join, it also helped Rice communicate with the larger membership about the renewing strength of the CCA.[21]

Although few associations were as moribund as the CCA, by the mid-1930s many associations had dwindled in size and significance and as a result had much rebuilding to do. The bulk of that rebuilding occurred in the postwar years, and, similarly to Colorado, associations in Montana, New Mexico, Arizona, and Wyoming began to gather new members into the fold. Ranchers participated in those drives in active and meaningful ways. For example, in their quest to rope new members during the 1950s, the MSGA deployed cow talk stories from ranchers, including celebrity testimonials from well-respected ranchers such as Wallis Huidekoper. As one of the oldest members of the MSGA, Huidekoper had the respect of ranchers across the state. Because of this respect, the MSGA believed him to be a perfect mouthpiece. Huidekoper represented one of the "real" ranchers whose large operation supposedly persisted because, as Bill Grieve discussed in the poem at the beginning of this chapter, he had taken care of the few he had. Interestingly, Huidekoper mobilized the ethic of individual achievement so prevalent in ranch culture to argue against it. He explained that "our Montana stockmen have the reputation of standing very squarely on their own feet and of being strong for 'self help' but there comes a time when they need an active association in back of them to be attuned to the bigger matters beyond their personal control." Being part of the larger collective of ranchers, Huidekoper explained, should not make ranchers feel self-conscious. They could be individuals and still recognize that some things simply moved "beyond their personal control."[22]

Active member ranchers as well as the executive secretaries, then, peddled membership in the associations. Both groups knew that in order to persuade ranchers to join the association, they had to convince them that theirs was a united community. Member ranchers and association personnel used the print culture of their magazines to sell to ranchers both the effectiveness of the associations and camaraderie among ranchers. With the help of office staff, executive secretaries (who tended to be the editors of the magazines) published each periodical and created a print culture grounded in the dominant values of ranch culture. Because of their roles as editors, the executive secretaries became responsible for selling the importance of organizing to the ranching community, and to accomplish that goal they relied on cow talk.[23]

As they drew on cow talk in articles they authored, association personnel also relied on unspoken requirements of cow talk in soliciting material for the periodicals. The editors' primary goal was to gather fodder of interest to their readership. For example, post-1935, the increasing presence of government regulatory and research agencies in range ranching required ranchers to at least try to keep their fingers on the pulse of government projects and rules. To address this need, association editors included in each of their periodicals recurring columns and articles written by government officials. These features related almost always to cow work and the ecological labor required in range ranching and gave ranchers news about grazing fees, range management, and scientific experiments with pesticides and herbicides. Additionally, state veterinarians consistently wrote columns updating ranchers about the latest in disease prevention and cures. In these columns government agents sold the modern to the ranching community in a way that was palatable to a skeptical audience.

The articles written by government agents and accepted for publication by the editors tended to depict happy relations among the bureaucrats and ranch folk. The decades of animosity over outsiders trying to manage the range rarely appear in the prose of government representatives, and time and again they are sure to thank ranchers for their cooperation. In March 1952 W. M. Beveridge, supervisor of the Prescott National Forest, contributed an article to the *Cattlelog* (a reprint of a speech he had given at an association meeting) on the success of juniper control on a section of the forest. Beveridge was "sure that all cattlemen are anxious to improve conditions on their ranges" or he "would not have been invited to talk on the subject." To speak to cattle ranchers in a language they would value, Beveridge assured them that it was their labor, and not that of the USFS, that enabled the "pioneering control work." He explained that "the Forest Service cannot claim credit for . . . this work. A number of progressive ranchers undertook this job at their own expense. . . . It was indeed fortunate that a number of . . . ranchers had gained experience in practical methods that enabled us to start off on a sound and efficient basis."[24] Beveridge clearly took his audience into consideration and wrote to appeal to them, but had he not chosen to do so, Abbie Keith easily could have refused to publish the piece. Beveridge engaged in cow talk through his promotion of "progressive" ranchers. Ranch publications across the mountain West included similar articles. The depiction of intelligent, hard-working cattle folk trying to operate diligently alongside the constantly present government gelled well with ranchers' own heroic constructions of their cultural group.[25] In their publications, then, ranchers got to be in control of which experts spoke; in this way they shaped not only the topics government representatives could cover but also the messages' content.

Many columns featured rural colloquialisms with particular relevance to the cattle business. For example, the CCA's *Cattle Guard* included a column in nearly every issue entitled "Irons in the Fire"—a title that played off branding lingo. Dick Goff placed a picture of branding irons in the fire accompanied by text that served to suggest work unfinished or ongoing. The column offered general information for ranchers on many of the issues discussed in this book—developments in cattle health and disease, government action (or inaction), land issues, sale of livestock, and other bits of news.[26]

Like Goff's use of the branding reference for the news column, the *Montana Stockgrower* also relied on cow talk in a feature column, "The Salt Lick," to update ranchers on various news items of interest in the state and the industry more broadly. As I wrote above, in ranch ecology, a salt lick ensures cattle receive enough sodium in their diet. Salt is necessary for all life forms, but it is particularly crucial for successful weight gain and overall digestive health in livestock. If cattle are not getting enough salt in their diets, they will seek it out. Ranchers often place salt licks throughout a pasture. Cattle roam in search of these licks and congregate around them in groups to get the much-needed mineral the licks provide. In the postwar years, ranchers began experimenting with salt-added feed (including rolled oats and barley or soy meal). Throughout the publications in these years, ranchers shared information (yet another kind of cow talk) about the efficacy of various kinds of salt-added feed. In 1952, for example, Ace Tyrrell wrote into *Cow Country* to explain to his fellow ranchers that his experiments with grain and salt feeding had been quite successful—he had doubled his herd's weight in just ten months.[27] Knowing that most ranchers would be interested in Tyrrell's success, Robert Hanesworth, the editor of *Cow Country*, chose to put a picture of cattle congregating around the salt feed on Tyrrell's ranch on the magazine's cover.[28]

When the MSGA decided to name the news column "The Salt Lick," they played on both cows' practice of herding around the lick for sustenance as well as ranchers' constant struggle to provide enough salt for their cattle in order to signal to ranchers that the news contained within the column was essential nourishment for them and their ranches. The news items sometimes included trivial facts, such as the amount of sugar consumed by Americans or a short history of a place of interest in Montana such as Blackfoot City. More often, however, the news items provided important information and advice of service to ranchers. In 1955, for example, the column warned ranchers that the combination of sawdust and arsenic meant to control grasshoppers proved fatal for thirty-five cattle who had consumed the mixture. The column's entire focus conveyed to ranchers that they could achieve control of the often-uncooperative ecological economy if they consumed enough information and enough cow talk.[29]

Additionally, "The Salt Lick" always provided a list of the visitors who had stopped in at the MSGA office in Helena during the month. The list visually created the sense that ranchers from all over the state wandered into the office to receive the nourishment that the MSGA's block of salt (which was its mere existence) could provide.[30] "The Salt Lick" provided intellectual as well as gossipy nourishment as it communicated to ranchers that they could manage their lives with information and that they were in good company as they attempted to do so. In a business in which ranchers often had little control, "The Salt Lick," both the columns and the actual licks, represented spaces over which owner-operators could hold dominion. The column serves as another example of the ways in which the editors of the publications introduced cow talk to communicate with ranchers using a language that conveyed collective values, insider knowledge, and tension-free unity.[31]

In addition to soliciting articles from sympathetic nonranchers and writing much of the copy themselves, the executive secretaries also asked ranchers who belonged to the associations to submit much of the magazines' cow talk. Editors such as Abbie Keith constantly solicited entries from ranchers.[32] In 1952 Wyoming ranchers encountered a plea in *Cow Country* to submit "typical" pictures from their ranches to be included in the magazine. To illustrate the kinds of images he was looking for, Bob Hanesworth included four photos he believed ranchers would recognize as typical, or, at the very least, cow-centered and interesting (figure 24).[33]

It should come as no surprise that the photos Hanesworth used as examples of "typical scenes" on Wyoming ranches centered on cows: cows

Figure 24. "Typical Pictures Taken on Wyoming Ranches," *Cow Country*, May 1952, 28. WSGA Papers, American Heritage Center, UW.

standing in snow, cows grazing, cows being branded, and cows being worked over by cowboys—all without a single sign of mechanization. Here, again, is another use, although a visual one, of cow talk. The message was that the most important element in ranch culture was the cow—and discussions and representations of cows could serve as emblematic of the entire ranching world. This reliance on the cow as consummate unifier of all Wyoming ranches was not unique to Wyoming: it appeared on nearly every cover and in the pages of all the association periodicals in the postwar decades.

Ranchers answered the calls for submissions and often took the opportunity to be creative with their submissions. They wrote thousands of letters they believed would be helpful and of interest to fellow ranchers in their individual states and in the region more generally. They submitted amateur poetry and photography that they hoped would resonate with their fellows in the ranching business. They sent in commonplace weather updates. They reported births and deaths and agreed to have the stories of their families' ranches published in the pages of the association chronicles (all for no remuneration). Creating unity and fellowship among ranchers required a good deal of labor and was a task that rested on sharing news of the everyday.

Through their submissions and those of their neighbors, ranchers participated in a community of membership through a culturally based poetics. Ranchers' literary tropes featured a kind of "cattle slang" that was supposed to be recognizable to any authentic rancher no matter her or his class position or level of education. Take, for example, the cartoon drawn by rancher Ray Nelson which appeared in *Cow Country* in January 1960 (figure 25). Not only did Nelson create inside humor around the reading of brands, which itself requires a specific cultural literacy, the Wyoming rancher also expected his rancher audience to understand the slang of "br-r-low"—which captured the way that cow folk supposedly slurred their words and did not speak "proper" English.

The cartoons of renowned cowboy artist Ace Reid represent another of the common rancher-authored features that employed insider knowledge of ranch culture by playing with ranch vernacular. Born and raised on a cattle ranch in Texas, Reid syndicated his humorous rural cartoons in the 1940s and all five of the mountain West cattle growers' associations picked up various editions of the cartoons to be published in their magazines.

Figure 25. A cartoon illustrating cow-talk vernacular. Drawn by Ray Nelson. "Br-r-low," *Cow Country*, January 1960. WSGA Papers, American Heritage Center, UW.

Reid's cartoons made visual the culture of ranching and captured the patterns of everyday life for range ranchers. Reid entitled his cartoon *Cowpokes*, which through image and prose followed the happenings on the Draggin' S Ranch. Reid, according to his wife Madge Reid, created *Cowpokes* to help ranchers laugh at themselves and laugh at difficult times.[34]

The major themes of Reid's cartoon echoed the issues dancing in the pages of the association publications. Cowboys Jake and Zeb, the main characters, constantly confronted the issues of politics, range health, banking, the price of real estate and feed, droughty conditions, and tourists (to mention a few). In addition to wrestling with the difficult circumstances of ranching in the postwar era, *Cowpokes* also depicted antiquated cowboys using the rural vernacular so prevalent in the imaginative discourse of ranchers. In an image from 1956, one of the worst years for drought and high feed prices, Reid shows a rancher receiving a bill in the mail. Another rancher atop a horse sympathetically exclaims, "Oh them feed bills!" Reid uses the grammatically incorrect pronoun "them" to describe the feed bills and depicts Jake and Zeb as old-fashioned cowboys (complete with chaps and spurs) who ride horses and dress in the traditional garb of the open range. Reid's use of cow talk and of ranch-specific plotlines may seem the product of one isolated artist, but the fact that each of the state associations used Reid's cartoons throughout the 1950s and 1960s indicates that the art resonated with ranchers across the mountain West in meaningful ways.[35] Perhaps one of the most important aspects of belonging to any community is being able to understand its particular language. Group exclusion and inclusion, therefore, can be based in the comprehension or ignorance of the group's cultural dialect. The ranching community could gloss over regional, classed, raced, and gendered divisions when they believed they all could understand and laugh at an image such as an Ace Reid cartoon. The commonality of "getting the joke" and of speaking the language helped to create cultural affinity.[36]

Perhaps no one utilized cow talk as effectively or popularly as did F. H. Sinclair, a.k.a. Neckyoke Jones. Sinclair, a native of Glendive, Montana, left a publishing career in New York City in 1943 and returned to Montana and began ranching. Interested in political events, Sinclair had written a letter in "the language of the cowboy" to one of Montana's state senators, Charles L. Scofield. Ribbing the senator about legislative matters generally, Sinclair's letter soon ran through the gossip channels of the Montana ranch world and came to the attention of Eddie Phillips, executive secretary of the MSGA. Phillips requested a similar letter from Sinclair, which was the beginning of a twenty-five-year column. By the mid-1950s Neckyoke, his "pardner" Greasewood, and countless other colorful neighbors had made their appearance in cattle publications across the mountain West. Sinclair's property straddled the Wyoming and Montana border, so the Greasewood column was most popular in the *Montana Stockgrower* and *Cow Country,* but it also appeared in Colorado, New Mexico, and Arizona.

Neckyoke pontificated on all sorts of issues in the letters (which were always addressed to the executive secretary of the state association).

Usually writing from his outfit on the fictive Long Pine Creek, he attacked labor unions, modernization, taxes, and "Washington buearycrats." He also argued for the necessity of association and community within the cattle industry. In 1949, presaging Ralph Miracle's sentiment quoted in the epigraph that introduced this chapter, Neckyoke explained to his readers:

> Fightin' is everybody's job—an' we all got to turn to an' make a hand. If the stockman wants to go on as a free American, he ain't goin' to set back an' yelp about 2c a day dues to build a fire guard around his out- fit. This is a age of organization. You'n me would probably like to go on independent—an' do as we damn please—but this ain't 1890, which is perhaps too bad. We live in a time when we got to travel in bunches or git the tar walloped outen us. It might cost 2c a day—but by crackey it's worth it![37]

Neckyoke Jones's discussion of the benefit of organization echoed many of the sentiments of cattle ranchers who actively participated in their asso- ciations. What is perhaps more important for our discussion of cow talk, however, is his use of cowboy language to communicate his ideas. Sinclair, a well-educated, well-connected rancher, used phonetic spellings, turns of phrase unique to ranching (such as "turn to an' make a hand," which means to become an indispensable laborer), and colloquial configurations of writing to communicate in a language he believed would reverberate in the dominant ranch culture of the mountain West. Even the clever name "Neckyoke" would have made sense culturally to his fellow ranchers: neckyoke is the part of the cow's neck where the yoke rubbed as the cow worked. When the cow was slaughtered for beef, the neckyoke was usu- ally the toughest part of the meat. Indeed, Neckyoke and his buddies were salty, curmudgeonly characters who attempted to represent the toughness required to live a ranch lifestyle and succeed at cow work. Additionally, whether they agreed with his take on the issues or not, the topics Neckyoke addressed surely stuck in ranchers' collective craws.

Neckyoke's rendition of ranch life included few women. When women did appear in Neckyoke's letters, they seemed to be unwelcome inter- lopers on masculine terrain. This is not to say that Neckyoke did not, at times, try to acknowledge the increasingly visible presence of women in the industry. In 1964 Neckyoke pontificated about the importance of the Cowbelles, even claiming that the "men folks" were getting wise to the "fack" that the Cowbelles did more than "the men folks ever did an' they [the Cowbelles] sure shows more savvy than the men did."[38] Regardless of this nod of recognition, however, the majority of Neckyoke columns excluded or denuded women—which, of course, served to reinforce the paternalistic and patriarchal foundation of the larger ranch culture. Still, even here ranch women asserted their power and demanded recognition; in 1957 Neckyoke was joined by a female counterpart in the pages of the *Montana Stockgrower*.

Written in the same vernacular as the Neckyoke column, "Maggie's" column came from a ranchwoman who wrote cow talk as enthusiastically as Neckyoke. Maggie usually appeared in the "She Stuff" section of the *Stockgrower*. "She Stuff," a phrase used in ranching vernacular, referred to anything dealing with female cattle. Not surprisingly, the MSGA reserved the "She Stuff" section of the *Stockgrower* for Cowbelle news and feminine concerns more generally. The Montana Cowbelles mascot, a heifer cow, appeared under the section heading. Thus, both the name "She Stuff" and the iconography connected the Cowbelle-ranchwomen section of the periodical into the larger industry despite its segregated appearance. In drawing on cow talk when creating the women's section of the periodical, the MSGA staff effectively separated Montana ranchwomen from the ranchmen, but they also gave women a space that had not existed prior to 1955. "She Stuff" contained the reports from the local Cowbelle chapters, recipes, notices of upcoming Cowbelle activities, and a letter from the state Cowbelle president on the status of the organization; and, in 1957, it began to run the sporadic Maggie column.

Maggie's real identity, unlike that of Neckyoke, remains a public mystery. A 1982 memory book, produced by the MSGA to commemorate the longevity of the *Montana Stockgrower*, dedicates an entire section to honor Neckyoke and F. H. Sinclair. Maggie, however, appears nowhere. Even the pages of the *Stockgrower* of the 1950s and 1960s never mentioned Maggie's real identity. It is true that Maggie's column appeared less regularly than the Neckyoke column. This could account for the lack of attention she received both then and later. Her anonymity is telling in that it again underscores the privileging of the masculine so prevalent in ranch culture.

When Maggie's column did appear in the postwar decades, it usually chronicled some gathering of cattle growers from a gendered (ranch-woman's) perspective. The first column, published in 1957, explained how Maggie had finally "let them termater plants" go for a week and attend a stock growers' convention. She was excited because usually she was stuck at home while "Pa" went. The reasons for her immobility ranged from having to watch the kids to having "bum lambs" to attend to. She recalled the surprise (and joy) she felt at seeing so many ranchers in one place and explained that she was even more surprised to see a horse in a corral "right in the middle of that big hotel" lobby. Before she knew it, she had tickets to attend all of the events at the convention—from the Cowbelles fashion show to the coed cocktail hour—and had been signed up as an official member of the Cowbelles. The roping of Maggie into the various activities at the convention and her retelling of it is yet another example of the physical experience and later literary interpretation of cow talk.

After the convention was over, Maggie wrote to report how attending it had done much for her self-esteem as a rancher. She explained to "Secetery" Miracle, "I think I gained enough in new outlook to set me up for the year, and I've got enthusiasm for about every job I tackle now. I can see there's a lot of people in the same fix I'm in, and if we all work for the same thing and stay united we're bound to come out all right."[39] The next year, 1958, Maggie attended the convention for a second time. This time she was thrilled because she had made a new dress to wear with the "Keep Slim, Eat Beef" slogan sewn on the back. (The following year, as she prepared to attend the 1959 convention, Maggie appeared in the *Montana Stockgrower* in her dress—unfortunately with her back turned so we cannot see her face.)[40] She explained:

> We are lookin' forward to seein' everybody and talkin' a lot and gettin' some new ideas or brushin' off some old ones and probably agreein' we have been on the right track all the time. I sure think Neckyoke has somethin' when he says we cowmen is stubborn. But the longer I live the more I think stubborness is the answer to a lot of things if'n . . . [it] . . . is used to stick to what we know is right. . . . It's goin' to take some real nerve and stubbornness to resist the pressures we're apt to meet.[41]

The ranch vernacular Maggie uses in her report includes herself (a ranch-woman) in the masculine normative cow*men*, and, like Neckyoke, Maggie slurs her words to position herself, and her message, within the broader ranch culture. The modern appears (although not explicitly named) in Maggie's column as something against which cowmen need to be stubborn. And, most importantly, Maggie suggests that individual, stubborn ranchers will be safer if they unite.

Maggie's columns suggest the labor that went into creating unity through stock growers' conventions. Each state association in the years covered in this study hosted an annual convention (usually sometime after branding in the spring or before the autumn sales when the weather was expected to be decent and the demands for cow work slackened). Hundreds of ranchers attended and hundreds more attended the quarterly meetings of the executive committees.[42] In addition to the state-sponsored events, ranchers also gathered in untold numbers for meetings of their local livestock associations.

These group meetings were, of course, political. At the annual convention ranchers chose representatives for standing committees, listened to speakers on various issues of the day (including cattle health and the latest agency, policy, and legislative news from Washington), and adopted resolutions on everything from predator control to beef promotion.[43] However, the conventions, like most rancher events, were more than political gatherings; they also encompassed the social and cultural. As ranchers participated in the political aspects of convention-going—as they discussed marketing, legislation, federal regulation, and production issues—they also participated in a convention culture steeped in cow talk. That culture informed and buoyed the political.

Those ranchers responsible for organizing the gatherings conscientiously created the convention rituals and relied extensively on cow talk to convince one another of the importance of participating in these ostensibly social but in fact very deeply political gatherings. Both before and after the meetings (especially the annual state conventions), the associations published detailed accounts of the meetings. The "Call to Convention" issue appeared the month before the state convention and included the convention schedule as well as a letter from either the association president or the executive secretary urging ranchers to attend—all the

while using cow talk to convince ranchers of the importance of participating. In 1965, for example, Bob Barthelmess, president of the MSGA,
urged ranchers to attend the May convention in Billings. To get ranchers to saddle up, Barthelmess explained that prices would most certainly
be poor in 1965, exacerbating the problem of a rough winter and high
production costs. By attending the convention, he assured his readers,
they could learn from the MSGA what the "many capable individuals willing to invest time, energy, and brains" were doing about the troubles of
the industry. Despite rugged leadership, Barthelmess suggested that the
MSGA needed the attendance of as many members as possible to "meet
the formidable tasks ahead." And to remind ranchers of their commonality, Barthelmess ended his call with a cow-talk analogy: "Come to Billings
May 20–22 and help us out. A short-handed crew might spill the head. We
can't take that chance."[44] The labor necessary to confront the needs of
ranchers (the head) could not be conducted by only a few (short-handed
crew). The conventions existed so the collective group of ranchers could
pass resolutions that addressed issues important to ranchers' quest for
continued political, environmental, economic, and cultural power. Local
and state organizations, therefore, relied on cow talk—visual and written
manifestations of ranching culture—to promote unity and participation at
the conventions and to ultimately advance ranchers' desire for unshared
ecological space and uncontested politics.

The dominant and mostly unchallenged ranch culture showed itself
in countless and sometimes unquantifiable ways during ranchers' conventions and meetings. Of course, informal networking occurred outside
of the formal convention meetings. As ranchmen and -women mingled
in the hotel lobbies and convention halls, they engaged in cow talk as
they shared news of rain, range health, and the latest gossip about their
cows. Convention-goers attended dinners and cocktail hours and the big
dance (usually held on the last night of the convention). But convention
participants also imbibed ranch culture visually and obviously as they
embodied their culture through their dress. Ranchers wore their best
hats, shined their boots, donned leather bow ties, purchased or made
new dresses, and on more than one occasion displayed his or her brand
on a belt buckle. Like other displays of cow talk, ranchers' dress figured
prominently in their public advertisement of their culture. Seeing one

another in ranch-specific garb connoted, as surely as slurred language and phonetic spelling, that they mingled among members of the same community.

One of the most peculiar and interesting exhibitions of cow talk in rancher meetings was the decoration of the meeting sites with ranching iconography such as a horse in a corral in the hotel lobby. At various times from 1945–65, the state association convention committees decorated the lobbies of the convention sites with bales of hay, display booths, brand paraphernalia, and, every now and then, a cow or two.[45] Convention planners also asked permission to "brand" the walls of their meeting halls.[46] Using iconography and language that centered around the things ranchers had in common, ranchers could convince one another of their commonality of experience and thus overlook issues that could potentially divide them. When all was said and done with the political aspects of the meetings, ranchers could simply look at the branded wall and know they were, at their core, like-minded people with similar values and goals.

After the conventions and the bigger meetings (like the quarterly and executive committee meetings) had concluded, associations would devote entire editions of their periodicals to convention and meeting news.[47] This postconvention reporting mimicked other organizations' conferences, but importantly, the postmeeting articles in cow culture peppered the discussions of the political aspects of the gathering with a constant murmur of cow talk. Ralph Miracle used this language to describe stock growers' convention culture in 1955. He explained:

> There's something about a Stockgrowers convention that's hard to put your rope on. Something intangible would be the fancy word for it. There's serious business at these meetings. There's fun. And there's something that is just being with people. The right kind of people. . . . They [ranchers] like people. Particularly their own kind of people. They live with real things, weather, growing grass, cattle and horses. They like to talk about them with others who understand their language. . . . When you come right down to it, it defies description, but the true value and enjoyment of a stockgrowers meeting is hunkering down with your neighbors who may live hundreds of miles from you but have the same interest and the same set of standards.[48]

In mentioning the "right" kind of people, Miracle intended to set cattle ranchers apart from lesser workers (which included almost all nonranchers). Importantly, it was ranchers' experiences with the ecological labor and cow work—their living with real things like "weather, growing grass, cattle and horses"—that in Miracle's mind clearly set ranchers apart from other occupational groups.

Importantly, real ranchers often contributed articles about cultural gatherings of cattle folk to the pages of the association publications. In addition to chronicling events, ranchers wrote in to discuss any number of day-to-day operational issues. Some wrote to ask questions, others to share what they had learned through various experiments on their ranches. This information sharing provided valuable rallying space for ranchers' unity. Ranches, in these large western states, were often located hundreds of miles from one another, and ranchers experienced great distance from one another in their day-to-day lives. Each ranch differed according to its land use pattern, the number and type of head grown, the number of hands hired, and the nonhuman factors involved in growing cattle (weather, topography, etc.). To successfully come together in their associations and create an image of group unity and strength to the outside world, ranchers had to believe they understood one another despite the vast distances and differences that could and did separate them.

Ranchers' sharing of everyday news most often appeared in sections of the periodicals created for the purpose of learning about one's neighbors, but columns like "Neighborly Gossip" in the *Arizona Cattlelog* and the "Letters from Members" section in *Cow Country* were created from actual letters written to the executive secretaries in the course of transacting some sort of business, such as the paying of dues.[49] The sections visually and discursively negate differences because the letters never mention the number of head a rancher ran or the number of acres he or she owned, and the editors printed only the locale with the rancher's name. Thus, a small rancher's newsy update existed side-by-side with a large rancher's similar gossip. The commonality of experience across space, time, and economic position strikes readers as they peruse the letters. It could appear that all ranchers are doing in these letters is talking about the weather, but when one thinks more carefully about ranchers' use of certain mundane topics, such as the weather, in their correspondence to one another, it becomes clear that ranchers are using the discussions of rain, winter, and heat to create fellowship.[50]

Weather, for many people, can be a painfully trite discursive topic. For ranchers, however, the banality of weather was really a subject of life and death. As such, the weather, in all of its manifestations, served as a connective idiom that drew cattle folk into a common frame of reference throughout the arid region of the mountain West. The ecological economy of cattle ranching could not exist without precipitation. Thus, everywhere the weather blew ranchers together.

This use of weather as a topic of commonality appears in ranchers' personal papers as much as in the pages of the association periodicals. In Arizona and New Mexico, the language of drought played a particularly important role in the creation of cow talk. Throughout the desert southwest, "no two ranches are alike in terms of vegetation, soils, rainfall, elevation or topography," but ranchers everywhere in the arid state, especially in the drought-ridden years from 1952–56, could relate to the need for rain.[51] Eulalia Bourne, who ran a midsized ranching operation in south-central Arizona beginning in the 1930s, explained the infatuation with rain in the following way: "Rain is a touchy subject in this country. In the 'spotted showers' season, ranchers meet, and tactfully, sympathetically inquire about each other's rainfall. There are many among us who might be called rain worshipers, so excessive is our reverence for pennies from heaven."[52] Most ranchers ended letters with a rain update from their region, but when these people discussed rain, they were not just talking about the weather. In fact, rain symbolized for range cattle folk the green of both pastures and cash—as is illustrated by Bourne's reference to "pennies from heaven."

Ranchers were well aware of the economic importance of rain for their ranches and the range cattle industry. Ranchers in the Southwest particularly were desperate for rain so they could grow palatable feed for their cattle. For desert ranchers, rain symbolized both healthy ranges and economic viability.[53] Ranchers infused even topics that had nothing to do with feed, grass, or cattle with discussions of rain. Jo Flieger, from Painted Cave Ranch in Winkelman, Arizona, sprinkled her discussion of a recipe for green corn tamales with an explanation of rain and the status of range feed. She wrote, "As I am writing this, we are having a good slow rain; started last night and rained all night and is raining today. Coming on the heels of two other recent rains, it will keep the feed growing and put out plenty of water on the ranges."[54]

And it was not just ranchers in the desert Southwest who prayed for the pennies from heaven. While rain references were not as prolific in Wyoming and Montana, they were present. In 1959, when George Snodgrass wrote to accept an appointment on the Game and Wild Life Committee of the WSGA, he explained to Bob Hanesworth that in Natrona County they had "been getting some rain lately" and that several of their reservoirs had caught some water "for the first time in ten years."[55] In the northern Great Plains states, rain existed alongside severe weather as core elements of ranchers' cow talk.[56]

But nothing connected ranchers through cow talk more than cows. The tendency to mention their cows every chance they could allowed ranchers to overcome regional variations and promote collectivity as cow folk. As ranchers in the mountain West states experienced their identities as rural people living in an increasingly urbanized West, they relied on their connections to the nonhuman world of their ranches (and especially to their cows) to make sense of their identities—both as individuals and as a community.

To conclude, we return to the intrepid J. D. Craighead in southeastern Colorado for a final illustration of ranchers' privileging of their cows. In nearly every letter he penned (that was preserved), Craighead mentioned his cows and his concern for them. Certainly, this mentioning of cows was partly an economic concern, but it also shows a concern for the greater community of ranchers, as Craighead explained in a letter to a fellow rancher who had hit dry times in 1945. The rancher, Earl Kelly, hoped to be able to send his cows to Craighead, just until the rains came. Kelly would either rent some pasture from Craighead or would trade grazing time once the grass returned to his range. The informal economy and the concern for the health of both the cows and the ranches is palpable in Craighead's response. He wrote:

> I was glad to hear from you, but sorry to learn that you were having such dry weather and that you wished to move some of your cattle. I certainly can sympathize with you as I had to do that in 1934. . . . I could take care of 50 head of cows and heifers if they could be run in one pasture as I have at present plenty of grass. The thing that bothers

me is the continual lack of rain here. We had several wet snows in December and January that went off in a few days and the grass from these got a good start and is still green and growing but if we do not have rain soon . . . the grass will stop. For this reason I hesitate to say I can take care of them. We are very short of help, have only part of the crop planted and are right up to cutting the first alfalfa. . . . I would need one more saddle horse. . . . I hope by the time you receive this you will have had rain, but if not, you may wire or telephone me so that I shall know what you decide about coming up and can meet you. . . . My experience has been that next to losing cattle the worst thing is moving them away from home.[57]

Craighead, like so many ranchers in the mountain West, believed his cows were better off at home and knew that the owner-operator to whom he was writing would share this belief and his emotional attachment to the animals.

Even when things were going well in the ecological economy of range ranching, ranchers could not help but talk about and worry about their cows. In the early 1950s the Craighead ranch was doing great, and Craighead wrote to update the officers of the American Hereford Association on the progress of his breeding program. He ended the letter by saying, "Conditions here have improved wonderfully in the last ten days following our long drought. Several gentle rains have changed the appearance from grey to green. It looks like we can forget the old cows for a few days."[58] Of course he, and all owner-operators in the West, could never *really* forget the cows—for if they did, it would mean forgetting what it was that made them who they believed they really were.

Shutting the Gate
Concluding Thoughts

> There will be another roundup, you can rest assured.
> —Betty Accomazzo, Pioneer Ranch Histories, 1968

When I first began this work, I wanted to do two things. First, I wanted to make an original contribution to environmental and agricultural history by tracking changes during the postwar years regarding ranchers' attitudes about and actions toward the nonhuman world of their ranches. Second, I wanted to lend insight into the contemporary issues facing the interior West by finding the roots of the Sagebrush Rebellion. Both things happened, but not in ways I would have predicted.

In the early 2000s, when this work first commenced, the region had just come out of the increasingly tense decade of the 1990s. The rebellion, which had "officially" started in the 1970s when Jimmy Carter asserted federal government control over western lands in unprecedented ways, had gotten a new shot in the arm during the Clinton administration. Being from rural western Colorado (not far from San Juan County, Utah, which is now the epicenter of Sagebrush III), I was fascinated by the increasingly violent rhetoric and strangely disconnected ideologies of the rebels. My mom had worked with Gov. Richard Lamm, and I had grown up hearing about an increasingly "angry west." The governor's book, *The Angry West*, sat on our coffee table, for heaven's sake! But the roots of that anger seemed to exist somewhere in the long history of the twentieth century, and no one could quite tell me what they were. I thought maybe I could begin to excavate those roots with this study. Of course, sagebrush is notoriously tough to dig up, and I did not find simple answers in the course of my research.

What did emerge was the unexpected story this book chronicles. As the previous chapters have shown, ranchers in the mid-twentieth century were trying to find themselves as they simultaneously tried to hang on to who they thought they had always been. The new political and material contexts of the postwar decades brought ranchers' understandings of their land, their cattle, and their culture into question, and they spent those decades seeking to strengthen their ecological knowledge and their cultural confidence.

Ranchers' attitudes about and actions toward the ecology of the range and their work with cows did not seem to shift significantly in these years. They always believed in the centrality of cattle, the importance of husbandry, and the soundness of lived experience. So I did not really find the change over time I was expecting. Instead, I found evidence, throughout the years covered here, to suggest they did not want to overgraze their lands, but neither did they want some "monkeyward" scientist telling them what overgrazing meant. They did not despise coyotes, but they would shoot any they believed to be threatening their cattle (not unlike the response of many urbanites today to wildlife who wander into spaces they are not wanted). Ranchers in these years wanted government help but not government regulation, and, mostly, they wanted to be left alone to tend to their cows and wait for rain. Thus, I may not have found the "ah-ha" moment of change in ranchers' land-use ideologies or ecological labor strategies. What I found instead was a community of agriculturalists that was deeply committed to curating a group identity based in unique ecological and work experiences.

To achieve my second goal for the study—to find the roots of the Sagebrush Rebellion—I expected to find documented vitriol in the thousands of pages of archives I read. I did not find that. Instead, I found a group of landowners cultivating an image of victimhood and fear as they sought the attention and respect they believed they deserved. To do both, they persistently mobilized the cultural glue of cow talk that I have described in this book. Central to the cow talk narrative was the power and agency of the nonhuman world in ranchers' lives. They loved their cows and worried about nearly everything from bugs to wolves to even, ironically, sagebrush.

While the ranchers in this study recognized a changed and changing West, and while they clearly feared all that entailed, their responses were relatively peaceful. They joined their collective associations to engage in discourse with each other and with outsiders and to advocate for public policies and legislative initiatives that benefited their ranches. Whether they were in agreement or whether they were in debate, ranchers talked with one another and even with chosen outsiders about their ecological and material worlds. Especially via their formal associations, ranchers engaged in conversations and negotiations about the things they valued and feared. Government agents, sportsmen, tourists, and even conservationists were part of these conversations with ranchers on a host of issues during these years. And despite sometimes profound differences of opinion, the discussions continued for the decades covered in this book. That kind of ongoing dialog would become increasingly rare after the 1970s.

While I do not feel confident that I found *the* roots of the rebellion as it manifested in the decades after the 1970s, I do think the foundation laid by ranchers in these years provided the footing for the later sagebrush rebels. My study of ranchers' archives unearthed the presence of cow talk, and while that may not have included the social and political militancy that coalesced in the 1970s, it does illuminate the means through which ranchers continued their quests for power after the glory days of the open range. This "in between" part of the story is important and is something no other historians have investigated. Ranchers' publishing of ranch iconography, their recording of ranch lingo, their accounting of community organizing strategies, and their gathering of ranch stories of hardship and endurance all combined to create a formidable identity that later rebels would use toward their own violent ends. In this way, the study begins to unveil what Governor Lamm called the taproot of the Sagebrush movement, and it did indeed grow deep in the history of the twentieth century.[1]

The larger contribution of this study was something I was not seeking when I set out with my research agenda. Namely, the book shows the raw material and the laborious process required in the creation of a group identity. As I read ranchers' perspectives in the archives and analyzed their cultural values and practices, it became ever more apparent that ranchers were very much focused on and enthused by publicly and privately celebrating themselves. Their sense of entitlement to common resources

(e.g., public lands and water resources) and their assurance of the critical contributions they were making to society, in general, never wavered.
These beliefs became as strong and unyielding as the oldest sagebrush in
the West. As they repeated these strident beliefs about themselves, their
cultural unity strengthened and manifested in a politicized identity as a
community that was becoming marginalized, slighted, and discounted.
Whether that increasing marginalization was true can be debated. But the
fact that they believed it and, through the sharing of cow talk, emphasized
it at every opportunity is what is important here, as it seems that that sense
of themselves created cause for anger. Perhaps this study's universal contribution, then, is to further our understanding of how to create politicized
community by repeating cultural tropes—over and over again.

Just after the years covered in this book, dialog and discourse among
stakeholder groups in the mountain West seemed to wane. Ranchers began
to talk much less frequently with government officials and conservationists and turned ever inward. Environmentalists seem to almost never talk
with ranchers. (There are excellent exceptions to this, such as the Quivira
Coalition, but these exceptions are far too few.[2]) Historians and journalists
have increasingly sought to write what Joseph Taylor calls "adversarial" history. Indeed, in a book review titled "As Though Bunkerville and Malheur
Are the West," Taylor argues that too much current scholarship features
debates "according to the terms" set by the most radical in the Sagebrush
movement (most recently Cliven and Ammon Bundy).[3] I think this adversarial history might be exactly what I expected to write initially, but the
ranchers in the archives from the postwar decades had other ideas. The
archival material—ranchers' words and thoughts—asked me to consider
their perspectives in ways I had not expected. I may not have gotten their
entire story, but it's a start.

Ranchers continue to lose ground (quite literally) in the modern West.
Their successful experiences at creating commonality, comradery, and
political unity in the 1940s, 1950s, and 1960s were born from a sense of
loss that has only increased over the last half century. By understanding
these decades, perhaps we can also have a deeper understanding of the
tactics they used in their first and subsequent sagebrush rebellions. But
for now, this study simply meets ranchers where they were in the middle
decades of the last century. My hope is that the perspectives given here

will germinate interest in future studies of ranching in the 1970s and beyond. When future scholars turn to those studies, I hope they do so with a commitment to put away adversarial motives in order to open avenues to empathetic dialog among all the stakeholders in the West. The future of the region depends on it. And I, for one, desire that future to be more collaborative and less angry.

Notes

1. Epigraph quote from Anderson, *Imagined Communities*, 6. The *Montana Stockgrower* was the official publication of the MSGA. Each of the state stock growers' associations considered in this work (Arizona, Montana, New Mexico, Colorado, and Wyoming) used a monthly publication to communicate with the community of cattle ranchers in their state and their region: *Montana Stockgrower*, Montana Stockgrowers Association Papers, Montana Historical Society Research Center Archives, Helena; *Arizona Cattlelog*, Arizona Cattlegrowers' Association Manuscript Collection, Arizona Historical Society, Tempe; *Cow Country*, Wyoming Stockgrowers Association Papers, American Heritage Center, University of Wyoming, Laramie; *New Mexico Stockman*, George F. Ellis Papers, University of New Mexico Center for Southwest Research and Special Collections; [Colorado] *Cattle Guard*, Western History Collection, Denver Public Library.

2. There is a long history of discussion about what and where "the West" is. Is it process? Is it a place? Is it a fluctuating frontier or a coherent region? As David Emmons, William Cronon, and others have so rightly pointed out, both potential definitions of the West (process and place) are problematic. For clarity, I have decided to offer a rather simple and inexact definition of the West. For the purposes of this book, when I refer to the West, I mean the region west of the 98th meridian that has, at certain moments in time, experienced historical phenomena differently from other regions of the United States. The examples of these historical phenomena are resource-based and include things like bison and grassland ecological systems (the term "ecological systems" includes American Indian interactions with the bison, grasses, etc.), hard-rock mining, open-range cattle ranching, and the creation of massive irrigation systems, to name only few. My definition, then, is that the West is a region of place-based processes that are not the same as those encountered in other regions of the nation-state. While I do consider the West a distinct region, at the same time I recognize that culturally, politically, environmentally, and socially the region is profoundly diverse. And while I do agree that

213

"the" West is a place, I agree with Patricia Limerick, Richard White, and William Cronon: that place has been linguistically, culturally, and historically constructed. This book undertakes to examine one of those resource-based historical phenomena at a particular moment in time. For discussions about defining the West, see Cronon, "The West"; Emmons, "Constructed Province"; Limerick, *Legacy of Conquest*; White, *"It's Your Misfortune."*

3. Lucille Anderson, cover poem, *Arizona Cattlelog*, September 1946, Arizona Historical Society (hereafter cited as AHS), Tempe; Fain, "Cottonseed Meal-Salt Mixture," *Arizona Cattlelog*, October 1949, 8–10; "Jack Brenner, "President's Convention Address," *Montana Stockgrower*, June 1958, 34–35, Montana Historical Society (hereafter cited as MHS) Research Center Archives, Helena.

4. In subsequent chapters I explore more critically the gendered and racialized dimensions that existed in ranch work culture as well as the classed relationships between owners and hired hands. Because of the sources I used, however, I have mostly the voices of ranchers who either owned deeded property or utilized grazing permits to run large to mid-sized herds or of managers who ran larger ranches on the Native lands that pepper the West. Many American Indians ran substantial operations, but the nature of these enterprises (many were tribally owned) make them different from nonreservation ranches. As a result, I have included American Indians whenever they belonged to the general stock growers' associations (as in the case of Alvin Tso, a Navajo rancher in Arizona). I did not, however, address associations on the reservations (such as the San Carlos Apache Cattlegrowers' Association). A comparison of the two would make interesting future research. Despite my inability to incorporate the reservation aspect of twentieth-century ranching, Peter Iverson's work seems to indicate that American Indian ranchers very much engaged in cow talk as well. For discussions of Native ranching see Getty, *San Carlos Indian Cattle Industry*; and Iverson, *When Indians Became Cowboys.* Regarding class as a category of analysis, at times it was impossible to tell the economic position of any given rancher (especially in the correspondence files of the state association papers). What was interesting was that ranchers rarely discussed the size of any rancher's holdings, thus serving to homogenize the group in noteworthy ways. When I could discover the size of the ranch, the source base tended to come from larger ranches. I used these sources to read against the grain, looking for the voices of those less commonly represented in the archives (especially female ranchers, ranch hands, and domestic wage laborers). For examples of those papers of prominent ranchers that have been kept safely in the archives across the West, see Conrad K. Warren Papers, Grant-Kohrs National Historic Site, Deer Lodge, Mont.; and George F. Ellis Papers, Center for Southwest Research, University of New Mexico, Albuquerque.

5. I include in that latter group wives and daughters of ranchers who may not have considered themselves owner-operators but who did consider themselves to be ranchers. The gendered contours of ranch life will be a continuous lens of analysis throughout this book.

6. It is important to note that all five associations based their membership numbers on the ranch. A membership total of four thousand meant, generally, four thousand ranches, which could mean that multiple individuals running the ranch were members. Most members paid dues based on the number of head the ranch ran. "Membership in the New Mexico Cattle Growers Association," *New Mexico Stockman*, January 1960, 61; "Membership Reaches All-Time High," *Montana Stockgrower*, May 1951, 28. Because of the state's sparser population, the Wyoming Stock Growers Association (WSGA) had the fewest members (2,700 in 1957). Even so, in the mid-1950s the WSGA was adding as many as 70 members per month. See "Honor Roll," *Cow Country*, February 15, 1958, 17, WSGA Papers, Box 251, Folder 6, American Heritage Center, University of Wyoming, Laramie (hereafter cited as UW); Burroughs, *Guardian of the Grasslands*, 338. Similar things were happening in Colorado; see "Bob Schafer's 12,000-Mile Tour," *Cattle Guard*, May 1956, 12, Denver Public Library. Much of the increase in numbers came thanks to the tireless efforts of the executive secretaries and committee members of the various associations. I discuss these professionals further in chapter 7.

7. These numbers decreased in the latter twentieth century. Today, for example, the MSGA has approximately two thousand members and the ACGA reports having about fifteen hundred. In many ways, then, the 1940s, 1950s, and 1960s were the heyday of membership in the cattle growers' associations. See Montana Stockgrowers Association, accessed April 29, 2022, http://www.mtbeef.org/; Arizona Cattle Growers' Association, accessed April 29, 2022, https://www.azcattlegrowers.org.

8. The Cowbelles formed in Arizona in 1939, but the most substantial membership increases occurred from the late 1940s through the late 1960s. See Berry, "Be Shure to Fix the Fence."

9. Carr-Childers, *Size of the Risk*; and Merrill, *Public Lands and Political Meaning*. Two of the more well-known books on the Sagebrush Rebellion include Cawley, *Federal Lands, Western Anger*; and Makley, *Open Space, Open Rebellions*.

10. I am aware that some may think my use of the word "language" in this setting does not do justice to linguistic anthropological methodologies. I am not attempting to engage with that academic discipline, but I do believe that ranchers' cow talk can be considered a language in the broadest sense. In this case, I define "language" as the critical mechanism for forming social identity and group membership. My analysis suggests that cow talk (as a specific language) allowed ranchers to organize cultural beliefs and ideologies on a large scale in a similar vein to theories in sociolinguistics and linguistic anthropology. In this book I am most interested in shining light on the means that ranchers used to communicate about their work and their understanding and appreciation of natural spaces, cattle's bodies, and ecological systems. For a good introduction to linguistic anthropology, see Duranti, *Linguistic Anthropology*.

11. Hersey and Brady, "New Directions in Environmental History."

12. For examples that offer exceptions to the rule by doing an excellent job blending the environmental and agricultural, see Fiege, *Irrigated Eden*; Knobloch,

Culture of Wilderness; and Walton, *Western Times and Water Wars*. Donald Worster's *Dust Bowl* attempts to connect a people's (agri)culture and their agrarian practices, but the culture of Great Plains farmers becomes staid in Worster's hands, and the people emerge as unfettered, one-dimensional capitalists. I hope my story about western cattle folk's culture is more nuanced by being particularly aware of the paradoxes under which ranchers lived every day. Nathan Sayre's book, *Ranching, Endangered Species, and Urbanization in the Southwest*, is an excellent account of the intersections between ranching and the environment of the borderlands, but it does not address the culture of ranchers in any meaningful way. James A. Young and B. Abbott Sparks's *Cattle in the Cold Desert* weds the human and the nonhuman but addresses only the early period of ranching in the Great Basin desert. Richard L. Knight, Wendell C. Gilgert, and Ed Marston have edited an anthology that is one of the most thoughtful works regarding the important intersections of ecology, economics, and culture; although it is informed by a certain kind of historicity, it mainly addresses policy making and contemporary range management strategies. See Knight, Gilgert, and Marston, *Ranching West of the 100th Meridian*. Other agricultural histories tend to be focused more on rural sociology, on issues of rural policy, or both. This literature is enormous. For some of the best twentieth-century agricultural history, see Daniel, *Breaking the Land*; Hahamovitch, *Fruits of Their Labor*; Hurt, *American Agriculture*; Hurt, *Rural West since World War II*; Neth, *Preserving the Family Farm*.

13. White, "Are You and Environmentalist?" For an excellent look at post-1945 agricultural solidarity, see Divine, *On Behalf of the Family Farm*. We need similar studies for agricultural special interest groups in the West. My work also answers both Richard White's and Donald Worster's calls to wed the fields of labor, agricultural, and environmental history; see Worster, "Transformations of the Earth." In this study I use the word "culture" to denote the shared beliefs and values of a group that are represented through language, rituals, and images. In conducting my research, I considered both the material culture of range ranchers as well as the nonmaterial—the perceptual.

14. Several excellent studies treat the subject of range policy over time, especially regarding the federal government, but most end with the 1930s and the passage of the Taylor Grazing Act. See, for example, Carr-Childers, *Size of the Risk*; and Merrill, *Public Lands, Political Meanings*.

15. I chose not to begin the study in 1935, when the Taylor Grazing Act passed, mainly because the decade between 1935 and 1945 was exceptional for most ranchers. Prices were the lowest they had been in years in the late 1930s and the droughts the worst. Furthermore, wartime for the cattle industry (like almost all industries in the United States) was unusual due to government-controlled production and prices. Several studies address the Taylor Grazing Act, both its creation and its immediate aftermath. See Cawley, *Federal Land*; Merrill, *Public Lands and Political Meaning*; Rowley, *U.S. Forest Service Grazing and Rangelands*.

16. See Homer J. Berkshire, "New Mexico's Livestock Business," *New Mexico Stockman*, December 1939, 10; William Chapman, Commissioner of Agriculture, to Mrs. William E. Dover, October 7, 1953, WSGA Papers, Box 183, Folder 8, American Heritage Center, UW.

17. See Friedberger, "Cattle Raising and Dairying in the Western States"; White, *"It's Your Misfortune,"* 520–21; Gray, *Ranch Economics*, 6–10; and Schlebecker, *Cattle Raising on the Plains*,185–86. The aggregate numbers of cattle in each of the five states covered in this study increased in these decades, due in part to technological developments in the raising of cattle. For numbers of aggregate livestock, see agricultural statistical reports for the years 1945–65 (for example, Richard K. Smith, *Agricultural Statistics 1949*).

18. A note about terminology: here I enclose "cowboys and Indians" in quotes to denote that historians long used that phrase and others like it that are now considered both dated and racist. Still—it is what Anglo historians of the U.S. West and ranchers themselves used for several generations as shorthand for a complex racial frontier. But please note—there are instances in this text where I repeat problematic or culturally loaded terms as they appear in the archival sources I consulted. Additionally, ranchers during the period covered in this study had ideas about concepts such as "progress," "control," and even "conservation" that are today understood very differently.

19. For an enduring and broad discussion of the importance of the mythic West in both culture and scholarship, see Athearn, *Mythic West*. See also Henry Nash Smith, *Virgin Land*. The better known and most important of scholarly treatments of the late nineteenth century in the West are Billington, *The Far Western Frontier*; Lamar, *The Far Southwest*; Slotkin, *The Fatal Environment*; Utley, *The Indian Frontier*; Webb, *The Great Frontier*. Those works dealing specifically with the cattle boom are Allmendinger, *The Cowboy*; Dale, *The Range Cattle Industry*; Dykstra, *The Cattle Towns*; Igler, *Industrial Cowboys*; Young and Sparks, *Cattle in the Cold Desert*. Terry Jordan examines the earliest years of cattle ranching in his sweeping book, *North American Cattle-Ranching Frontiers*, but he also devotes considerable time to the "cattle boom" of the late nineteenth century. The comparative transnational turn in U.S. historiography has also tended to focus on the colonial period through the 1930s. See Dewey, "Ranching across Borders"; and Morris, "Disturbed Belt or Rancher's Paradise?"

20. The winter of 1886–87 brought unprecedented blizzards to most parts of the Great Plains and had been preceded by a prolonged drought. These two ecological phenomena, coupled with the arrival of cheap barbed wire (invented in the 1870s) and the shifting environmental ethics of the progressive federal government in the early 1900s, meant the end of open-range ranching. For Arizona and eastern New Mexico, the end of the open range came a bit later. The "big dry up" of the 1890s brought the ultimate demise of the open-range phase of ranching in the Southwest.

21. Paul Starrs quotes Stegner in *Let the Cowboy Ride*, 155. Starrs's book is one exception to the dearth of literature on ranching in the West post-1945. For other exceptions that focus, at least partially, on the postwar decades, see Cawley, *Federal Land, Western Anger*; Grosskopf, *On Flatwillow Creek*; Hess, *Visions upon the Land*; Schlebecker, *Cattle Raising on the Plains*; Sharp, *Big Outfit*.

22. For three more contemporary studies, see Lynn Jacobs, *Waste of the West*; Wuerthner and Matteson, *Welfare Ranching*; Rifkin, *Beyond Beef*. Like the other books listed here, Eric Schlosser's best-selling book is also generally antiranching in orientation, but he does lend what appears to be a less biased view of the use of the range for the growing of red-meat protein products. See Schlosser, *Fast Food Nation*.

23. I have chosen here to focus on beef cattle rather than dairy cattle because the two industries had little in common. On a cow-calf operation, the primary goal is the breeding of mature cows and heifers. (Mature cows are females that have produced at least one calf, and heifers are females that have not yet produced offspring.) The calves can be used as either future breeding stock or feed stock. Steer operations were less common in range country. Generally, steers (castrated bulls) were fattened either for finishing at feedlots or for slaughter. Many ranchers in the postwar decades blended both kinds of operations—resulting in a diverse business focus. (Some ranchers even had a few dairy cows to supplement the family's diet.) All range ranchers in this study raised beef cattle. The primary breeds grown in the five states in this study were Hereford, Angus, and Brahman.

24. The ecological biogregions of this broader mountain West region are complex and comprise numerous species of both shrubby plants and grasses. The Great Plains, for example, features four grassland types and is dominated by four species of grass in the central and southern sections: *Andropogon gerardii*, *Schizachyrium scoparium*, *Panicum virgatum*, and *Sorghastrum nutans*. In the northern portions of the region the dominant grass is *Stipa spartea*. Southwestern desert grasslands obviously vary. For discussions of the myriad of grasses found throughout the region and for descriptions of the climatological and topographic differences between ecological bioregions, see Phillips and Comus, *Natural History of the Sonoran Desert*; U.S. Forest Service, *The Western Range*; Vavra, *Ecological Implications of Livestock Herbivory*.

25. For an excellent discussion of the intersections between and the opportunities for joining labor and environmental history, see Peck, "Nature of Labor." Despite the nuggets of wisdom in this article, farmers and ranchers are almost not mentioned at all. Here, then, lies expanding opportunities for thinking about labor and the environment.

26. I am inspired by and draw on the theorizations about power from Michel Foucault. In the 1970s and 1980s, Foucault suggested that power exists everywhere and emanates from all places. Foucault and other adherents of a literary turn in the study of history observed a methodology that suggested that power can and should

be studied by focusing on the discourses contained within a diversity of texts. Foucault might be surprised to find his work being applied to a cultural group far from his time, place, and interests. But his ideas encourage us to take seriously the many texts produced by ranchers in the postwar decades (including letters, articles, cartoons, plays, autobiographies, images, and even events). These texts reveal the ways in which ranchers constituted their understandings of themselves and in so doing also unveil how they understood their power relations with outsiders—those Others who were not in the ranching business.

27. For examples, see Associated Press Wire, "Ranchers Ride into the Sunset: Cowboys Can't Afford Land," *Denver Post*, November 17, 2003, 1E; Leo Banks, "Under Seige," *Tucson Weekly*, March 10, 2005, 23–28; Brian Maffly, "Independent Ranchers Fight Corporate Control," *High Country News*, September 30, 2002, 4; Tim Vanderpool, "Klump Country Blues," *Tucson Weekly*, May 20, 2004, 23–28; Ann Wendland, "Fewer Hats . . . More Heads: Ruminations on the Quivera Coalition Trying to Find Harmony between Agriculture and Environmentalism," *Canyon Country Zephyr*, June/July, 2003, 22; Dennis Wagner, "Border Ranchers, in a World without a Wall," *USA Today*, accessed January 13, 2019, https://www.usatoday .com/border-wall/story/us-ranchers-deal-with-migrants-border-crossers-mexico /559702001/; Mateusz Pertowski, "Ranchers Prevail in Idaho Grazing Dispute," *Capitol Times*, accessed January 13, 2019, https://www.capitalpress.com/state /idaho/ranchers-prevail-in-idaho-grazing-dispute/article_99b719d7–0ecd-5a37 –9358-f61f1dee2fb6.html.

28. Brian Calvert, "The Political Power of the Cowboy," *High Country News*, July 23, 2018, 2; Carrie Stadheim, "Hammonds Are Home: Dwight and Steven out of Prison and Back to Oregon," *Tri-State Livestock News*, July 11, 2018, https://www .tsln.com/news/hammonds-are-home-dwight-and-steven-out-of-prison-and-back -to-oregon/.

29. This idea come from Nancy MacLean, who argues that the bulwark of conservative power in the 1920s KKK came from a "remarkable synchronicity" of ideas and values; see MacLean, *Behind the Mask*, xvi.

CHAPTER 1

1. The term "rancher" is, in some ways, difficult to define. Throughout this work, when I refer to ranchers I mean generally the people who owned a ranch and saw to the day-to-day operations on a range cattle ranch. This group includes small, large, and midsized ranching operations. Furthermore, the term owner-operator includes women. Most ranches in this era were family operations in which the owners both owned and operated the ranch. There were, of course, exceptions— especially for the very large ranches whose owners used hired labor to run the day-to-day operations. The Bell Ranch in New Mexico is an example of the latter. Still, even in these situations, while the operators were waged labor, they often owned

some cattle of their own and owned or leased smaller plots of land near their place of employment to grow their own herds. For example, George Ellis, manager of the Bell Ranch, ran cows for the Bell as well as owning a small herd of his own. The dominant ranch culture that solidified itself in the postwar years was, generally speaking, created and reinforced by this owner-operator class. When I refer to "ranchers" in this chapter, I employ the term more broadly. Modernization affected ranch hands, as well as owner-operators, on any size of ranch; all felt the effects of modernization acutely. The decision about which forms of modernized mechanization to bring to the ranch (which I discuss in chapter 2) concerned a more focused group of ranchers: namely the owner-operators.

2. For discussions of the emergence of the idea of the New West in the historical discipline, see the anthology edited by Limerick, Milner, and Rankin, and especially Limerick's essay, "What on Earth Is the New Western History?," in *Trails: Toward a New Western History*. See also McGerr, "Is There a Twentieth-Century West?" For discussions specifically on developments in the twentieth-century West, see Malone and Etulain, *The American West*; Fernlund, *Cold War American West*; Lamar, "Westering in the Twenty-First Century"; Nash, *American West Transformed*; Nash, *World War II and the West*.

3. For interesting discussions of modernization, including the definition I apply here, see Yoshiie Yoda and Radtke, *Foundations of Japan's Modernization*.

4. The idea that interest groups can and do form during times when a group's welfare is threatened by changing socioeconomic and environmental circumstances is a well-known theory of group formation in political science circles. The first to suggest this theory was David Truman in his 1951 *The Governmental Process*. See also Olson, *Logic of Collective Action*; and Sabatier, "Interest Group Membership."

5. J. D. Craighead to Dr. Bessie Metz, October 26, 1943, Craighead Papers, Box 5, Folder 1, Huntington Library, San Marino, Calif. For a recent study on Craighead's general region, see Sheflin, *Legacies of Dust*.

6. The passage of this act was not as simple as I make it sound here. Passage of legislation removing the public domain from open access to ranchers has a long, convoluted history. Because it is not the purpose of this book to chronicle the changing circumstances of public lands grazing, I will not go into great detail about that history, but there has been much written about it, and I will give a quick overview here. Karen Merrill has written the best book chronicling the policy debates and divisiveness engendered by the government's removal of public domain from resource use in the late decades of the nineteenth and early decades of the twentieth centuries (*Public Lands and Political Meaning*). She argues, quite convincingly, that the general conflicts about public lands grazing policy and the specific conflicts over the workings of the Taylor bill stemmed from two different views of property rights—ranchers held the view that they were entitled to access to public resources (invested through historical usage and through rights as members of the public), and the federal government believed itself to be the ultimate steward (and owner)

of those lands. In spite of these tensions, the Taylor Grazing Act passed, and, on the whole, ranchers approved of it because in its final form the act gave considerable power to ranchers at the local level. It set up advisory boards to distribute the initial permits and to cooperate with the Grazing Service to decide carrying capacity of the range. The livestock associations were intimately involved in this and were often in charge of appointing the rancher representatives on the local advisory boards. Because they had such an active part in the regulatory enforcement of the act, ranchers did not generally complain about it in the early years. In the 1940s, in fact, ranchers' ire was directed much more at the Forest Service (because of its heavy-handedness in deciding animal unit months of grazing on Forest Service lands) than at the Grazing Service. The Grazing Service, while not wholeheartedly loved by all, avoided much of ranchers' anger until the early 1950s when, under its new title as the Bureau of Land Management, it began to threaten fee increases. For the best sources on the history of and problems surrounding public lands grazing, see Donahue, *Western Range Revisited*; Hirt, *Conspiracy of Optimism*; Peffer, *Closing of the Public Domain*; Rowley, *U.S. Forest Service Grazing Lands*. For works specifically on the Taylor Grazing Act, see Calef, *Private Grazing and Public Lands*; Foss, *Politics and Grass*; Libecap, *Locking Up the Range*. For another fantastic study of the federal government's heavy-handed intrusion into traditional grazing cultures, see Weisiger, *Dreaming of Sheep in Navajo Country*.

7. Other policies wrought on livestock communities in the West were not nearly as popular as the Taylor Grazing Act. For example, John Collier's decision to slaughter millions of Navajo sheep without full support from the Diné undermined the tribe economically and brought cultural hardship. Policies such as herd reductions, however, were very different from the creation of a permit-based grazing system, which was the outcome of the Taylor Act. For a discussion of the New Deal's impacts on Navajo sheep ranchers, see White, *Roots of Dependency*; and Weisiger, *Dreaming of Sheep in Navajo Country*. For a general discussion of American Indian cattle ranching, see Iverson, *When Indians Became Cowboys*. In the later twentieth century, Hispanic and American Indian pastoralists in northern New Mexico and southern Colorado began groundbreaking cooperative ranching efforts both to curb negative environmental effects of grazing and to aid in the cultural and economic viability of the region. See Pena, *Chicano Culture, Ecology, and Politics*; Pulido, *Environmentalism and Economic Justice*.

8. Nash, *The Federal Landscape*.

9. Graf, *Wilderness Preservation*, 45.

10. For discussion on the intellectual reaction of ranchers to the rise of conservation in the early twentieth century, see Merrill, *Public Lands and Political Meaning*; and Rowley, *U.S. Forest Service*. For the seminal discussion of conservationist values, see Hays, *Conservation and the Gospel of Efficiency*. Ranchers did indeed possess an instrumentalist view of natural resource usage—rather than supporting the preservationist agenda of setting aside nature to view from afar (a political stance that

began in the late nineteenth century, gained currency in the 1950s, and really took off in the 1960s), they supported political movements that promoted management of those resources for use in present and future generations.

11. See Graf *Wilderness Preservation*, as well as Merrill, *Public Lands and Political Meaning*, and Rowley, *U.S. Forest Service*. See also Sayre, *Politics of Scale*. Paul Hirt also discusses some early Forest Service history in his excellent book *Conspiracy of Optimism*. For older (but still useful) studies on grazing politics, see Foss, *Politics and Grass*; Peffer, *Closing of the Public Domain*; Robbins, *Our Landed Heritage*; Steen, *U.S. Forest Service*.

12. Ralph Miracle, "Tangled Twine," *Montana Stockgrower*, April 1938, 4. See also Farrington Carpenter, "The Federal Range Code," ibid., 2–4. The idea that the regulatory impulse of New Dealers was not completely misplaced but did become unreasonable over time continued to surface years after the New Deal. See, for example, Safford, Jack Brenner Oral History, September 11, 1976, MHS Research Center Archives, Helena.

13. The 1979 Nevada state legislature's demand that the federal government hand the public domain over to the individual states is probably the most familiar manifestation of this discussion. As William Graf explains, however, the 1979 Sagebrush Rebellion had many precedents. As early as the late nineteenth century, states' rights advocates rebelled against the idea of a federal government landlord. The 1940s hearings and rancher-led attacks against Forest Service officials were simply two instances in a long string of land rebellions in the West. See Graf, *Wilderness Preservation*, 155–70. For the ways in which the 1970s movement was situated in a larger context of environmentalism, see chapter 7 in Rothman, *Saving the Planet*. For two other excellent studies about the sagebrush rebels' ideology and tactics, see Cawley, *Federal Land, Western Anger*; and Switzer, *Green Backlash*. For an interesting global examination of the reaction to green politics, see Rowell, *Green Backlash: Global Subversion*.

14. Bernard DeVoto's essays on what he termed "the western land grab" are the most well-known of this coverage in the mid-to-late 1940s and appeared mostly in his column in *Harper's Weekly*. The columns, called "The Easy Chair," were collected in a book of the same name in 1955. For ranchers' perspectives, see the editorial written by Wyoming rancher Elmer Brock to the *Denver Post*, February 2, 1947. For the best example of eastern depictions of ranchers' enacting environmental harm to promote their self-interest, see DeVoto, "The Anxious West," *Harper's Monthly* 93 (December 1946): 481–91; and DeVoto, "The West Against Itself," *Harper's Monthly* 94 (January 1947): 231–56. See also Jonathan Thompson, "First Sagebrush Rebellion," *High Country News*, January 14, 2016.

15. A rich oral history collection documents some of the encounters ranchers had during the mid-1940s with the U.S. military. See White Sands Missile Range Oral History Legacy Project, Manuscript Collection 346, Rio Grande Historical Collections, New Mexico State University Library, Las Cruces. An overview of this

oral history project has also been published as Eidenbach and Morgan, *Homes on the Range*. For an institutional history of the White Sands National Monument, see Welsh, *Dunes and Dreams*. An exciting and growing subfield of inquiry in western history focuses on the atomic West. For some of the best works, see Ackland, *Making a Real Killing*; Amundson, *Yellowcake Towns*; Goin, *Nuclear Landscapes*; Hevly and Findlay, *The Atomic West*; Hunner, *Inventing Los Alamos*; Ringholz, *Uranium Frenzy*.

16. Approximately ninety-seven New Mexico ranch families lost their land to the federal government during the mid-late 1940s; see Eidenbach, *Homes on the Range*, xiii.

17. For an interesting discussion of the mentality behind western support of the defense industry, see Chambless, "Pro-Defense, Pro-Growth." Once the ranchers' lands had been confiscated by the military, the testing began. The increasing numbers of tests at the White Sands range are staggering. In 1948, a year after Boyd's protest, the military was testing seven projects and conducted a total of fifty-two tests. In 1950 there were still only seven projects firing sixty-three projectiles into the New Mexico desert. But by 1955 those numbers had, quite literally, sky-rocketed. In 1955, thirty-six projects conducted 1,251 firings; ten years later the numbers had increased to seventy-eight projects firing 2,400 tests. "White Sands Missile Range History," White Sands Missile Range Museum. It is beyond the scope of this work to consider the environmental and cultural impacts of this kind of intensive testing, but fortunately journalists in the West and scholars of the West have been theorizing the effect of atomization on the region for decades. For good and sometimes painfully sad discussions of this, see Hevly and Findlay, *The Atomic West*; Montoya, "Landscapes of the Cold War West"; Udall, *The Myths of August*; Terry Tempest Williams, *Refuge*.

18. Beginning with Gerald Nash in the 1980s, scholars have generally agreed that the militarization of the American West had far-reaching effects on its social, cultural, economic, and political development. For ranchers, it appears that developments during the war years and the postwar decades changed their lifeways forever. See Malone and Etulain, *The American West*; Fernlund, *Cold War American West*; Nash, *American West Transformed*; Nash, *World War II and the West*.

19. White, *"It's Your Misfortune,"* 500–503, 562–65. See also Milner, O'Conner, and Sandweiss, *Oxford History of the American West*, 454–56.

20. Census material reveals that the highest involuntary changes in land and farm ownership in the states under consideration occurred, not surprisingly, in the 1930s. During the Depression decade, thirty-five out of a thousand farms changed hands through delinquent taxes, foreclosures, bankruptcies, and administrator sales. This outpaced the voluntary sales and trades category, which shows twenty-eight out of a thousand farms changed hands in this manner. It is important to note that ranches were not considered a separate category from farms in the census during these years. In the five states here, however, it is clear that the majority of both private and federal agricultural lands were used, at least partially, for raising

and grazing cattle. In the 1940s and 1950s land exchanged hands more voluntarily, but the trend toward less acreage used for agriculture simply accelerated. For the former statistics, see U.S. Department of Agriculture, *Agricultural Statistics* (1949), 569. For the latter statistics, see USDA, *Agricultural Statistics* (1957), 427.

21. I borrow the phrases "warm winter" and "cold winter" from Kevin Leonard. Population growth in the northern mountain West states in fact declined during the war. Both Montana and Wyoming lost people in the war years, but after the conclusion of the war both states joined the warm-winter states in experiencing population growth. See Leonard, "Migrants, Immigrants, and Refugees," 36–37.

22. Jones, *Farm Real Estate, 1950–92*.

23. Jones.

24. Letters from J. D. Craighead to J. F. Gauger, March 19, 1950, and April 16, 1950. Craighead Papers, Box 5, Folder 8, Huntington Library, San Marino, Calif.

25. U.S. Department of Agriculture, *Agricultural Statistics* (1963), 435.

26. See O'Conner, "A Region of Cities," 554–55. Much of the urban growth in Montana and Wyoming occurred in the 1970s and 1980s, but the process of urbanization, if not metropolinization, began in the immediate postwar years.

27. Dias, "The Great Cantonment," 71–84.

28. See Sayre, *Politics of Scale*, 3.

29. While many ranchers continually referred to all outsiders as "dudes," most also referred to urban interlopers as tourists and recreationists. I will refer to those who sought leisure in the rural and wild spaces of the mountain West interchangeably, as both tourists and recreationists.

30. Rothman, *Devil's Bargains*.

31. William Chapman to Mrs. William E. Dover, October 7, 1953, WSGA Papers, Box 183, Folder 8, American Heritage Center, UW. Dover was the public relations committee chair in 1953 and had written to Chapman requesting statistics on the modernization of Wyoming ranches in order to illustrate to the broader public how difficult Wyoming ranchers had it. While ten miles may not seem like a long distance, most of the roads were simply graded dirt paths that were not paved. Traveling ten miles could very easily take forty-five minutes to an hour. In the rough Wyoming, Colorado, and Montana winters, roads could, and often did, become impassable. Additionally, ranch families rarely owned more than one transportation vehicle, and that vehicle often was needed for work on the ranch and thus only infrequently could be used to get ranch families to town.

32. Evelyn Perkins, "Life on a Cattle Ranch," *Arizona Cattlelog*, April 1950, 23.

33. J. E. Magnum to NMCGA, September 24, 1947, George Godfrey Papers, Box 6, Folder 3, Rio Grande Historical Collections, New Mexico State University, Las Cruces.

34. William Willey to Abbie Keith, March 29, 1956, ACGA Manuscript Collection, Box 5, Folder 3, AHS, Tempe. See also Abbie Keith to Thomas A. Beaham, June 15, 1956, Box 5, Folder 4, ibid.; Ernest Chilson to Thos. Beaham, April 26, 1956, ibid.

35. For a good anthology of the peculiar manifestations of masculinity in the trans-Mississippi West, see Basso, McCall, and Garceau, *Across the Great Divide.* For a broader overview of the crisis in masculinity in the 1950s, especially as it manifested itself in cultural forms, see Cohan, *Masked Men.* Elaine Tyler May also grapples with gender roles in the 1950s and is particularly insightful regarding how ideas about masculinity were reflected in and reflective of the domestic politics of the decade; see May, *Homeward Bound.* There is some debate about women's acceptance of the gendered ideals of the 1950s. For an excellent anthology that adds women's agency to the discussions of their objectification in these years, see Meyerowitz, *Not June Cleaver.*

36. Rothman, *Devil's Bargains,* 143–52. Rothman is far from the only historian to discuss this trend, and it is important to note that while the automobile was essential in making the West ever more accessible to tourists, other modes of transportation laid the foundation for the western tourist industry. For the latter, see Schwantes, "No Aid and No Comfort"; Dilworth, "Tourists and Indians." For other works on the intersections of tourism and automobiles, see Belasco, *Americans on the Road*; Hyde, "From Stagecoach to Packard"; Jakle, *The Tourist*; Scharff, *Taking the Wheel*; Sutter, *Driven Wild.* See also Margaret Jacobs, *Engendered Encounters.*

37. White, *"It's Your Misfortune,"* 552.

38. The dude ranchers in the West experienced these changes acutely. As revenues increased as more guests arrived, dude ranchers also noted that these guests came mostly to ride, to fish, and to hike. In earlier years, these same tourists would have most likely expected to be exposed to the spectacle of cattle ranching *on the ranch* rather than expecting to experience the natural world surrounding the ranch. See Dude Ranchers' Association Papers, Surveys, Box 4, Folder 8, American Heritage Center, UW. For discussions of the early dude ranching business, see chapter 5 in Rothman, *Devil's Bargains*; and chapter 7 in Athearn, *The Mythic West.* See also Borne, *Dude Ranching.*

39. These attempts were met with impressive and sometimes successful resistance. For discussions of some of these encounters, see Warren, *Hunter's Game.* See also Harmon, *Indians in the Making*; Jacoby, *Crimes against Nature*; McEvoy, *The Fisherman's Problem*; Spence, *Dispossessing the Wilderness.*

40. Warren, *Hunter's Game,* 85.

41. "Antelope Hunting Season Controversy," *Montana Stockgrower,* October 15, 1953, 14; D. W. Wingfield, "Neighborly Gossip," *Arizona Cattlelog,* June 1946, 9.

42. Paul Christensen, "Range Management from the View of Recreationists and Dude Ranchers," Dude Ranchers' Association Records, Box 3, Folder 4, AHC, UW.

43. John Babbitt, "Cattleman Refutes 'Anti-Game' Claim," *Arizona Daily Sun,* September 28, 1951.

44. We will discuss wildlife control further in later chapters. For the purposes of this chapter, it is important to note that ranchers were not against hunting, per se. They were against a particular type and category of hunter. "Of Interest to

Southwestern Livestock Growers and Farmers," *New Mexico Stockman*, January 1960, 48, shows that New Mexico was slated to receive $430,000 in wildlife and fish restoration funds from the U.S. government because of the concern that deer, antelope, quail, and certain species of fish were fast disappearing due to adverse hunting and fishing pressures. Thus, overhunting seemed a real threat for many ranchers and partly explains their opposition to nonlocal hunters. Despite their conservationist concerns, they still clung to the sport as an important part of their masculine identity. For the celebratory articles and notes regarding successful hunting, see Marvin Glenn, "Hunting Lions," *Arizona Cattlelog*, April 1952, 40–41; Clyde Riggs (Mrs. F. D.) Perkins, "We Lick the Cats," *Arizona Cattlelog*, July 1949, 32–29; Henry Smith, "Rattlesnakes," *Arizona Cattlelog*, March 1948, 42–43; "Livestock Commission Report," *Montana Stockgrower*, March 1956, 12.

45. Image drawn by Melvin Miller, 1959, Box 192, WSGA Records, AHC, UW.

46. Porter to NMCGA, May 1953, George Godfrey Papers, Correspondence, Rio Grande Historical Collections, New Mexico State University, Las Cruces.

47. "Questionnaire to Ranchers Concerning Game," WSGA Papers, Box 57, Folder 7, American Heritage Center, UW.

48. WSGA Papers, "Film," Box 57, Folder 7, American Heritage Center, UW.

49. The Bell Ranch had a long history dating back to Spanish colonization. It comprised over 130,000 acres during the 1940s, 1950s, and 1960s. It was a prime area for antelope hunting. The Bell Ranch figures prominently in later chapters of this book.

50. Because of the Bell Ranch's size and central location for antelope migrations, the game warden coordinated with Ellis to decide on numbers of licenses issued for the Bell Ranch area. See George Ellis to Ralph Keeney, August 30, 1949, Ellis Papers, Box 1, Folder 1, Center for Southwest Research, University Libraries, University of New Mexico.

51. Warren, *Hunter's Game*, 71–103.

CHAPTER 2

1. The rise in demand for agricultural commodities with the coming of World War I led the federal government to increase support for research and development for industrial agriculture. For the best sources on this phenomena and on how technological developments affected farmers' business, the land's ability to produce, and the social relations within rural America, see Daniel, *Breaking the Land*; Hurt, *American Agriculture*; Jellison, *Entitled to Power*; Neth, *Preserving the Family Farm*; Robert C. Williams, *Fordson, Farmall, and Poppin' Johnny*.

2. From 1938 to 1945 the size of ranches increased while the number of ranchers decreased—changes greater than at any other time in U.S. history. However, they were not profoundly significant. In 1940 the average ranch contained 3,559 acres of deeded land; by 1945 the average ranch contained 3,667 acres. The farm population

throughout the postwar decades continued its twentieth-century decline—but that decline was slow, and for those in ranch country it often seemed imperceptible. See Hurt, *American Agriculture*; Schlebecker, *Cattle Raising on the Plains*, 185.

3. See Bonnifield, *The Dust Bowl*; Worster, *Dust Bowl*.

4. Craighead to Metz, 1943, Craighead Papers, Box 5, Folder 1, Huntington Library, San Marino, Calif.

5. J. D. Craighead to Wyatt Mfg. Co., February 10, 1950, ibid.

6. Interestingly, labor costs continued to increase for ranchers across the West. This was largely because the cost of labor in all areas and industries increased astronomically during the postwar years. Southwest cattle ranches saw an increase in expenditures for labor of 110 percent from 1940 to 1963, while northern ranches experienced an increase of over 400 percent. See Gray, *Ranch Economics*, 192.

7. Gray, *Ranch Economics*, 187.

8. Frank Krentz, "Neighborly Gossip," *Arizona Cattlelog*, December 1951, 56.

9. Mrs. Ott Dixon, *Arizona Cattlelog*, December 1951, 56.

10. Georgia Baker, *Arizona Cattlelog*, December 1951, 56.

11. See, for example, George Ellis's efforts in the Western Research Association in the early 1950s on cloud seeding, Ellis Papers, Box 3, Folder 14, Center for Southwest Research, UNM. See also "Quay County Rancher Offers $100 an Inch for Artificial Rain," the *New Mexico Stockman*, December 1947, 88.

12. The list is in Research Committee Correspondence Folder, Ellis Papers, Box 2, Folder 11, Center for Southwest Research, UNM.

13. Note that while Ellis managed the Bell Ranch for its absentee owners, he also owned his own cows and leased land from a neighbor for grazing. Thus, Ellis was both an owner *and* an operator.

14. Ellis, *Bell Ranch*, 81.

15. "Head" refers to the number of cattle: a herd of one hundred head consists of one hundred animals. Many range cattle ranches not only used deeded property (private property owned by the rancher or business corporation) but also leased land from the federal or state governments. See Remley, *Bell Ranch*; and Rowley, *U.S. Forest Service*.

16. George Ellis also discusses Apache and Comanche utilization of the region, but reserves most of his history for the use of the land for the growing of cows based on grazing. For hundreds of years before the arrival of the Spanish and Anglos, Native peoples had left their marks on the land in the places they used most often: in canyons where they hid and hunted; and near watering holes where they lived or found respite and rest during long journeys. The land that encompassed the Bell, then, has a long and rich history, including that of Apache and Comanche peoples. Following Spanish invasion and occupation, the land was surveyed into two Mexican land grants: the Baca Location No. 2 and the Pablo Montoya Grant of 1824. After the United States' war with Mexico in 1846–48, the heirs of Pablo Montoya applied for confirmation of their grant. As with so many Spanish

land-grant disputes, an Anglo, John S. Watts, acted as the "legal representative" for the Montoyas in the confirmation process. Watts took a large part of the grant as his legal fee and later acquired the adjoining Baca Location No. 2. Watts later sold this property to Wilson Waddingham. By 1885 Waddingham was running large herds of cattle on the range in the way of the Anglo cattle kings of the day. Waddingham overused the range, and by 1893 overstocking and grazing of stock from other ranches combined with drought to leave the range deeply depleted. Financial hardship and mismanagement caused Waddingham to sell the ranch in 1898 to E. G. Stoddard, president of the New Haven Bank, who founded the Red River Valley Company in order to buy the Bell Ranch. From then until 1946 this company, headed first by Stoddard and, after 1923, by Julius G. Day, survived the ups and downs of the cattle markets of the 1920s and 1930s. In 1932 Bell Ranch manager Charles O'Donel retired but stayed on as vice president of the Red River Valley Company. In January 1933 Albert K. Mitchell took over the management of the Bell and ran it until the Red River Valley Company sold it in 1947. This sale broke the Bell Ranch into seven smaller ranches. Harriet E. Keeney bought the headquarters unit (130,855 acres) and acquired the rights to the Bell brand. It was Harriet Keeney and her husband Ralph D. Keeney who hired George Ellis to manage the Old Headquarters Unit of the Bell Ranch. Because the Keeneys maintained rights to the Bell brand, the unit Ellis managed continued to be referred to as the Bell Ranch. For an excellent history of the Bell from the nineteenth century through 1947, see Remley, *Bell Ranch.*

17. Ellis, *Bell Ranch*, 81.

18. Ellis, 83.

19. Mattie Ellis was a prolific writer. For discussions of her life as a ranchwoman, see Mattie Ellis, *Bell Ranch: Peoples and Place*; *My Dishpan*; *Bell Ranch Recollections.*

20. Stella (Mrs. Cort) Carter, "Neighborly Gossip," *Arizona Cattlelog*, January 1952, 42–43.

21. In the 1970s and 1980s feminist scholars increasingly began to demand that historians reclaim women's contributions to the economic workings of societies. For the best overviews and examples of Marxist-feminist theorizing and revisioning of labor history, see Baron, "Gender and Labor History," 1–47; Boydston, *Home and Work*; Cowan, *More Work for Mother*; Johnson, "Memory Sweet to Soldiers"; Scott, *Gender and the Politics of History*; Strasser, *Never Done.*

22. Marion Moore to Walter Nye, May 1945, Dude Ranchers' Association Papers, Box 3, Folder 4, American Heritage Center, University of Wyoming.

23. What historian Nancy Grey Osterud has found true for nineteenth-century women in the Nanticoke Valley in upstate New York seems to hold true for 1950s female ranchers as well: namely that "women strove to create mutuality in their marriages . . . and reciprocity in their performance of labor." See Osterud, "She Helped Me Hay It," 91. Dee Garceau's work reveals that Wyoming ranchwomen in the early decades of the twentieth century associated their labor identity with their

sense of "group partnership," but they also were aware of their individual contributions to the ranch's success. Postwar ranchwomen illustrate this same pull between individualism and communalism but seem to emphasize their individual triumphs. In the public projects of 1950s (a topic discussed more in chapter 5), ranchwomen seem distinct from Garceau's early twentieth-century ranchwomen. See Garceau, *Important Things*, 89–111.

24. See Rosa Ronquillo Rhodes, Rhodes Diaries, 1964–1982, AHS, Tucson.

25. Jordan, *Cowgirls*.

26. Jeffers, *Ranch Wife*, 68.

27. "T-Bone News," Montana Cowbelles Records, Box 4, Folder 13, pg. 1, MHS Research Center Archives, Helena.

28. Ellis, *Bell Ranch*, 81.

29. Bourne, *Woman in Levi's*, 10.

30. Josefina Badilla, Oral History, AHS, Tucson. In the original Spanish: "Le dije a mi esposo no—yo no quiero estar aquí en este rancho sola porque un rancho, mira, es una cosa muy dura, muy triste, no? Porque por ejemplo mira, una, la mujer se queda en el rancho todo el día. El hombre se levanta temprano, se desayuna, se asilla su caballo y se va. . . . Y nosotros las mujeres no mas en el rancho . . . no mas hacer la comida para mis esposo cuando venia, lavar, planchar mi ropa y toda del, no mas pasaba el día sola y es muy triste, es muy duro. . . . En el rancho muy solo. La gente muy lejos, lejos, así que no es, para mi no era nada bonito." My thanks to Maritza de la Trinidad for helping me with aspects of the oral history I could not hear or understand and for helping me with writing the Spanish and English transcripts.

31. The chuckwagon also implicitly symbolizes the disparities that existed between ranches in the mid-twentieth century. Few ranches were large enough to require the use of such a wagon by that time. With over a hundred thousand acres to roam during branding season, the Bell was one of those large ranches.

32. Ellis, *Bell Ranch*, 89.

33. Jeffrey J. Jack Brenner Oral History, September 11, 1976, pp. 23, 27, MHS Research Center Archives, Helena.

34. Shorty Wallins to Frank M. King, May 1950, Frank M. King Papers, Box 1, Shorty Wallins Folder, Huntington Library, San Marino, Calif.

35. Shorty Wallins to Frank M. King, May 1950.

36. Bell Ranch list of employees, Ellis Papers, Box 2, Folder 26, Center for Southwest Research, University Libraries, UNM.

37. 1951 expense book, Godfrey Papers, Box 2, Folder 10, Rio Grande Historical Collection, New Mexico State University, Las Cruces; Warren Hereford Ranch Employer's Tax and Information Return for Agricultural Employees, Conrad K. Warren Collection, Box 15, Folder 4, Grant-Kohrs National Historic Site, Deer Lodge, Mont. By 1967 the wages at the Bell had increased significantly: a cowboy earned as much as $275 per month (or $1.05/hour), while the cook was earning $200 a month. Ellis himself received $500 a month. On the Warren Hereford Ranch

in 1961, wages had increased similarly: cowboys were earning approximately $12.50 a day (or $1.25 an hour).

38. Shorty Wallins to Frank M. King, c. 1950, Frank M. King Papers, Box 1, Shorty Wallins Folder, Huntington Library, San Marino, Calif.

39. Brenner Oral History, September 11, 1976, p. 25, MHS Research Center Archives, Helena.

40. Godfrey expense book, Godfrey Papers, Box 2, Folder 10, Rio Grande Historical Collection, New Mexico State University, Las Cruces. I have chosen to exclude the labor of both of Godfrey's sons because it appears to have been sporadic. I also excluded labor expenses paid to J. A. Brittain and W. H. Brittain for hauling, welding, and windmill work because I could not ascertain whether these men earned $120 per day or per month or how the remuneration was calculated, and I did not want the obscure numbers to inaccurately influence the calculations.

41. For an excellent discussion of the nineteenth-century phenomenon of wages of whiteness in the northeastern United States, see Roediger, *Wages of Whiteness*. For wages of whiteness in a southwestern agricultural industry (cotton) see Foley, *White Scourge*. In Arizona, Colorado, and New Mexico, a large proportion of waged labor tended to be drawn from Mexican and Mexican American workers. This tendency in the Southwest for the labor force to be predominately non-Anglo did not exist as noticeably in the northern states of Montana and Wyoming. While many American Indians continued to work for wages on cattle ranches in the latter states, sources indicate that a majority of employees in these states were Anglos. See Warren Hereford Ranch Receipt Books and Tax Information, Conrad K. Warren Papers, Box 15, Folder 4, Grant-Kohrs National Historic Site, Deer Lodge, Mont. While ranch records indicate that most ranch laborers had Anglo names, other sources indicate that ranchers in Montana and Wyoming, especially during and just after World War II, hoped to rely extensively on Mexican and Japanese American labor. For example, in 1942 the MSGA conducted a labor questionnaire to "get together some actual facts" about their "work problems." Question no. 11 was: "Would you be able to use Japanese evacuee or Mexican labor on your ranch?" And if so: "Seasonal Only or Year Around?" See Labor Questionnaire, *Montana Stockgrower*, October 1942, 4. No responses to the questionnaire appear to have survived.

42. 1951 Ranch expense book, Godfrey Papers, Box 2, Folder 10, Rio Grande Historical Collections, New Mexico State University, Las Cruces.

43. As was hinted at by Jo Jeffers and Eulalia Bourne, these tasks were not always undertaken by males. Female laborers as well as the wives and daughters of owner-managers completed the common labor of maintenance.

44. I have benefited from a number of works in thinking through the ways in which the controlling classes create cultural and social standing and power through valuation of particular kinds of labor. See Kathleen Brown, *Good Wives, Nasty Wenches*; Johnstone, "Virtuous Toil, Vicious Work"; Liu, *The Weaver's Knot*.

45. Lillian Riggs, "Chicago Girl Spreads a Loop," *Arizona Cattlelog*, September 1946.
46. Jeffers, *Ranch Wife*, 68. See also Dan Fain, "Four Generations of Fains," *Arizona Cattlelog*, January 1946, 16. For other examples of this, see C. E. Hellbusch, "Field Day at White Mountain Hereford Ranch," *Arizona Cattlelog*, September 1947, 3–5. It is interesting to note that even in articles about hired hands, this honoring of cow work (by both genders) is prevalent. In an article about a Mexican American foreman on the X9 ranch in Arizona, Abbie Keith explained that Frank Figueroa was a "first class cowman" and that he had "three sons and one daughter, and they all ride and rope, break horses and round up cattle just as their dad [does] in much the same country." See Abbie Keith, "Cowboy Corner: Frank Figueroa," *Arizona Cattlelog*, April 1952, 38–39.

47. The covers of the association periodicals comprised another cultural production that celebrated cow work most the time. In many cases ranchers submitted photographs to be printed on the cover. In my survey of the publications, I found no cases of domestic labor being depicted. (The exceptions are the occasional pictures of cooked steak.)

48. Note that these images, while simple and heroic, are not really romantic in the sense of romantic agrarianism. These ranchers were not romantics or idealists. They were realists. And the rugged and difficult experiences of life as a rancher in these years dominate their representations of themselves. The sources are full of cow talk that centers around hardship and ecological challenges, and these are more prevalent than are stories pining for an idyllic rural past (although this tendency does show up in the material covered in chapter 6). This study moves us beyond simple romantic agrarianism to understand rural peoples' embrace of rural life in all its beauty and hardship. For an excellent general history of rural America (focusing mostly on farming, not ranching) that offers some discussion of romantic agrarianism, see Danbom, *Born in the Country*.

49. Harry Day was the father of Sandra Day O'Conner, and the Lazy B has been the subject of an autobiographical history by O'Conner and her brother H. Alan Day. See O'Conner and Day, *Lazy B*; Harry Day to Abbie Keith, May 1954, ACGA Papers, AHS, Tempe.

50. This reliance on chemicals to control the bodies of plants, insects, and even predatory animals increased exponentially in American agriculture (including cattle ranching) following World War II, a topic I will cover further in chapter 3. The pesticide 2,4-D was invented in 1946, and by the mid-1950s it was being used prevalently throughout the United States. In the 1960s 2,4-D was one of the major components of Agent Orange (the compound used by the U.S. military to defoliate thousands of acres of Vietnamese land). Today, 2,4-D remains one of the most commonly used herbicides in the endless, global war against weeds. Industry Task Force II on 2,4-D Research Data, accessed May 6, 2022, www.24d.org.

51. Day to Keith, May 1954, ACGA Papers, AHS, Tempe. Day, like many ranchers, had to grapple with control of noxious weeds on his private land, but he also had

to worry about weeds on public lands. In 1952 the MSGA passed a resolution asking Congress to appropriate funds for the control of noxious weeds on public lands. See "Resolutions Adopted by the 68th Annual Convention," *Montana Stockgrower*, June 15, 1952, 15.

52. Day to Keith, May 1954.

53. Human exposure to a toxic chemical capable of killing the bodies of plants suggests one of the environmental costs of modernization. Day may not have had information about the toxicity of certain pesticides at the time, but certainly the mingling of human bodies and toxic chemicals brings up interesting issues about environmental justice for agricultural workers. Hazardous working conditions were not uncommon in range country. An examination of that aspect of labor is outside the scope of this work, but it would be an interesting topic for a future study. For some of the literature on occupational health, generally centered in factory settings, see Gottlieb, *Forcing the Spring*; Sellers, *Hazards of the Job*.

54. Ellis, *Bell Ranch as I Knew It*, 74.

55. George Ellis to Colonel and Mrs. Keeney, July 15, 1957, Ellis Papers, Box 3, Folder 2, Center for Southwest Research, UNM.

56. George Ellis to Colonel and Mrs. Keeney, July 15, 1957. The Bell apparently carried unemployment insurance for their long-term employees. Despite this private social safety net, however, the amount would have still left Buster Taylor's wife quite destitute.

CHAPTER 3

1. The chapter title is from Carl Sandburg's poem "Grass." I use this intentionally. Sandburg's poem is an ode for recovery from war—a poem about healing from combat. Ranchers saw the protection of grass and their livelihood as a defensive battle that they waged, together, every day. For eradication of the prickly pear in Australia, see "The Prickly Pear Story," Department of Agriculture and Fisheries, State of Queensland, 2016, accessed August 8, 2018, https://www.daf.qld.gov.au /__data/assets/pdf_file/0014/55301/prickly-pear-story-.pdf. This publication features photos of properties infested with the non-native cactus in Australia.

2. Mrs. Walter Meyer, "Prickly Pear vs. Australian Beetle," *Arizona Cattlelog*, May 1946, 31.

3. S. A. Raney, "Prickly Pear vs. Australian Beetle," *Arizona Cattlelog*, March 1946, 10.

4. Mrs. Y. S. Olea, "Prickly Pear vs. Australian Beetle," *Arizona Cattlelog*, March 1946, 8.

5. See Ingold, *Perception of the Environment*; Latour, *Pandora's Hope*; Gerald Nash, "Agency of Nature," 67–69. Thanks to Doug Weiner for pointing me to these ideas and works. See also Weiner, "Presidential Address."

6. White, "Are You an Environmentalist?"

7. Peck, "Nature of Labor."

8. Thomas D. Rogers, *The Deepest Wounds.* Mark Fiege has a similar argument for cotton in the antebellum U.S. South; see *The Republic of Nature.*

9. Linda Nash, *Inescapable Ecologies.*

10. In 1749, when Carolus Linnaeus first began to formalize the ideas of the discipline of ecology (which would not be fully formed in the United States until the early 1900s), he called his work the "economy of nature" (*Oeconomia Naturae* 1749). Ecology, then, is primarily concerned with "the relations of organisms to one another and to their physical surroundings." Linnaeus and his proteges came to believe that ecological relations are predicated on a fight for existence. In this way, ranchers were "true" ecologists as they understood that the organisms of the ranch—cows, grass, insects, wildlife, and human beings—were all connected, and they recognized well how those connections affected the continued health and existence of the ranch, themselves included.

11. C. K. Warren, "Convention Address," *Montana Stockgrower,* June 1951.

12. Hadley, Mills, and Ahlstrom, *El Rio Bonito;* Gibson, *Grasses and Grassland Ecology.*

13. E. G. Hayward, "The Livestock Industry, Harvester of Nation's Greatest Crop—Grass," *Cow Country,* February 1951, 13.

14. *Cow Country,* February 1956, 14.

15. W. M. Beveridge, "Juniper Control," *Arizona Cattlelog,* March 1952, 52–56. See, for example, "New and Cultivated Grasses: Various Types of Cultivated Grasses Are Becoming More Important to Cattlemen," *Cow Country,* December 1950, 6, 18.

16. W. M. Beveridge, "Juniper Control."

17. H. P. Alley, "Weed Poisoning and Eradication," *Cow Country,* March 15, 1960, 18; Harold Alley, "Larkspur Control on Stock Ranges," *Cow Country,* May 15, 1960, 7.

18. *Xanthium* is the genus name for a group of plants commonly known as cockleburs. Many species occur throughout the United States, and while they are native to North America, botanists have classified them as invasive. USDA, NRCS, PLANTS database, Version 3.5, accessed May 8, 2022, http://plants.usda.gov/home/plant Profile?symbol=XANTH2.

19. Harry A. Day to Abbie Keith, September 1, 1954, ACGA Manuscript Collection, AHS, Tempe.

20. Harry A. Day to Abbie Keith, September 1, 1954.

21. Harry A. Day to Abbie Keith, September 1, 1954.

22. See note 50 in chapter 2 on the development of 2,4-D. For an interesting discussion of the history of "weeds" in the United States and a history of the USDA's approach to eradication, see Knobloch, *Culture of Wilderness.* For an excellent discussion of increasing use and development of chemicals in agriculture post–World War II, see Vail, *Chemical Lands.*

23. Day to Keith, September 1, 1954, ACGA Manuscript Collection, AHS, Tempe.

24. Studies on the toxicity of 2,4-D in humans and animals show conflicting results. A National Cancer Institute study shows that 2,4-D has been found to be carcinogenic in dogs, but the official EPA position claims that 2,4-D has a "moderate to low acute toxicity" in humans. Academic sources and industry sources both report the same information. See the National Pesticide Information Center at Oregon State University, accessed August 12, 2018, http://npic.orst.edu/factsheets/24Dgen .html#cancer; see also the Industry Task Force on 2, 4-D, accessed August 12, 2018, https://www.24d.org/is-24d-safe.php.

25. See "Resolutions Adopted by the 68th Annual Convention," *Montana Stockgrower*, June 15, 1952, 15.

26. Harry Day to Abbie Keith, April 17, 1955, Box 5, Folder 2, ACGA Manuscript Collection, AHS, Tempe. The number of times rain appears in the sources is too numerous to explain. Precipitation (especially rain) seemed all-powerful in most of the sources—it could "make everything better."

27. Douglas Cumming to Abbie Keith, February 19, 1954, ACGA Manuscript Collection, AHS, Tempe.

28. "Five-Year Demonstration," *Cattle Guard*, October 1957, 12, 13.

29. For a good overall history of the U.S. Agricultural Extension Service, see Rasmussen, *Taking the University to the People*. See also Hirt, *Conspiracy of Optimism*; Worster, *Dust Bowl*; and Hurt, Agricultural Technology in the Twentieth Century." By the late 1970s ranchers were becoming increasingly associated with the Sagebrush Rebellion, wherein their loathing of the federal government seemed to be the only relationship they wanted to claim. This shift in the fifteen-plus years following this story is fascinating but beyond the scope of this study. Future studies on that topic should be aware that the public relationship between the ranching communities in the states examined here was largely positive. How that relationship was re-remembered and re-presented by the Sagebrush Rebels is worth investigating.

30. "Mountain Meadow Grazing Results Told at Field Day," *Cow Country*, October 1952, 32.

31. "Mountain Meadow Grazing Results Told at Field Day."

32. "Mountain Meadow Grazing Results Told at Field Day."

33. B. W. Allred, "It Pays to Graze Correctly," *Montana Stockgrower*, April 1952; Ben S. Slanger, "Range Condition Classes," *Montana Stockgrower*, November 15, 1952; E. J. Woolfolk, "Crested Wheatgrass Grazing Values," *Montana Stockgrower*, May 1951. See also F. A. Chisholm, "New and Improved Cultivated Grasses," *Cow Country*; "Howard Major's Deferred Grazing Pays-Off in Rehabilitation of Valencia County Ranch," *New Mexico Stockman*, January 10, 1955.

34. Wilma Turley, "Good Range Management . . . And Some of the Pay-Off," *Arizona Cattlelog*, December 1949, 24.

35. Brewster's concept of conservation has its roots in the conservation ethics of the Progressive Era, when conservation meant avoiding wastefulness and inefficiency.

Abandoned, dry land would have appeared to this kind of conservationist to be a waste; by reseeding, Brewster believed he had brought useless land back into grazing productivity—which for most ranchers was the highest, best, and only use befitting the grasslands of the high plains and the arid West more generally. See Lyman Brewster, "My Personal Experiences in Ranching for Profit and Conservation" *Montana Stockgrower*, October 15, 1953, 38–40. See also George Ellis, "Problems of Ranching on Privately Owned Land"; Hays, *Conservation and the Gospel of Efficiency.*

36. Day to Keith, April 17, 1955, Box 5, Folder 2, ACGA Manuscript Collection, AHS, Tempe.

37. A steady source of water was an essential component for all ranchers in the arid West. For background on reclamation in the West, see Pisani, *To Reclaim a Divided West*; Pisani, *Water and American Government*; Reisner, *Cadillac Desert*; Walton, *Western Times and Water Wars*; Worster, *Rivers of Empire.*

38. "J. D. Craighead Pioneered Valley Hereford Industry," *Arkansas Valley Journal*, January 17, 1952.

39. Buffelgrass is now considered a noxious weed in the Sonoran Desert and other arid spaces of the Southwest, and much energy and resources are being devoted to eradicate it. See, for example, Saguaro National Park, "Buffelgrass," accessed June 29, 2021, https://www.nps.gov/sagu/learn/nature/buffelgrass.htm.

40. Grasshoppers have long been a nemesis to agriculturalists on the Great Plains. For a narrative history, see Schlebecker, "Grasshoppers in American Agricultural History," 85–93. I look at insects that threatened cattle in the next chapter.

41. "Hopper Control Program All Set to Go," *Cow Country*, May 19, 1950.

42. Lyman Brewster to Ralph Miracle, June 13, 1949, Montana Brands Enforcement Division Records, Box 1, Folder 8, MHS, Helena.

43. "Hopper Control Program," *Cow Country*, May 19, 1950. See also "Operation Grasshopper," *Cow Country*, March 30, 1950.

44. Abbie Keith, "Our Page," *Arizona Cattlelog*, February 1952, 73–74.

45. Bourne, *Woman in Levi's*, 111.

46. Bourne, 160–61.

47. Most histories of the Forest Service examine the bureaucratic perspective of the service itself and ignore the perspective of the livestock industry, which comes across as being a particularly monolithic special interest group. I hope to conduct future research specifically on the perspective of ranchers regarding ecology, environmentalism, and the federal government. For an excellent history of the U.S. Forest Service, see Rowley, *U.S. Forest Service*; and Hirt, *Conspiracy of Optimism*. And for an informative study on the multiple-use doctrine that forced ranchers and government officials into their tenuous relationship, see Carr-Childers, *Size of the Risk.*

48. Lillian Riggs, "Neighborly Gossip," *Arizona Cattlelog*, August 1956, 37–38.

49. Ernie Richards, "Arizona's Vanishing Cowboys," *Arizona Cattlelog*, August 1952, 6–8.

CHAPTER 4

1. Day to Keith, September 1, 1954, ACGA Manuscript Collection, AHS, Tempe.

2. This information was well known by ranchers in the 1940s and 1950s. For an excellent overview of the cattle grub's economic effects, its life cycle, and present-day efforts to control the grub, see the University of Florida's entomology department's publication on grubs, accessed September 4, 2018, http://edis.ifas.ufl.edu /in146.

3. Some diseases affected different regions differently. For example, brucellosis was a chronic problem in Montana, Colorado, and Wyoming, while FMD was more of a concern for southwestern states because of the 1947 and 1950 outbreaks of the disease in Mexico. Cancer eye tended to be more of a problem for Hereford ranchers in sunnier states, because the white faces of the cattle attracted the intense sun. I chose to discuss cattle grubs because, like many insecticidal infections, grubs affected ranchers in the different bioregions very similarly. For a brief but excellent discussion on disease in the cattle industry, see Mortensen, *In the Cause of Progress*.

4. J. P. Corkins, "Cattle Grub Control," *Montana Stockgrower*, February 1951. See also J. N. Roney, "Cattle Grub Control," *Arizona Cattlelog*, September 1949. Roney's article assures ranchers that rotenone is compatible with DDT and thus may be used in combination with it if the ranchers are spraying for both grubs and lice. For an excellent discussion of the advent of DDT during World War II, see Russell, "Speaking of Annihilation." There was almost no discussion in the sources I reviewed regarding concerns for the health of those using DDT. Rachel Carson was in the midst of her research, and *Silent Spring* was not released until 1963. As a result, I conclude that ranchers, despite some available information about toxicity, chose to ignore any warnings about the potential for ill side effects of chemical applications for pest control.

5. Corkins, "Cattle Grub Control," *Montana Stockgrower*, February 1951.

6. Rotenone is considered safe by the EPA because of its status as an organic (as opposed to synthetic) chemical. It occurs in the roots of some tropical and subtropical plants. For an excellent discussion of this chemical, see the Oregon Department of Fish and Wildlife, accessed September 17, 2018, https://www.dfw.state.or .us/fish/local_fisheries/diamond_lake/FAQs.asp.

7. J. P. Corkins, "Cattle Grub Control," *Montana Stockgrower*, February 1951.

8. John Greer, "Letters," *Arizona Cattlelog*, July 1948, 26.

9. Bennett, *Vibrant Matter*, 31.

10. Nash, *Inescapable Ecologies*, 1–11.

11. Dusenberry, "Foot and Mouth Disease in Mexico," 84; "Foot and Mouth Situation," *Montana Stockgrower*, July 1949, 8. For a good discussion of the background on the zebu breed of cattle and its role in the FMD outbreak in the 1940s, see Wilcox, "Zebu's Elbows," 218–47.

12. Dr. Manuel Chavarria, "Mexican National Committee for the Prevention of Hoof and Mouth Disease," ACGA Manuscript Collection, Box 29, Folder 2, AHS, Tempe.

13. George Godfrey to Mr. Gillworth, February 1, 1947, Godfrey Papers, Box 6, Folder 2, Rio Grande Historical Collections, New Mexico State University, Las Cruces.

14. George Godfrey to Mr. Gillworth, February 1, 1947.

15. Abbie Keith to H. R. Sixk, February 19, 1947, ACGA Manuscript Collection, Box 29, Folder 2, AHS, Tempe.

16. Dan C. McKinney to Congressman Ernest K. Bramblett, ACGA Manuscript Collection, January 28, 1947, Box 29, Folder 2, AHS, Tempe.

17. Public Law 8, U.S.C. §568 (1947).

18. Mary Mendoza has done an excellent study on race and cattle growers and the first federally funded border fence, built in the early 1900s to combat tick problems. C. J. Alvarez has added interesting discussions about the kinds of fencing (barbed wire) erected to keep cattle from Mexico (supposedly infected with FMD) out of the U.S. borderlands in the late 1940s. Only about 115 miles of ranch fencing had been added by 1951, when Congress stopped funding. The U.S.-Mexico border in ranch country—Arizona, New Mexico, and Texas—is approximately 1,800 miles long. See Mendoza, "Treacherous Terrain"; Alvarez, "Police, Waterworks, and the U.S.-Mexico Border"; U.S. Department of Agriculture, "Foot and Mouth Disease Situation in Mexico" ACGA Manuscript Collection, Box 29, Folder 2, AHS, Tempe.

19. McKinney to Bramblett, ACGA Manuscript Collection, January 28, 1947, Box 29, Folder 2, AHS, Tempe.

20. See F. E. Mollin, Bulletin on Foot and Mouth to State and Local Associations, March 7, 1947, ACGA Manuscript Collection, Box 29, Folder 2, AHS, Tempe. Ranchers were not the only ones to call for the construction of a fence. Officials in the Bureau of Animal Industry also supported the idea. See Agricultural Research Administration, *Summary of Developments*. Of the hundreds of sources I examined, not one voiced a concern for the Sonoran, Mojave, or Chihuahua Desert ecosystems that would be affected by the construction of a fence.

21. Montana Cattlemen's Association, c. October 1959, Press Release, Box 1, Folder 12, Montana Cattlemen's Association Manuscript Collection, MHS Research Center Archives, Helena.

22. J. S. Jack Brenner, "Control and Eradication of Brucellosis in a Range State," *Montana Stockgrower*, January 15, 1955, 30–32; G. H. Good, "Let's Control and Eradicate Brucellosis from Our Herds," *Cow Country*, April 15, 1956, 14; G. H. Good, "Brucellosis . . . First in a Series of Articles on Bang's Disease," *Cow Country*, December 1950, 14; "Statewide Brucellosis Certification Drive Launched," *Cattle Guard*, April 1957, 26–27; "New Federal Brucellosis Regulations Announced," *Cow Country*, October 15, 1956, 7.

23. See J. W. Safford, Speeches, Montana Livestock Sanitary Board Records, Box 8, Folder 19, MHS Research Center Archives, Helena.

24. "Modified-certified brucellosis free" basically meant that less than 1 percent of all herds in the county were infected with the disease. The cattle sanitary boards in each state hired veterinarians to test the herds in each county and then granted the certificate to those counties achieving less than 1 percent infection rate. This certification helped ranchers from the county to sell their cows, as they could claim that their animals were relatively safe from possible infection.

25. Safford Speeches, Montana Livestock Sanitary Board Records, Box 8, Folder 19, MHS Research Center Archives, Helena.

26. "1950 Convention Resolutions," *Montana Stockgrower*, June 1950, 18. Concerns over diseases and their control were prevalent throughout the 1940s and 1950s in all four states under consideration here. In addition to addressing specific issues annually, even the guiding principles of the associations indicated the primacy of disease in ranchers' ecological economy. One of the MSGA's six guiding principles, for example, included the organizational goal of leading "the fight against diseases in livestock within Montana." See Paladin, *Montana Stockgrower*, 10–13.

27. The government programs regarding animal control are varied and too numerous to discuss in detail here. Generally speaking, each state cooperated with the federal government's division in charge of animal control to trap, poison, and hunt undesirable animals. This division has changed names numerous times since its inception in 1886 as the Bureau of Biological Survey under the umbrella of USDA—the division is now called the Fish and Wildlife Service and is located in the Department of the Interior; there is also the Wildlife Services agency in the USDA, which in 2018 alone killed 1.5 million mammals (both native and non-native species). See "The Secretive Government Agency," *The Guardian*, accessed June 26, 2020, https://www .theguardian.com/environment/2020/jun/26/cyanide-bombs-wildfire-services -idaho. Each of the five states discussed here used a bounty system for big predators at one time or another; some programs, like that in Arizona, lasted well into the 1950s. And each state government, in cooperation with the livestock commissions and game commissions, worked to utilize the newest technology in animal eradication. See my discussion of the compound 1080 in this chapter; and Mortensen, *In the Cause of Progress*, 71–77. See also Arizona State Legislature, "Relating to Predatory Animals; Providing for a Reward for the Destruction Thereof, and Prescribing Penalties Therefore," 1947. There is a rich literature looking at predator control efforts in the United States. See, for example, Dan Flores, *Coyote*; Goldfarb, *Eager*; Bergstrom et al, "License to Kill: Reforming Federal Wildlife Control to Restore Biodiversity and Ecosystem Function," USDA, 2014, accessed July 2018, https://onlinelibrary.wiley .com/doi/pdf/10.1111/conl.12045.

28. Elliott Barker to George F. Ellis, August 10, 1949, Ellis Papers, Center for Southwest Research, University of New Mexico, Albuquerque.

29. George F. Ellis to Elliott Barker, August 12, 1949, Ellis Papers, Center for Southwest Research, University of New Mexico, Albuquerque.

30. George F. Ellis to Elliott Barker, August 12, 1949.

31. Jeffers, *Ranch Wife*, 242.

32. Art Nelson, "Central Montana's View on Game Problem," *Montana Stockgrower*, November 15, 1954.

33. For an excellent discussion on current approaches to mammalian predator management, see Shivik, *The Predator Paradox*. Perhaps the best long history of the coyote is Flores, *Coyote*.

34. Cabral, "Meaningful Clearings."

35. Each state livestock association had standing committees on wildlife and predator issues throughout the 1940s and '50s. See ACGA Papers, AHS, Tempe; *Montana Stockgrower*, MHS Research Center Archives, Helena; NMCGA Papers and the *New Mexico Stockman*, Rio Grande Historical Collection, New Mexico State University, Las Cruces; and the WSGA Papers, American Heritage Center, UW.

36. This style of cover, with publication name, date, and some sort of image regarding the cattle industry, was used in all four states under consideration here. *Montana Stockgrower*, June 1956.

37. A brand marks the cow as belonging to a particular ranch and to a particular work culture. Importantly, branding was one of the few elements of ranch work that remained largely nonmechanized in these years and so, in some ways, continued to be a highly "organic" aspect of the industry.

CHAPTER 5

1. By 1959 ranchers were receiving as much as $31 per hundredweight (cwt), whereas in the 1956 prices had been on average $17 cwt. See USDA, National Agricultural Statistics Service, "Average Prices Received by Farmers and Ranchers," for the states of Wyoming, Arizona, New Mexico, Montana, and Colorado, accessed July 4, 2022, https://www.nass.usda.gov/.

2. "Words of Warning," *Montana Stockgrower*, July 1959, 11. The artist of this cartoon is unknown.

3. *Montana Stockgrower*, July 1959, 11.

4. Lubar, "Men/Women/Production/Consumption." See also Frank, *Purchasing Power*.

5. Gray, *Ranch Economics*, 453.

6. For trucking in the ranching industry, see Gray, *Ranch Economics*. For an interesting discussion of the business history of trucking in the United States more broadly, see Schwartz, *J. B. Hunt*. By the 1950s trucking had come to largely replace railroad shipping for ranchers who could easily access roads (yet another way the ranching industry benefited from highway construction). Some ranchers continued to ship via railroad, but no matter which transportation ranchers used, the cost

of getting cows to market was something every rancher had to take into consideration. For interesting discussions of the transformation from rail to truck and the effect it had on the industry, see Laurie Mercier, Julian Terrett Oral History, 1982, Oral History 226, MHS Research Center Archives, Helena.

7. For discussions about the conflicts over water in the twentieth-century West, see Pisani, *Water and American Government*; Walton, *Western Times and Water Wars*; Worster, *Rivers of Empire*. For discussions on conflicts over grass, see Merrill, *Public Lands and Political Meaning*; Rowley, *Grazing*; and Hirt, *Conspiracy of Optimism*.

8. Cattle theft was one of the primary reasons for the creation of the state cattle growers' associations in the nineteenth century. For the early histories of the associations, refer to Burroughs, *Guardian of the Grasslands*; Mortensen, *In the Cause of Progress*; Goff, *Century in the Saddle*; and Paladin, *Montana Stockgrowers*.

9. Montana Brand Enforcement Division, Box 5, Folder 4, MHS Research Center Archives, Helena.

10. See, for example, William Cheney, "Livestock Commission Report," *Montana Stockgrower*, June 15, 1955, 25.

11. Advertisement, *New Mexico Stockman*, January 1960, 61.

12. In 1955 the Montana Livestock Commission reported in the *Montana Stockgrower* that Jerry Stein, a Helena "laborer," and Keith Morley, a "state employee" allegedly stole and killed a calf from George Diehl. Both of the other cases under investigation that month involved urban residents. William Cheney, "Livestock Commission Report," *Montana Stockgrower*, August 15, 1955.

13. Leo Overfelt, "District Report," April 25, 1958, Montana Brands Enforcement Division Records, Box 1, File 27, MHS Research Center Archives, Helena.

14. Leo Overfelt, "District Report." There is no evidence to indicate that Show was a member of either tribe. And it is impossible to tell if the other parties involved were Native or Anglo. These kinds of stories abound in the archives and would make an interesting future study.

15. F. E. Mollin, "Agricultural Adjustment Program as the Cattle Producers View It," *The Producer*, November 1933. Protective legislation had been around long before the New Deal. Tariffs on cattle, which had existed since the late nineteenth century, became truly protective when the Emergency Tariff of 1921 imposed a 30 percent ad valorem tax on live cattle entering the United States. The following year the tariff became more stringent—33 percent on beeves under one thousand pounds and 43 percent on those over that weight. See Schlebecker, *Cattle Raising*, 119–52; Skaggs, *Prime Cut*, 134–40.

16. J. D. Craighead is one example of a rancher who had a long side career in the loan business. Craighead, as noted in chapter 3, served as president of the La Junta Production Credit Association for over a generation.

17. USDA, National Agricultural Statistics Service, statistics for Wyoming, Arizona, New Mexico, and Colorado, accessed January 12, 2022, https://quickstats.nass .usda.gov/.

18. The beef industry was not the only industry to fall under the price regulations of World War II. For discussions on government intervention in the U.S. economy during World War II, see Hooks, *Forging the Military-Industrial Complex*; Koistenen, *Military-Industrial Complex*; Sparrow, *From the Outside In*; Winkler, *Politics of Propaganda*. For excellent treatments of agriculture and its specific role in the war effort, as well as the gendered elements of that role, see Jellison, *Entitled to Power*; Bentley, *Eating for Victory*.

19. Schlebecker, *Cattle Raising*, 204–6.

20. See Historical Drought Palmer Indices at the National Centers for Environmental Information from the National Oceanic and Atmospheric Administration, accessed January 4, 2022, https://www.ncdc.noaa.gov/temp-and-precip/drought/historical-palmers/maps/psi/195312–195611.

21. USDA, Bureau of Agricultural Economics, Division of Crop and Livestock Estimates, "Estimated Prices Received by Farmers, New Mexico," New Mexico Agricultural Statistics Service, Las Cruces. The same kinds of price declines and rebounds occurred in each of the states under consideration here. The drought lifted at different times in different locales during the mid-1950s, but in each state the years 1952–56 were some of the driest on record and resulted in low feed for ranchers and caused ranchers to dump their inventory on the market, thereby saturating it.

22. "Words of Warning," *Montana Stockgrower*, July 1959, 11.

23. In 1950 Americans ate an average of 71.4 pounds of beef and veal. This was up 6 percent from the 1939 average. The high prices of 1951 and 1952 reduced consumer demand. But by 1955 it was up again to a gastronomical level—91.4 pounds of beef per person annually. As with all supply-and-demand situations, it is difficult to ascertain whether the drought and the saturation of the market with cheap beef inspired increased consumer demand, but the issue of causation really is moot. People were eating meat in the 1950s more than at any time prior in U.S. history, and ranchers were desperate to capitalize on that demand. See Schlebecker, *Cattle Raising*, 205; and Fite, *American Farmers*.

24. This "working-out" system was not new to rural households in this era. Tessie Liu has found similar occurrences in nineteenth-century French artisan households. The same is true for farm families in the United States throughout the twentieth century. See Liu, *Weaver's Knot*; and Elbert, "Amber Waves of Gain"; Osterud, "'She Helped Me Hay It."

25. Ranchers' associations took official positions supporting government tariffs long before the New Deal. Import tariffs are, of course, a kind of price support, but ranchers rarely referred to them as such. See Schlebecker, *Cattle Raising*, 126–27, 220–25.

26. Lloyd Taggart, Convention Address, June 1952, Box 250, Folder 2, WSGA Papers, American Heritage Center, UW. Of course, Taggert joined his fellow ranchers in accepting a good deal of help from USDA extension agents whenever it was beneficial to do so.

27. "Price Support Poll," *Montana Stockgrower*, December 15, 1953. See also the October 1953 issue of the *Montana Stockgrower* for the original price-support poll. Interestingly, of those ranchers answering the Montana poll, 75 percent were small operators who ran fewer than 250 head. A mere 4 percent were large operators who owned more than a thousand head. These numbers may indicate that the issue of price supports was more salient for small operators who had less leeway in their operations and so were hit harder during tough times. Fite argues that in the farm support programs of the 1930s, 1940s, and 1950s, the larger operators tended to receive more aid than smaller operators. Still, the possibility of having an increase in demand for beef products (through government purchasing) would not have necessarily favored large producers over small ones. Fite, *American Farmers*, 143–47.

28. The NMCGA also took a poll at their annual convention in 1953. The New Mexico cattle growers agreed almost exactly with the ranchers in Colorado and Montana. Seven out of twenty-three ranchers wanted full price supports on cattle, while two out three supported some kind of government assistance just short of full price support. The group voted 65 percent to 35 percent to take an official stand against full price supports and to not convene a special convention to discuss the issue further. See Mortensen, *In the Cause of Progress*, 37.

29. Doug Cumming to Abbie Keith, September 24, 1953, ACGA Manuscript Collection, Box 5, Folder 2, AHS, Tempe.

30. Horace H. Hening to Abbie Keith, October 6, 1953, ACGA Manuscript Collection, Box 5 Folder 2, AHS, Tempe. See also Albert K. Mitchell to Abbie Keith, October 7, 1953, ACGA Manuscript Collection, Box 5, Folder 2.

31. Mitchell to Keith, October 7, 1953.

32. Alvin C. Tso to Abbie Keith, October 29, 1956, ACGA Manuscript Collection, Box 5, Folder 9, AHS, Tempe; Abbie Keith to Irven Taylor, October 10, 1956, ACGA Manuscript Collection, Box 5, Folder 9.

33. Mrs. Jo Flieger to Abbie Keith, October 13, 1953, ACGA Manuscript Collection, Box 5, Folder 2, AHS, Tempe.

34. MCGA, March 1950, "Special Resolution," Ellis Papers, Box 3, Folder 5, Center for Southwest Research, University Libraries, UNM.

35. *American Cattle Producer* 28 (May 1947): 7.

36. *American Cattle Producer* 28. See also Dan Hanson, "Hat Creek Rancher Replies to Budd Letter," *Cow Country* June 15, 1956, 18–19.

37. Jim Smith, "Speech before the Greenlee County Cattle Growers Association," August 29, 1953, ACGA Manuscript Collection, Box 5, Folder 2, AHS, Tempe.

38. The Conrad Kohrs Company Ranch was part of the Conrad Kohrs Company, which had been run by family members, including Con's stepfather, Frank Bogart, since Conrad Kohrs's death in 1920.

39. National Park Service, "Biography," Warren Papers, Grant-Kohrs National Historic Site, Deer Lodge, Mont.

40. The annual sales of A. C. Bayers of Twin Bridges, Montana, serve as another wonderful example of a place in which ranchers came together to witness the fruits of their labor as producers and to engage in conversations about their similarities as entrepreneurs. See A. C. Bayers, "Bayers Hereford Ranch: Spring News Letter," *Montana Stockman*, May 1946.

41. Abbie Keith to Alvin Tso, September 17, 1955, ACGA Manuscript Collection, Box 5, Folder 9, AHS, Tempe.

42. In New Mexico, for example, news about ranchers' comings and goings and about their land and cattle made regular appearances in the "News Notes of Interest to Southwestern Livestock Growers" section of the *New Mexico Stockman*. In 1947 the editors of the *Stockman* informed interested readers that "Rutherford Brothers of Folsom, New Mexico, have shipped 93 cars of steers from Union County to Ortea, California." Here ranchers could read of the Rutherfords' successful sale and could, perhaps, dream of their own coming day of marketing their cows. See "News Notes," *New Mexico Stockman*, December 1947, 88. For other examples of the sharing of celebratory market news, see "Cattleman's Calendar," *Cow Country*, June 15, 1956, 19. See also "Reviewing the November Market," *Montana Stockgrower*, December 1961, 30; "Market News," *Montana Stockgrower*, March 1963, 26–27. Mrs. Howard Grounds to Abbie Keith, July 17, 1954, ACGA Manuscript Collection, Box 5, Folder 2, AHS, Tempe.

43. Mitchell to Keith, October 7, 1953, ACGA Manuscript Collection, Box 5, Folder 2, AHS, Tempe.

44. My thanks to Steve Baratt at the Cattlemen's Beef Board for helping me to ferret out the obscure history of beef councils across the nation. Personal correspondence. Montana's Beef Council was the earliest in the mountain West, forming in 1954. The Wyoming Beef Council began in 1971. For information on Colorado's council, see Colorado Beef Council, accessed May 13, 2022, https://www.cobeef .com/about-us. Arizona created its beef council in 1970, and New Mexico's arrived nine years later. See Arizona Beef Council, accessed May 13, 2022, http://www .arizonabeef.org/. For an overall history of beef promotion, see Ball, *Building the Beef Industry*. There is a fascinating history here, but its scope is too wide to include in this work.

45. Eulalia Bourne, "Kids and Cows," *Arizona Cattlelog*, October 1951, 6.

46. Lil' Dudette ads in *Arizona Cattlelog*, March 1955, 35–52. The image of Lil' Dudette consuming a hamburger appeared on page one of the *Arizona Cattlelog* in the same year and also began turning up in other media across the state. See, for example, the *Bisbee Daily Review*, October 30, 1955, 1.

47. Elizabeth Johnson, "Four Generations of Cooks: In the Cattle Business at Willcox since 1893," *Arizona Cattlelog*, November 1955, 16. Connie Cook also made headlines in Arizona; see, for example, *Bisbee Daily Review*, January 1956, 1.

48. Montana Cowbelles Manuscript Collection, MHS Research Center Archives, Helena.

49. Accomazzo, *Arizona Cowbelles*, 17.

50. For information on Cowbelles' beef promotion activities in Wyoming, see WSGA Papers, Wyoming Cowbelles Records, Box 183, Folders 3–8, American Heritage Center, UW. For the same in Colorado, see Colorado Cattlewomen, Inc., Records, Beef Promotion Activity Materials, Box 2, Denver Public Library.

51. For interesting and important discussions of the gendered ideals of the 1950s and women's responses to those ideals, see Harvey, *The Fifties*; Kaledin, *Mothers and More*; May, *Homeward Bound*; Meyerowitz, *Not June Cleaver*; Rupp, *Survival in the Doldrums*.

52. Mrs. Jack Brooks to Mrs. Graham, February 10, 1966, WSGA Papers, Box 183, Folder 8, American Heritage Center, UW.

53. Cody Cowbelles, Minutes, Barbie Q Committee Report, December 1962, WSGA Papers, Box 183, Folder 8, American Heritage Center, UW. The Wyoming Cowbelles also attempted to convince the public relations committee of Swift and Co. (one of the largest meat packing companies in the United States) to adopt Barbie Q for their own use. The Swift executives were fearful of using just one kind of species (Hereford) for meat advertising but still admitted that Barbie Q was catchy and thought they might use the idea with different animals (pigs, for instance). I can find no information as to whether Swift ever utilized the mascot.

54. Rubie K. Dover, "Barbie Q's," *Cow Country*, September 15, 1961, 19.

55. Accomazzo, *Arizona Cowbelles*; and Goff, *Century in the Saddle*, 341.

CHAPTER 6

1. Ranchers and their associations began chronicling ranch history in the mountain West even earlier than 1945. Many ranchers and cowboys wrote their memoirs in the 1920s and 1930s as the Old West slipped further and further away. The postwar decades witnessed more of the same as ranchers turned to the past to draw inspiration from the tradition that informed their identities as cattle ranchers. For examples of the early memory productions see Burt, *Diary of a Dude Wrangler*; Cleveland, *No Life for a Lady*; Lavender, *One Man's West*; Rak, *A Cowman's Wife*; Russell, *Good Medicine*. In this partial list, I have included autobiographical accounts of life on ranches in the five states under consideration here. The list would expand exponentially if one included histories and biographies of ranches and ranchers in other western states, especially Texas. For two examples of this latter kind of memory production, see Collings, *The 101 Ranch*; and Greer, *Early in the Saddle*.

2. Wrobel, *Promised Lands*.

3. Mrs. John (Lucille) Anderson, "The Anderson Story," *Arizona Cattlelog*, October 1948. In 1991 Anderson self-published another memory production. She had arrived as a young bride on the Crescent Ranch, near Hayden, Arizona, never having lived on a cattle ranch before. The book, based on her diaries and memories,

chronicles her induction into the ranch way of life. See Lucille S. Anderson, *Bridle-Wise*, x. See also Sharp, *Big Outfit*, 1–5.

4. Veracini, *Settler Colonialism*.

5. Nixon, *Slow Violence*, 153.

6. The first, written by Agnes Wright Spring, was published in 1942 and was given as a souvenir brochure at the Seventieth Anniversary Convention in 1942. See Spring, *70 Years Cow Country*. The associations of four of the five states being discussed here produced at least one official history. Arizona is the lone state that never has, but personal ranch histories and the Arizona National Ranch Histories of Living Pioneer Stockman series often wove the history of the ACGA throughout. See Burroughs, *Guardian of the Grasslands*; Goff, *Century in the Saddle*; Mortensen, *In the Cause of Progress*; Paladin, *The Montana Stockgrower*.

7. Frink, *Cow Country Cavalcade*.

8. Frink, 209.

9. Cawley, *Federal Land, Western Anger*.

10. George Amos Godfrey, "New Mexico Rancher Urges Sale of Federal Grazing Lands to Users," newspaper clipping, paper unknown, c. 1947, Godfrey Papers, Box 4, Folder 4, Rio Grande Historical Collections, New Mexico State University, Las Cruces.

11. Godfrey, "New Mexico Rancher Urges Sale of Federal Grazing Lands to Users." This is another example of settler colonial history: Godfrey and others created the sense that they had claims to the land that paralleled Indigenous rights, which preceded government structures meant to enforce certain limits on land use.

12. Burroughs, *Guardian of the Grasslands*, 305.

13. See Minutes of Wyoming Stock Growers Association Forest Advisory Committee, 1947–51, WSGA Papers, Box 56, Folder 1, American Heritage Center, UW.

14. Sayre, *Politics of Scale*, 114.

15. It is interesting and important to note that the epigraph is from Sandburg's poem "Grass," which is an ode to war. The poem is available online at many sites.

16. The notion that ranchers and their collective associations had protected the range was not unique to Montana and Wyoming; for similar language and interpretations, see Dick Goff, "Guardian of the Grass Country," *Cattle Guard*, May 1957, 11–17.

17. Burroughs, *Guardian of the Grasslands*, 8. For discussions of conservation, see Hays, *Gospel of Efficiency*; and Roderick Nash, *Wilderness and the American Mind*. Remember, Taggert was interested in non-native grass cultivation—a topic covered in chapter 3 in this work.

18. For early discussions about the rise of grassland ecology, see Clements, *Plant Succession*; McIntosh, "Ecology since 1900"; Odum, *Fundamentals of Ecology*; Tobey, *Saving the Prairies*; Worster, *Nature's Economy*. For discussions about the numbers of cattle driven in the open-range days, see Igler, *Industrial Cowboys*; Skaggs, *Cattle-Trailing Industry*; Young and Sparks, *Cattle in the Cold Desert*. For a detailed discussion

of how much of this science failed in the grasslands of the West, see Sayre, *Politics of Scale.*

19. Burroughs, *Guardian of the Grasslands,* 9.

20. Burroughs, 9. See also Coburn, *Pioneer Cattleman in Montana.*

21. Van Cleve, *40 Years' Gatherin's,* xv.

22. Many historians and ranchers believed that blizzard began the decline of the cattle baron era. See, for example, Coburn, *Mavericks;* Mattison, "The Hard Winter."

23. This included Conrad Kohrs. Kohrs suffered less than most because of his access to the Deer Lodge Valley, which experienced a milder winter. Still, the Grant-Kohrs Ranch suffered tremendous losses.

24. Frink, *Cow Country Cavalcade,* 196.

25. Goff, *Century in the Saddle,* 2–3.

26. Note that despite this aspect of ranchers' collective memory (of performing labor in common with the cattle baron era), as we saw in the first chapter, the modernization of ranching also served to unite ranchers in current experience.

27. Accomazzo, *Arizona Cowbelles,* 34.

28. Morgan, "Sense and Sentiments of Cowmen," *Echoes of the Past,* 107.

29. Morgan, "Sense and Sentiments of Cowmen." Half of the stories in the book are of pioneer women. Women did work as hired hands, although it was rare (especially on the open range), but their stories are generally absent in the memory productions. Whereas cowboys (who were hired hands employed by owner-operator ranchers) appear in the memories in important roles, memory chroniclers almost always overlook or underemphasize female employees. See chapters 2 and 5 for more on the producer identities of women connected to the owning class.

30. Morgan, "Sense and Sentiments of Cowmen."

31. Morgan, "Nell Ritter," *Echoes of the Past,* 83.

32. Mrs. Harry Hooker, "Five Generations of Hookers: On the Sierra Bonita Ranch," *Arizona Cattlelog,* December 1949.

33. Hooker, "Five Generations of Hookers: On the Sierra Bonita Ranch." Mrs. Hooker never discusses how the Anglo owner-operators came to own (or control) the land or the ramifications that open grazing had on Native lands in the late nineteenth century, although the Native use of land for hunting does make appearances in some discussions of what ranchers called "prehistory."

34. McChristian, *Ranchers to Rangers.*

35. Nell Warren is completely absent from this spatial record. And even today, the Wikipedia entry about the Con Warren era of the ranch is blank.

36. Ellis, *Bell Ranch as I Knew It,* 64.

37. Ellis, 64.

38. Russell Thorp, "Presentation of Wyoming Stock Growers Association—Russell Thorp Historical Collection to the State of Wyoming," May 22, 1945, WSGA Papers, Box 213, Folder 11, American Heritage Center, UW.

39. For interesting discussions on the importance of collecting historic objects in the making of collective identity, see Crane, *Museums and Memory*; and Kaplan, *Museums and the Making of Ourselves*.

40. Crane, *Museums and Memory*, 3.

41. We know that the glory days were rife with conflicts between large and small ranchers as well as between Native peoples and Anglo imperialists thanks more to historians than to rancher memories. For the historical perspective, see Igler, *Industrial Cowboys*. For one of the best analyses of the inter-Anglo conflict with regard to the Johnson County War of 1892, see Belgrad, "Power's Larger Meaning." Belgrad argues that the Johnson County War was fought largely between two groups (cattle barons against smaller ranchers and homesteaders) due to environmental circumstances that created the differentiated ecological strategies among the disputants. See also Richard Maxwell Brown, "Violence," 369, 399, 402–3.

42. Winner, *Whale and the Reactor*, chapter 2.

43. T-Bone Cowbelles, *1962 Brand Book*, MHS, Helena.

44. T-Bone Cowbelles.

45. T-Bone Cowbelles.

46. The evidence I have been able to gather indicates that the state Cowbelle organizations in four of the five states covered here utilized brands in some way in the creation of their cultural productions (including historical publications and collective memory artifacts). New Mexico, the state for which Cowbelle evidence is sparsest, may have used brands as well, but I have no evidence of that. See Colorado Cowbelle activities in the 1960s as chronicled in the Chapter Reports, Box 2, Colorado Cowbelle Records, Denver Public Library; and Brand Book Reproduction, Wyoming Cowbelles, 1962, WSGA Papers, Box 183, American Heritage Center, UW.

47. Phillips County Livestock Association, *Brand Book Phillips County, State of Montana* (Phillips County Livestock Association, Mont., 1957).

48. Pat Gudmundson, "Miles City Turns Clock Back 75 Years," *Great Falls Tribune*, May 17, 1959. A fascinating play was performed at the Jubilee, the analysis of which I removed for space considerations. I plan to write a stand-alone article about that cultural moment of racialized cow talk.

CHAPTER 7

1. Epigraph from Ralph Miracle, *Montana Stockgrower*, May 1955, 1; Anderson, *Imagined Communities*, 35–36.

2. Bill Grieve, "The Cattleman's Job," *Montana Stockgrower*, March 1965, 26.

3. John R. Hogg to WSGA, October 15, 1956, WSGA Papers, Box 251, Folder 2, American Heritage Center, UW; Agnes Bishop, "Neighborly Gossip," *Arizona Cattlelog*, December 1949, 48. See also "Letters from Members," columns in *Cow Country*, January 15, 1956, 18; and Letters to Abbie Keith, ACGA Manuscript Collection,

Box 5, Folder 8, AHS, Tempe. I found little evidence of ranchers critiquing the associations or their larger political projects. When critical evidence did turn up, it usually centered on personal animosities and less about the larger goals or the existence of the associations. Such an example occurred in New Mexico in 1947 when Lon Merchant, owner-operator of the Bridle Bit Ranch near Capitan, withdrew his membership in the NMCGA because he was angry that he had not been nominated by the group to serve a second term on the Cattle Sanitary Board. Merchant apparently protested some policy the majority of the board and the association supported. The officers of the NMCGA, to whom the governor turned for nominations, left Merchant's name off their nomination list. As a result, Merchant wrote a scathing letter to George Godfrey (then president of the NMCGA) accusing the association of being run by "no more than six identical men." The concentration of power, in Merchant's mind, meant that he needed to drop his membership (although clearly Merchant was one of those in power in the NMCGA at the time of the conflict). Even Merchant, however, was saddened by his decision to leave the organization as it would mean he would have to "forego the pleasure of mingling with and enjoying the society of a great many people with whom I . . . have every thing in common interest." Merchant recognized, however, that "the association managed to worry along somehow before I showed up and that it can very well continue to grow and to follow a course determined by its full membership, and that one less in membership today will probably result in ten new arrivals tomorrow." Importantly, Godfrey responded to Merchant's letter by refusing to accept Merchant's resignation from the association. Godfrey informed Merchant that contrary to his request, Godfrey had reappointed Merchant as the chairman of the Brand and Theft Committee and as a member of the NMCGA executive committee. Aside from the major break in the late 1950s in Montana, which resulted in the forming of the Montana Cattleman's Association (see chapter 4), this anecdote is one of the few surviving stories in the archives showing intense animosity among ranchers within the associations. Stories about irreconcilable rancher-to-rancher conflicts (aside from the reports of theft) appear rarely if ever within the association public periodicals. See Lon Merchant to George Godfrey, Godfrey Papers, March 28, 1947, Box 6, Folder 2, Rio Grande Historical Collections, New Mexico State University, Las Cruces; Godfrey to Merchant, April 2, 1947, Box 6, Folder 2, ibid.

4. Clemens, *The People's Lobby*, 147–80. For more on the creation of agrarian interest group political structures in the United States, see also Hansen, "Creating a New Politics." For broader discussions on interest group politics see Baumgartner, *Basic Interests*; Field, *Harvest of Dissent*; Shaiko, *Interest Group Connection*.

5. This mentality of an individual's right to free labor being protected by unions stretches back into the nineteenth century. For one of the best works that deals with the topic of the rise of unions to protect craft independence in the nineteenth century, see Wilentz, *Chants Democratic*. For works that grapple with twentieth-century union mentalities, see Cohen, *Making a New Deal*; Faue, *Community of Suffering and*

Struggle; Lichtenstein, *Labor's War at Home*. Lichtenstein focuses more on the institutional structures, which changed considerably due to political conditions during World War II. However, he chronicles the motivations of the rank and file in attempting to maintain autonomy through collectivity.

6. See, for example, Wallis Huidekoper's argument for membership later in this chapter.

7. See "Letters," *Montana Stockgrower*, May 1950, 54; and Abbie Keith to Rulon Langston, September 26, 1956, ACGA Manuscript Collection, Box 5, Folder 8, AHS, Tempe. See also membership lists for each association. The holdings of the remaining 16 percent of the NMCGA membership are unknowable.

8. Wayne Walker to Abbie Keith, April 7, 1956, ACGA Manuscript Collection, Box 6, Folder 1, AHS, Tempe; W. A. Winder to Abbie Keith, September 5, 1956, ACGA Manuscript Collection, Box 6, Folder 1.

9. The spirit of organization that overtook much of the United States in the postwar years has been studied by many scholars, especially as it occurred among white-collar workers in postwar cities. William Whyte asserted in 1956 that as these workers joined various organizations, they simultaneously lost their individuality. Something more interesting was going on with ranchers, at least in their own minds. See Whyte, *The Organization Man*.

10. The exception to the hiring of executive secretaries from the inner community of ranchers was Robert Hanesworth in Wyoming. The WSGA hired him from the Cheyenne Chamber of Commerce, and Hanesworth had little ranch experience. His hiring, according to John Rolfe Burroughs, did not come "without a good deal of soul searching . . . and some skepticism among the members." The WSGA ultimately hired Hanesworth because he was an "organizer par excellence." See Burroughs, *Guardian of the Grasslands*, 337.

11. Ralph Miracle is a good example of a secretary who had diverse work and life experiences but whose connection to ranching was hailed by other ranchers as his most important qualification. Miracle was born to a family of ranchers, graduated from Harvard Military Academy in Los Angeles, and later attended Dartmouth College. He met and married a New York woman named Lillian Shaw in 1934 and returned to Montana shortly thereafter to manage his family's ranch upon the death of his father. The tough times of the 1930s forced Miracle out of the business, and after liquidating the ranch holdings he worked at odd jobs before joining the service. He returned from World War II to manage briefly the Westwood Ranch before becoming the executive officer for the Montana Livestock Commission and Recorder of Marks and Brands. It was from this powerful administrative position that Miracle became the executive secretary of the MSGA in 1954. See Paladin, *The Montana Stockgrower*, 121. The majority of the other executive secretaries had similar life histories and connections (however tenuous) to the cattle industry.

12. Ralph Miracle, *Montana Stockgrower*, May 1955, 1.

13. Bob Hanesworth to Membership, October 15, 1950, WSGA Papers, Box 250, Folder 12, American Heritage Center, UW.

14. In 1950, for example, the WSGA spent $2,000 on the publication of *Cow Country*, whereas in previous years the costs had been only in the hundreds of dollars. See Association Account Report, WSGA Papers, Box 250, Folder 10, American Heritage Center, UW.

15. Mortensen, *In the Cause of Progress*, 90.

16. "Why Should You Belong?," *New Mexico Stockman*, April 1952, 12.

17. Membership Advertisement, *Montana Stockgrower*, March 1965, 11.

18. Fred Fritz, "Organization—Its Purpose and Need," *Arizona Cattlelog*, September 1946 (title page)

19. Julian Terrett, "In Unity There is Strength," *Montana Stockgrower*, October 15, 1953, 5.

20. "A Man Working for the Cattle Business," *Cattle Guard*, November 1955, 11–12; and "Bob Schafer's 12,000-Mile Tour Brings 800 New Members Into CCA," *Cattle Guard*, May 1956, 12.

21. "Schafer's 12,000-Mile Tour," *Cattle Guard*, May 1956, 12.

22. See "In Unity there Is Strength," *Montana Stockgrower*, September 15, 1953, 5. See also Ralph Miracle, "Editor's Column," *Montana Stockgrower*, July 1956, 4, wherein Miracle explains to his readers that "most of us can't run an outfit and find time for much outside activity. There are always more jobs ahead right at home without going anywhere looking for more."

23. The one exception to the arrangement of executive secretaries also being editors-in-chief was in Colorado, where the first editor of the *Cattle Guard* was Dick Goff, who the CCA hired specifically for the purpose of maintaining the periodical. David Rice, the executive secretary of the CCA, assisted Goff in the publication until Goff left the CCA to continue his livestock advertising business in 1958. John Boyd replaced Goff as editor and also became executive secretary in 1963. See Goff, *Century in the Saddle*, 298–99.

24. W. M. Beveridge, "Juniper Control," *Arizona Cattlelog*, March 1952, 53.

25. For other examples of similar agricultural specialists writing for the publications and trying to be of help to ranchers by educating them in the ways of modern agriculture while still arguing that ranchers were, in fact, the real experts and were essential to the government's success, see A. A. Beetle, "Let's Judge Your Range," *Cow Country*, April 15, 1956, 6–7; N. A. Jacobsen, "Are Pine Needles to Blame? A Review of Studies on the Part Played by Pine Needles in Connection with Abortion in Range Cows," *Montana Stockgrower*, December 1961, 8–9; John L. Sears and Carmy G. Page, "The County Agent Speaks: A Review of 1949," *Arizona Cattlelog*, January 1950, 52–53; Dr. J. F. Ryff, "Have You Heard about Anaplasmosis?," *Cow Country*, April 15, 1956, 10.

26. See Dick Goff, "Irons in the Fire," *Cattle Guard*, April 1957, 19. In the *New Mexico Stockman*, the news column was simply titled "Notes of Interest to Southwestern

Livestock Growers" or "News Notes of Interest to Southwestern Livestock Growers and Farmers." "Notes" carried similar news items as the columns in other publications but utilized less iconography and cow talk than the others. Still, the "Notes" section often contained a cartoon specific to ranch or southwestern culture that often made gendered or racialized jokes. For an example of this, see "Notes of Interest," *New Mexico Stockman*, April 1955, 56. The *Arizona Cattlelog* subsumed news under its "Neighborly Gossip" column. See below for more information on the "Neighborly Gossip" section of the *Arizona Cattlelog*. See also Dick Goff, "Irons in the Fire," *Cattle Guard*, October 1957, 18–19.

27. Ace V. Tyrrell, "Grain and Salt Feeding: Weight Doubled in 10 Months," *Cow Country*, September 1952, 7.

28. *Cow Country*, September 1952, cover. See also M. Webb to Abbie Keith, ACGA Manuscript Collection, Box 6, Folder 1, AHS, Tempe.

29. "The Salt Lick," *Montana Stockgrower*, January 15, 1955, 24.

30. All of the publications considered here included a list of visitors to the association office. This strategy also helped to shrink the distance ranchers may have felt from one another and made it seem as though they were only a quick visit at the main office from their fellow ranch folk.

31. For a few examples of the "Salt Lick" column, see *Montana Stockgrower*, January 15, 1955, 24; July 1957, 24; April 1959, 23; and August 1959, 22.

32. At times Keith had difficulty in getting material, and she did a considerable amount of the writing herself. In 1949 she convinced Mary Kidder Rak, a prolific writer and rancher in southeastern Arizona, to write an article telling ranchers *how to* write—as they both worried that ranchers did not send as much material as they might for fear of not producing quality written work. Despite this, however, the *Arizona Cattlelog* in any given issue had four or five feature articles written by ranchers as well as the usual "Neighborly Gossip" section. Mary Kidder Rak, "Help Eliza Cross the Ice," *Arizona Cattlelog*, September 1949, 29–30.

33. "Typical Pictures Taken on Wyoming Ranches," *Cow Country*, May 1952, 28.

34. See Erickson, *Ace Reid, Cowpoke*. Examples of Reid's cartoons are widely available online.

35. In *Cowpokes* Reid often depicts women as nagging wives who tend to serve no purpose other than nitpicking the men around them. Thus, even in this broadly appealing art, there is gender tension that is almost naturalized. For an example of this, see Ace Reid, *Cowpokes*, *Cow Country*, April 15, 1956, 21.

36. I borrow much of this analysis from Mary Douglas, "Jokes."

37. Neckyoke Jones, "Greasewood Answers Powder River Pete," *Cow Country*, July 7, 1949, 8.

38. Paladin, *The Montana Stockgrower*, 83.

39. Maggie, "Maggie Reports on the Convention," *Montana Stockgrower*, July 1957, 15.

40. Maggie, "Minnie's Conventioning," *Montana Stockgrower*, May 1959, 31.

41. Maggie, "Maggie Promotes," *Montana Stockgrower*, May 1958, 27.

42. In 1958, for example, over five hundred Montana ranchers attended the annual convention; *Montana Stockgrower*, June 1958, 6. Other states reported similar numbers.

43. Committee appointments and convention resolutions were adopted by the membership through a majority vote. Anywhere from ten to forty ranchers participated on the standing committees—the numbers varied according to the type of committee and the state. The bulk of the committees' labor, however, was conducted by the officers of the committee (chair, vice chair, and secretary).

44. Bob Barthelmess, "Call to Convention," *Montana Stockgrower*, May 1965, 9.

45. For examples of various committee decorating ideas, see "Wyoming's Cowbelles," *Cow Country*, October 15, 1956, 9; "125 Attend Colorado Cowbelles Annual Stock Show Breakfast," *Cattle Guard*, February 1956, 10.

46. Ruth Stearns to Bill Cheney, July 22, 1961, Montana Brands Enforcement Division Records, Box 6, Folder 13, MHS, Helena. This practice of branding the convention halls continued throughout the 1960s.

47. For representative articles, see Abbie Keith, "48th Annual Convention," *Arizona Cattlelog*, February 1952, 11–19; Abbie Keith, "Our Holbrook Meeting," *Arizona Cattlelog*, December 1951, 59–64; "Resolutions," *New Mexico Stockman*, April 1955, 10–12; "Resolutions Adopted by Cattlemen in Clovis Meet," *New Mexico Stockman*, April 1959, 5–10; "Resolutions," *New Mexico Stockman*, March 1947, 36–39; "Convention Resolutions," *Montana Stockgrower*, June 15, 1955, 6–8; "Resolutions Adopted at the 67th Annual Convention," *Montana Stockgrower*, June 1951, 12–15.

48. Ralph Miracle, "Editor's Column," *Montana Stockgrower*, June 15, 1955, 4.

49. Such sections occurred regularly in all of the editions of the five periodicals. For representative examples, see "Letters from Members," *Cow Country*, November 1952, 11; and "Neighborly Gossip," *Arizona Cattlelog*, August 1946, 34–36.

50. Anderson, *Imagined Communities*, 187–97. Even those ranchers who chose not to contribute directly to the association publications could join in on the imagining of community through reading and subscribing to the periodicals.

51. Hadley, "Commercial Livestock Operations in Arizona," 387.

52. Bourne, *Woman in Levi's*, 136.

53. Keith subsequently published the letter in "Neighborly Gossip," *Arizona Cattlelog*, January 1953, 58.

54. See Mrs. Jo Fleiger to Abbie Keith, ACGA Manuscript Collection, Box 5, Folder 1, AHS, Tempe. Again, Keith published the letter; see Mrs. Jo Fleiger, "Home on the Range," *Arizona Cattlelog*, September 1951, 65. See also Deming Rancher W. A. Winder to Abbie Keith, September 5, 1956, ACGA Manuscript Collection, Box 6, Folder 1, AHS, Tempe.

55. Gorge Snodgrass to Robert Hanesworth, October 26, 1959, WSGA Papers, Box 57, Folder 7, American Heritage Center, UW.

56. Of course, the seasonality and the coming and going of hard weather dictated the number of discussions of bad weather that existed in ranchers' correspondence. Still, like the comings and goings of drought in the Southwest, the potential of a nasty winter served as a crucial topic in northern ranchers' cow talk. See, for example, Bob Barthelmess, "Your President Reports," *Montana Stockgrower*, January 1965, 18.

57. Craighead to Earl Kelly, June 6, 1945, Craighead Papers, Box 5, Folder 3, Huntington Library, San Marino, Calif.

58. Craighead to American Hereford Association, May 23, 1951, Craighead Papers, Box 4, Folder 9, Huntington Library.

EPILOGUE

1. Lamm and McCarthy, *The Angry West*, 282.

2. See the Quivira Coalition, accessed January 16, 2022, https://quivira coalition.org/.

3. Joseph Taylor, "As though Bunkerville and Malheur Are the West," H-Net Reviews in the Humanities and Social Sciences, November 2021, accessed January 17, 2022, https://www.h-net.org/reviews/showpdf.php?id=56763.

Bibliography

PRIMARY SOURCES

Accomazzo, Betty. *Arizona Cowbelles: This Is Your Life.* N.p.: Arizona Cowbelles, c. 1973.

Adams, Ramon F. *Western Words: A Dictionary of the Range, Cow Camp and Trail.* Norman: University of Oklahoma Press, 1946.

"Administration and Use of Public Lands." In *Committee on Public Lands and Surveys.* Casper, WY: United States Senate, 1945.

Agricultural Research Administration, Bureau of Animal Industry. *Summary of Developments in the Mexican Outbreak of Foot-and-Mouth Disease.* Washington, D.C.: U.S. Department of Agriculture, January 28, 1947.

Alley, Harold. "Larkspur Control on Stock Ranges." *Cow Country,* May 15, 1960.

———. "Weed Poisoning and Eradication." *Cow Country,* March 15, 1960.

Allred, B. W. "It Pays to Graze Correctly." *Montana Stockgrower,* April 1952.

Anderson, Lucille S. "The Anderson Story." *Arizona Cattlelog,* October 1948.

———. *Bridle-Wise.* Phoenix, Ariz.: Self-published, 1991.

"Antelope Hunting Season Controversy." *Montana Stockgrower,* October 15, 1953.

Arizona Cattlegrowers' Association Manuscript Collection. Arizona Historical Society, Tempe.

Arizona Cowbelles Records. Arizona Historical Society, Tempe.

Babbitt, John. "Cattleman Refutes 'Anti-Game' Claim." *Arizona Daily Sun,* September 28, 1951.

———. "Cattle or Elk?" *Arizona Republic,* September 29, 1951.

Baker, Georgia. "Neighborly Gossip." *Arizona Cattlelog,* December 1951.

Barthelmess, Bob. "Call to Convention." *Montana Stockgrower,* May 1965.

Bayers, A. C. "Bayers Hereford Ranch: Spring News Letter." *Montana Stockman,* May 1946.

Beetle, A. A. "Let's Judge Your Range." *Cow Country,* April 15, 1956.

Beveridge, W. M. "Juniper Control." *Arizona Cattlelog,* March 1952.

"Bob Schafer's 12,000-Mile Tour Brings 800 New Members into CCA." *Cattle Guard,* May 1956.

Bourne, Eulalia. *Woman in Levi's.* Tucson: University of Arizona Press, 1967.

Brenner, J. S. Jack. "Control and Eradication of Brucellosis in a Range State." *Montana Stockgrower,* January 15, 1955.

Burroughs, John Rolfe. *Guardian of the Grasslands.* Cheyenne, Wyo.: Pioneer Printing and Stationary Co., 1971.

Burt, Maxwell Struthers. *The Diary of a Dude Wrangler.* New York: Scribner's Sons, 1924.

"Cattleman's Calendar." *Cow Country,* June 15, 1956.

Cleveland, Agnes Morley. *No Life for a Lady.* Boston: Houghton Mifflin, 1941.

Coburn, Walt. *Mavericks.* New York: Century Co., 1929.

———. *Pioneer Cattleman in Montana: The Story of the Circle C Ranch.* Norman: University of Oklahoma Press, 1968.

Collings, Ellsworth. *The 101 Ranch.* Norman: University of Oklahoma Press, 1937.

Colorado Cattlewomen, Inc., Records. Denver Public Library. Denver, Colo.

Corkins, J. P. "Cattle Grub Control." *Montana Stockgrower,* February 1951.

Craighead, Jacob D. Papers of. Huntington Library. San Marino, Calif.

Culley, John. *Cattle, Horses, and Men of the Western Range.* Los Angeles: Ward Ritchie Press, 1940.

DeVoto, Bernard. *The Easy Chair.* Boston: Houghton Mifflin, 1955.

Dixon, Mrs. Ott. "Neighborly Gossip." *Arizona Cattlelog,* December 1951.

Dover, Rubie K. "Barbie Q's." *Cow Country,* September 15, 1961.

Dude Ranchers' Association Records. American Heritage Center, University of Wyoming, Laramie.

Ellis, George F. *Bell Ranch as I Knew It.* Kansas City, Mo.: Lowell Press, 1973.

———. Papers of. Center for Southwest Research, University of New Mexico, Albuquerque.

———. "Problems of Ranching on Privately Owned Land." In *Armour and Company Tour.* Albuquerque: n.p., 1950.

Ellis, Mattie. *Bell Ranch: Peoples and Places.* Clarendon, Tex.: Clarendon Press, 1963.

———. *Bell Ranch Recollections.* Clarendon, Tex.: Clarendon Press, 1965.

———. *My Dishpan and Other Items.* Clarendon, Tex.: Clarendon Press, 1963.

Etchart, Gene. "Call to Convention." *Montana Stockgrower,* May 1959.

Fain, Dan. "Cottonseed Meal-Salt Mixture," *Arizona Cattlelog,* October 1949, 8–10.

———. "Four Generations of Fains." *Arizona Cattlelog,* January 1946.

"Five-Year Demonstration Proves Value of Moderate Grazing." *Cattle Guard,* October 1957.

"Foot and Mouth Situation." *Montana Stockgrower,* July 1949.

Frink, Maurice. *Cow Country Cavalcade: Eighty Years of the Wyoming Stock Growers Association.* Denver, Colo.: Old West Publishing, 1954.

Fritz, Fred. "Organization—Its Purpose and Need." *Arizona Cattlelog*, September 1946.

Frohlicher, John. "Irrigation Ditch." *Arizona Cattlelog*, January 1946.

Glenn, Marvin. "Hunting Lions." *Arizona Cattlelog*, April 1952.

Godfrey, George Amos. "They Kicked Us off Our Land." *Lordsburg Liberal*, August 8, 1947.

———. Papers of. Rio Grande Historical Collections, New Mexico State University, Las Cruces.

Goff, Dick [Richard]. "Irons in the Fire." *Cattle Guard*, April 1957.

Goff, Richard, and Robert H. McCaffree. *Century in the Saddle.* Denver: Colorado Cattlemen's Centennial Commission, 1967.

Good, G. H. "Brucellosis . . . First in a Series of Articles on Bang's Disease." *Cow Country*, December 1950.

———. "Let's Control and Eradicate Brucellosis from Our Herds." *Cow Country*, April 15, 1956.

Greer, James. *Early in the Saddle.* Dallas: Dealey and Lowe, 1936.

Grieve, Bill. "Roundup Time." *Montana Stockgrower*, May 1965.

Griffin, Mrs. Laura (C. C.). "Reminiscences." *Arizona Cattlelog*, February 1950.

Gudmundson, Pat. "Miles City Turns Clock Back 75 Years." *Great Falls Tribune*, May 17, 1959.

Hanesworth, Robert. "Your New Magazine." *Cow Country*, October 15, 1950.

Hanson, Dan. "Hat Creek Rancher Replies to Budd Letter." *Cow Country*, June 15, 1956.

Hayward, E. G. "The Livestock Industry, Harvester of Nation's Greatest Crop—Grass." *Cow Country*, February 1951.

Hellbusch, C. E. "Field Day at White Mountain Hereford Ranch." *Arizona Cattlelog*, September 1947.

Hooker, Mrs. Harry. "Five Generations of Hookers: On the Sierra Bonita Ranch." *Arizona Cattlelog*, December 1949.

"Hopper Control Program All Set to Go." *Cow Country*, May 19, 1950.

"Howard Major's Deferred Grazing Pays-Off in Rehabilitation of Valencia County Ranch." *New Mexico Stockman*, January 10, 1955.

Huidekoper, Wallis. "The Story of the Range." *Montana Stockgrower*, January 1951.

"J. D. Craighead Pioneered Valley Hereford Industry." *Arkansas Valley Journal*, January 17, 1952.

Jacobsen, N. A. "Are Pine Needles to Blame? A Review of Studies on the Part Played by Pine Needles in Connection with Abortion in Range Cows." *Montana Stockgrower*, December 1961.

Jeffers, Jo. *Ranch Wife.* Garden City, N.Y.: Doubleday, 1964.

Johnson, Elizabeth. "Four Generations of Cooks: In the Cattle Business at Willcox since 1893." *Arizona Cattlelog*, November 1955.

Jones, John. *Farm Real Estate: Historical Series Data, 1950–92.* Statistical Bulletin #855. Microform. Washington D.C.: U.S. Department of Agriculture, Economic Research Service, 1993.

Jones, Neckyoke. "Greasewood Answers Powder River Pete." *Cow Country,* July 7, 1949.

Keith, Abbie. "A Real Cowman." *Arizona Cattlelog,* January 1947.

Kennedy, Michael, ed. *Cowboys and Cattlemen: A Round-up from Montana, the Magazine of Western History.* New York: Hastings House, 1964.

King, Frank M. *Longhorn Trail Drivers: Being a True Story of the Cattle Drives of Long Ago.* Los Angeles: Haynes Corp., 1940.

——. *Mavericks: The Salty Comments of an Old-Time Cowpuncher.* Pasadena, Calif.: Trail's End Publishing, 1947.

——. *Papers of.* Huntington Library, San Marino, Calif.

——. *Pioneer Western Empire Builders: A True Story of the Men and Women of Pioneer Days.* Pasadena, Calif.: Trail's End Publishing, 1946.

——. *Wranglin' the Past: Being the Reminiscences of Frank M. King.* Los Angeles: Haynes Corp., 1935.

King, Henry, dir. *The Gunfighter.* Beverly Hills, Calif.: 20th Century Fox, 1950.

Kratz, B. L. "A Cowboy's Life Ain't All Roses." *Montana Stockgrower,* February 1962.

Krentz, Frank. "Neighborly Gossip." *Arizona Cattlelog,* December 1951.

LaFont, Don. *Rugged Life in the Rockies.* Casper, Wyo.: Prairie Publishing, 1951.

Lambert, Fred. *Bygone Days of the Old West.* Kansas City, Mo.: Burton Publishing, 1948.

Lavender, David Sievert. *One Man's West.* Garden City, N.Y.: Doubleday, Doran & Co., 1943.

Maggie [no last name]. "Maggie Promotes." *Montana Stockgrower,* May 1958.

——. "Maggie Reports on the Convention." *Montana Stockgrower,* July 1957.

——. "Minnie's Conventioning." *Montana Stockgrower,* May 1959.

"A Man Working for the Cattle Business." *Cattle Guard,* November 1955.

"Market News." *Montana Stockgrower,* March 1963.

Mason, Oda, Papers of. American Heritage Center, University of Wyoming, Laramie.

"Mountain Meadow Grazing Results Told at Field Day." *Cow Country,* October 1952.

Mercier, Laurie. Julian Terrett Oral History, 1982. Oral History 226, Montana Historical Society Research Center Archives, Helena.

Meyer, Mrs. Walter. "Prickly Pear vs. Australian Beetle." *Arizona Cattlelog,* May 1946, 31.

Miracle, Ralph. "Your Secretary Reports to the Convention." *Montana Stockgrower,* June 15, 1955.

Mollin, F. E. "Agricultural Adjustment Program as the Cattle Producers View It." *The Producer,* November 1933.

Morgan, Learah Cooper, ed. *Echoes of the Past: Tales of Old Yavapai.* Prescott, Ariz.: Yavapai Cow Belles of Arizona, 1955.

Mortensen, Robert K. *In the Cause of Progress: A History of the New Mexico Cattle Growers' Association.* Albuquerque: New Mexico Stockman, 1983.

Montana Brands Enforcement Division Records. Montana Historical Society Research Center Archives, Helena.

Montana Cattlemen's Association Manuscript Collection. Montana Historical Society Research Center Archives, Helena.

Montana Cowbelles Records. Montana Historical Society Research Center Archives, Helena.

"Mountain Meadow Grazing Results Told at Field Day." *Cow Country,* October 1952.

Nelson, Art. "Central Montana's View on Game Problem." *Montana Stockgrower,* November 15, 1954.

"New Federal Brucellosis Regulations Announced." *Cow Country,* October 15, 1956.

"1950 Convention Resolutions." *Montana Stockgrower,* June 1950.

O'Conner, Sandra Day, and H. Alan Day. *Lazy B: Growing Up on a Cattle Ranch in the American Southwest.* New York: Random House, 2002.

Olea, Mrs. Y. S. "Prickly Pear vs. Australian Beetle." *Arizona Cattlelog,* March 1946.

"Operation Grasshopper." *Cow Country,* March 30, 1950.

Paladin, Vivian A. *The Montana Stockgrower: Montana Stockgrowers Association, 1884–1984: A Century of Service to Montana's Cattle Industry.* Helena: Montana Stockgrowers Association, 1984.

Perkins, Clyde Riggs (Mrs. F. D.). "We Lick the Cats." *Arizona Cattlelog,* July 1949.

Perkins, Evelyn. "Life on a Cattle Ranch." *Arizona Cattlelog,* April 1950.

"Price Support Poll." *Montana Stockgrower,* December 15, 1953.

Rak, Mary Kidder. *A Cowman's Wife.* Boston: Houghton Mifflin, 1934.

———. "Help Eliza Cross the Ice." *Arizona Cattlelog,* September 1949.

———. "A Kitchenful of Men." *Arizona Cattlelog,* January 1947.

Raney, S. A. "Prickly Pear vs. Australian Beetle." *Arizona Cattlelog,* March 1946.

"Reviewing the November Market." *Montana Stockgrower,* December 1961.

Rhodes, Rosa Ronquillo. Rhodes Diaries, 1864–1982, Arizona Historical Society, Tucson.

Riggs, Lillian. "Chicago Girl Spreads a Loop." *Arizona Cattlelog,* September 1946.

———. "Neighborly Gossip." *Arizona Cattelog,* February 1950.

Rollins, Philip Ashton. *The Cowboy; His Characteristics, His Equipment, and His Part in the Development of the West.* New York: Scribner's Sons, 1922.

Roney, J. N. "Cattle Grub Control." *Arizona Cattlelog,* September 1949.

———. "Grasshopper Control on Arizona Ranges." *Arizona Cattlelog,* June 1950.

Russell, Charles M. *Good Medicine: Memories of the Real West.* Garden City, N.Y.: Garden City Publishing Co., 1930.

Ryff, Dr. J. F. "Have You Heard about Anaplasmosis?" *Cow Country,* April 15, 1956.

Safford, Jeffrey J. Jack Brenner Oral History, September 11, 1976. Montana Historical Society Research Center Archives, Helena.

Sears, John L., and Carmy G. Page. "The County Agent Speaks: A Review of 1949."
Arizona Cattlelog, January 1950.

Sharp, Robert. *Big Outfit: Ranching on the Baca Float*. Tucson: University of Arizona
Press, 1974.

Slanger, Ben S. "Range Condition Classes." *Montana Stockgrower*, November 15,
1952.

Smith, Henry. "Rattlesnakes." *Arizona Cattlelog*, March 1948.

Spring, Agnes Wright. *70 Years Cow Country: A Panoramic History of the Wyoming Stock
Growers Association Interwoven with Data Relative to the Cattle Industry in Wyoming*.
Cheyenne: Wyoming Stock Growers Association, 1943.

Stokoe, Sonia. "American National Cowbelles' Cry for Rings for Promotion of Beef
Industry." *Arizona Republic*, July 21, 1957, C3.

Taylor Grazing Act of 1934. Title 43 of the U.S. Code, Public Rangelands Improvements, 1934. http://plainshumanities.unl.edu/encyclopedia/doc/egp.ag.071.

Tepoel, C. H. "Early Day Cow-Punching on Northern Ranges." *Arizona Cattlelog*,
February 1952.

Thorp, N. Howard (Jack). *Songs of the Cowboys*. Estancia, N.Mex.: News Print Shop,
1908.

Tyrrell, Ace V. "Grain and Salt Feeding: Weight Doubled in 10 Months." *Cow Country*, September 1952.

U.S. Department of Agriculture. "The Foot and Mouth Disease Situation in Mexico—Map, February 22, 1947." Box 29, Folder 2, ACGA Manuscript Collection,
Arizona Historical Society, Tempe.

Van Cleve, Spike. *40 Years' Gatherin's*. Kansas City, Mo.: Lowell Press, 1977.

Warren, Conrad K. "Convention Address of President C. K. Warren." *Montana
Stockgrower*, June 1951.

———. Papers of. Grant-Kohrs National Historic Site, Deer Lodge, Mont.

Wear, Peggy. "Willcox Cowbelles." *Arizona Cattlelog*, January 1948.

"White Sands Missile Range History." White Sands Missile Range Museum.
Accessed April 25, 2022, https://wsmrmuseum.com/history/.

White, Herbert P. "Typically Efficient Ranch Woman, Who Wins in Face of Wartime Barriers." *New Mexico Stockman*, December 1943.

Wingfield, D. W. "Neighborly Gossip." *Arizona Cattlelog*, June 1946.

Woolfolk, E. J. "Crested Wheatgrass Grazing Values." *Montana Stockgrower*, May
1951.

Wootan, J. F. "The Real Cowboy." *Arizona Cattlelog*, January 1946.

Wyoming Cowbelles Records. Wyoming Stock Growers Association Collection.
American Heritage Center, University of Wyoming, Laramie.

Wyoming Stock Growers Association Collection. American Heritage Center, University of Wyoming, Laramie.

SECONDARY SOURCES

Ackland, Len. *Making a Real Killing: Rocky Flats and the Nuclear West.* Albuquerque: University of New Mexico Press, 1999.

Allmendinger, Blake. *The Cowboy: Representations of Labor in an American Work Culture.* New York: Oxford University Press, 1992.

Alvarez, C. J. "Police, Waterworks, and the Construction of the U.S.-Mexico Border, 1924–1954." *Western Historical Quarterly* 50, no. 3 (Autumn 2019): 233–57.

Amundson, Michael A. *Yellowcake Towns: Uranium Mining Communities in the American West.* Boulder: University Press of Colorado, 2002.

Anderson, Benedict. *Imagined Communities: Reflections on the Origins and Spread of Nationalism.* New York: Verso Editions, 1983.

Argersinger, Peter. *The Limits of Agrarian Radicalism: Western Populism and American Politics.* Lawrence: University of Kansas Press, 1995.

Athearn, Robert G. *The Mythic West in Twentieth-Century America.* Lawrence: University of Kansas Press, 1986.

Baldwin, Robert. *The Political Economy of United States Import Policy.* Cambridge, Mass.: MIT Press, 1985.

Ball, Charles E. *Building the Beef Industry: A Century of Commitment 1898–1998.* Denver: National Cattlemen's Foundation, 1998.

Baron, Ava. "Gender and Labor History." In *Work Engendered: Toward a New History of American Labor,* edited by Ava Baron, 1–47. Ithaca, N.Y.: Cornell University Press, 1991.

Basso, Matthew, Laura McCall, and Dee Garceau, eds. *Across the Great Divide: Cultures of Manhood in the American West.* New York: Routledge, 2001.

Baumgartner, Frank. *Basic Interests: The Importance of Groups in Politics and in Political Science.* Princeton, N.J.: Princeton University Press, 1998.

Bederman, Gail. *Manliness and Civilization: A Cultural History of Gender and Race in the United States, 1880–1917.* Chicago: University of Chicago Press, 1995.

Belasco, Warren James. *Americans on the Road: From Autocamp to Motel, 1910–1945.* Cambridge, Mass.: MIT Press, 1979.

Belgrad, Daniel. "'Power's Larger Meaning': The Johnson County War as Political Violence in an Environmental Context." *Western Historical Quarterly* 33, no. 2 (Summer 2002): 159–77.

Bell, Margaret. *When Montana and I Were Young: A Frontier Childhood.* Lincoln: University of Nebraska Press, 2002.

Bennett, Jane. *Vibrant Matter: A Political Ecology of Things.* Durham, N.C.: Duke University Press, 2010.

Bentley, Amy. *Eating for Victory: Food Rationing and the Politics of Domesticity.* Urbana: University of Illinois Press, 1998.

Berkhofer, Robert F. *The White Man's Indian: Images of the American Indian from Columbus to the Present.* New York: Vintage Books, 1979.

Berry, Michelle K. "'Be Shure to Fix the Fence': The Arizona Cowbelles' Public Persona, 1950–1960." *Frontiers: A Journal of Women Studies* 25, no. 2 (2004): 151–75.

Billington, Ray Allen. *The Far Western Frontier, 1830–1860.* New York: Harper, 1956.

Black, Cyril Edwin. *The Dynamics of Modernization: A Study in Comparative History.* New York: Harper & Row, 1966.

Blunt, Judy. *Breaking Clean.* New York: Knopf, 2002.

Bogue, Allan. *From Prairie to Corn Belt: Farming on the Illinois and Iowa Prairies in the 19th Century.* Chicago: University of Chicago, 1963.

Bonnifield, Paul. *The Dust Bowl: Men, Dirt, and Depression.* Albuquerque: University of New Mexico Press, 1979.

Borne, Lawrence R. *Dude Ranching: A Complete History.* Albuquerque: University of New Mexico Press, 1983.

Boydston, Jeanne. *Home and Work: Housework, Wages, and the Ideology of Labor in the Early Republic.* New York: Oxford University Press, 1990.

Braunwald, Eugene, Anthony Fauci, and Dennis Kasper, eds. *Harrison's Principles of Internal Medicine.* 15th ed. New York: McGraw Hill, 2001.

Britz, Kevin. "Long May Their Legend Survive: Memory and Authenticity in Deadwood, South Dakota; Tombstone, Arizona; and Dodge City, Kansas." PhD. diss., University of Arizona, Tucson, 1999.

Brown, Kathleen. *Good Wives, Nasty Wenches, and Anxious Patriarchs: Gender, Race, and Power in Colonial Virginia.* Chapel Hill: University of North Carolina Press, 1996.

Brown, Richard Maxwell. "Violence." In *The Oxford History of the American West*, edited by Carol A. O'Connor, Clyde A. Milner II, and Martha A. Sandweiss, 393–427. New York: Oxford University Press, 1994.

Bush, Corlann Gee. "'He Isn't Half So Cranky as He Used to Be': Agricultural Mechanization, Comparable Worth, and the Changing Farm Family." In *"To Toil the Livelong Day": American's Women at Work, 1780–1980*, edited by Carol Groneman and Mary Beth Norton, 213–33. Ithaca, N.Y.: Cornell University Press, 1987.

Cabral, Diogo de Carvalho. "Meaningful Clearings: Human-Ant Negotiated Landscapes in Nineteenth-Century Brazil." *Environmental History* 26 (2021): 55–78.

Calef, Wesley. *Private Grazing and Public Lands: Studies of the Local Management of the Taylor Grazing Act.* Chicago: University of Chicago Press, 1961.

Carr-Childers, Leisl. *The Size of the Risk: Histories of Multiple Use in the Great Basin.* Norman: University of Oklahoma Press, 2015.

Cawley, R. McGreggor. *Federal Land, Western Anger: The Sagebrush Rebellion and Environmental Politics.* Lawrence: University Press of Kansas, 1993.

Chambless, Timothy K. "Pro-Defense, Pro-Growth, and Anti-Communism: Cold War Politics in the American West." In Fernlund, *The Cold War American West*, 101–19.

Chandler, Daniel. *Semiotics: The Basics.* New York: Routledge, 2001.

Clark, Christopher. *The Roots of Western Capitalism: Western Massachusetts, 1780–1860.* Ithaca, N.Y.: Cornell University Press, 1990.

Clark, Suzanne. *Cold Warriors: Manliness on Trial in the Rhetoric of the West.* Carbondale: Southern Illinois University Press, 2000.

Clemens, Elisabeth. *The People's Lobby: Organization Innovation and the Rise of Interest Group Politics in the United States, 1890–1925.* Chicago: University of Chicago Press, 1997.

Clements, Frederic. *Plant Succession: An Analysis of the Development of Vegetation.* Washington, D.C.: Carnegie Institution of Washington, 1916.

Cohan, Steven. *Masked Men: Masculinity and the Movies in the Fifties.* Bloomington: Indiana University Press, 1997.

Cohen, Lizbeth. *Making a New Deal: Industrial Workers in Chicago, 1919–1939.* New York: Cambridge University Press, 1990.

Coleman, Annie Gilbert. "Call of the Mild: Colorado Ski Resorts and the Politics of Rural Tourism." In *The Countryside in the Age of the Modern State: Political Histories of Rural America,* edited by Catherine McNicol and Robert D. Johnston Stock, 281–304. Ithaca, N.Y.: Cornell University Press, 2001.

Collier, Gaydell, ed. *Leaning into the Wind: Women Write from the Heart of the West.* Boston: Houghton Mifflin, 1997.

Confino, Alon. "Collective Memory and Cultural History: Problems of Method." *American Historical Review* 102, no. 5 (December 1997): 1386–1403.

Cowan, Ruth Schwartz. *More Work for Mother: The Ironies of Household Technology from the Open Hearth to the Microwave.* New York: Basic Books, 1983.

Crane, Susan, ed. *Museums and Memory.* Stanford, Calif.: Stanford University Press, 2000.

——. "Writing the Individual Back into Collective Memory." *American Historical Review* 102, no. 5 (December 1997): 1372–85.

Cronon, William. *Nature's Metropolis: Chicago and the Great West.* New York: Norton, 1991.

——. "The West: A Moving Target." *Western Historical Quarterly* 25, no. 4 (1994): 476–81.

Curry, Lynne. *Modern Mothers in the Heartland: Gender, Health, and Progress in Illinois, 1900–1930.* Columbus: Ohio State University Press, 1999.

Dale, Edward E. *The Range Cattle Industry.* Norman: University of Oklahoma Press, 1930.

Danbom, David. *Born in the Country: A History of Rural America.* Baltimore: Johns Hopkins University Press, 2006.

Daniel, Pete. *Breaking the Land: Transformation of Cotton, Tobacco, and Rice Cultures.* Urbana: University of Illinois Press, 1985.

Darnton, Robert. *The Great Cat Massacre and Other Episodes in French Cultural History.* New York: Basic Books, 1984.

Davis, Natalie Zemon. *Fiction in the Archives: Pardon Tales and Their Tellers in Sixteenth-Century France.* Stanford, Calif.: Stanford University Press, 1987.

———. *Society and Culture in Early Modern France.* Stanford, Calif.: Stanford University Press, 1975.

Deloria, Philip J. *Playing Indian.* New Haven, Conn.: Yale University Press, 1998.

Dewey, Alicia "Ranching across Borders: The Making of a Transnational Cattle Industry in the Texas-Mexico Borderlands." In *Farming across Borders: A Transnational History of the North American West,* edited by Sterling Evans, 221–47. Chapel Hill: University of North Carolina Press, 2017.

Dias, Ric. "The Great Cantonment: Cold War Cities in the American West." In Fernlund, *The Cold War American West,* 71–87.

Dilworth, Leah. "Tourists and Indians in Fred Harvey's Southwest." In Wrobel and Long, *Seeing and Being Seen,*142–65.

Dippie, Brian. *The Vanishing American: White Attitudes and U.S. Indian Policy.* Middletown, Conn.: Wesleyan University Press, 1982.

Divine, Jenny. *On Behalf of the Family Farm.* Iowa City: University of Iowa Press, 2013.

Dobie, J. Frank. *The Longhorns.* Boston: Little, Brown, 1941.

Donahue, Debra. *The Western Range Revisited: Removing Livestock from Public Lands to Conserve Native Biodiversity.* Norman: University of Oklahoma Press, 1999.

Douglas, Mary. "Jokes." In *Rethinking Popular Culture: Contemporary Perspectives in Cultural Studies,* edited by Chandra Mukerji and Michael Schudson, 291–311. Berkeley: University of California Press, 1991.

Dowd Hall, Jacquelyn. "'You Must Remember This': Autobiography as Social Critique." In *Gender and the Southern Body Politic,* edited by Nancy Bercaw, 1–29. Jackson: University of Mississippi Press, 2000.

Dunlap, Thomas R. *DDT: Scientists, Citizens, and Public Policy.* Princeton, N.J.: Princeton University Press, 1981.

Duranti, Alessandro. *Linguistic Anthropology: A Reader.* Malden, Mass.: Wiley-Blackwell, 2009.

Dusenberry, William. "Foot and Mouth Disease in Mexico, 1946–1951." *Agricultural History* 29, no. 2 (April 1955): 82–90.

Dykstra, Robert R. *The Cattle Towns: A Social History of the Kansas Cattle Trading Centers, Abilene, Ellsworth, Wichita, Dodge City and Caldwell, 1867–1885.* New York: Atheneum, 1976.

Dyson, Lowell K. *Farmers' Organizations.* New York: Greenwood Press, 1986.

Eidenbach, Peter, and Beth Morgan, eds. *Homes on the Range: Oral Recollections of Early Ranch Life on the U.S. Army White Sands Missile Range, New Mexico.* Tularosa, N.Mex.: Human Systems Research, 1994.

Eisenstein, Zillah, ed. *Capitalist Patriarchy and the Case for Socialist Feminism.* New York: Monthly Review Press, 1979.

Elbert, Sarah. "Amber Waves of Gain: Women's Work in New York Farm Families." In Groneman and Norton, *"To Toil the Livelong Day,"* 250–69.

Emmons, David. "Constructed Province: History and the Making of the Last American West." *Western Historical Quarterly* 25, no. 4 (1994): 437–59.

Erickson, John. *Ace Reid, Cowpoke.* Perryton, Tex.: Maverick Books, 1984.

Fabry, Judith. "Agricultural Science and Technology in the West." In *The Rural West since World War II,* edited by R. Douglas Hurt, 168–90. Lawrence: University Press of Kansas, 1998.

Faragher, John Mack. *Sugar Creek: Life on the Illinois Prairie.* New Haven, Conn.: Yale University Press, 1986.

Faue, Elizabeth. *Community of Suffering and Struggle: Women, Men, and the Labor Movement in Minneapolis, 1915–1945.* Chapel Hill: University of North Carolina Press, 1991.

Fernlund, Kevin J., ed. *The Cold War American West, 1945–1989.* Albuquerque: University of New Mexico Center for the American West, 1998.

Fiege, Mark. *Irrigated Eden: The Making of an Agricultural Landscape in the American West.* Seattle: University of Washington Press, 1999.

———. *The Republic of Nature: An Environmental History of the United States.* Seattle: University of Washington Press, 2013.

Field, Bruce. *Harvest of Dissent: The National Farmers Union and the Early Cold War.* Lawrence: University Press of Kansas, 1998.

Findlay, John M. *Magic Lands: The Western Cityscapes and American Culture.* Berkeley: University of California Press, 1992.

Fink, Deborah. "Sidelines and Moral Capital: Women on Nebraska Farms in the 1930s." In *Women and Farming: Changing Roles, Changing Structures,* edited by Wava G. Haney, 55–72. Boulder, Colo.: Westview Press, 1988.

Fisher, John R. "Cattle Plagues Past and Present: The Mystery of Mad Cow Disease." *Journal of Contemporary History* 33, no. 2 (1998): 215–28.

Fite, Gilbert C. *American Farmers: The New Minority.* Bloomington: Indiana University Press, 1981.

———. *The Farmers' Frontier, 1865–1900.* New York: Holt, Rinehart and Winston, 1966.

Fitzgerald, Deborah. "Beyond Tractors: The History of Technology in American Agriculture." *Technology and Culture* 32 (January 1991): 114–26.

———. *Every Farm a Factory: The Industrial Ideal in American Agriculture.* New Haven, Conn.: Yale University Press, 2003.

Fleischner, Thomas L. "Land Held Hostage: A History of Livestock and Politics." In *Welfare Ranching: The Subsidized Destruction of the American West,* edited by George Wuerthner and Mollie Matteson, 33–38. Sausalito, Calif.: Foundation for Deep Ecology, 2002.

Flores, Dan. "Bison Ecology and Bison Diplomacy: The Southern Plains, 1800–1850." *Journal of American History* 78, no. 2 (1991): 465–85.

———. *Coyote: A Natural and Supernatural History.* New York: Basic Books, 2018.

———. *The Natural West: Environmental History in the Great Plains and Rocky Mountains.* Norman: University of Oklahoma Press, 2001.

Foley, Neil. *The White Scourge: Mexicans, Blacks, and Poor Whites in Texas Cotton Culture.* Berkeley: University of California Press, 1997.

Foss, Phillip O. *Politics and Grass: The Administration of Grazing on the Public Domain.* Seattle: University of Washington Press, 1960.

Foucault, Michel. *The History of Sexuality.* New York: Pantheon Books, 1978.

——. *Power/Knowledge: Selected Interviews and Other Writings, 1972–1977.* Brighton, Sussex, UK: Harvester Press, 1980.

Frank, Dana. *Purchasing Power: Consumer Organizing, Gender, and the Seattle Labor Movement, 1919–1929.* New York: Cambridge University Press, 1994.

Freeman, Mark. *Rewriting the Self: History, Memory, Narrative.* New York: Routledge, 1993.

Friedberger, Mark. "Cattle Raising and Dairying in the Western States." In *The Rural West since World War II*, edited by R. Douglas Hurt, 190–213. Lawrence: University Press of Kansas, 1998.

Friedmann, Harriett. "World Market, State, and the Family Farm: Social Bases of Household Production in the Era of Wage Labor." *Comparative Studies in Society and History* 20, no. 4 (1978): 545–86.

Furman, Necah Stewart. *Caroline Lockhart: Her Life and Legacy.* Cody, Wyo.: Buffalo Bill Historical Center, 1994.

Garceau, Dee. *The Important Things of Life: Women, Work, and Family in Sweetwater County, Wyoming, 1880–1929.* Lincoln: University of Nebraska Press, 1997.

Gates, Paul Wallace. *The Farmer's Age: Agriculture, 1815–1860.* New York: Holt, Rinehart and Winston, 1960.

Geertz, Clifford. *The Interpretation of Cultures.* New York, 1973.

Getty, Harry. *The San Carlos Indian Cattle Industry.* Tucson: University of Arizona Press, 1963.

Gibson, David. *Grasses and Grassland Ecology.* Oxford: Oxford University Press, 2009.

Goin, Peter. *Nuclear Landscapes.* Baltimore: Johns Hopkins University Press, 1991.

Goldfarb, Ben. *Eager: The Surprising, Secret Life of Beavers and Why They Matter.* White River Junction, Vt.: Chelsea Green Publishing, 2019.

Goldstein, Judith. *Ideas, Interests, and American Trade Policy.* Ithaca, N.Y.: Cornell University Press, 1993.

Good, Charles M. "Salt, Trade and Disease: Aspects of Development in Africa's Northern Great Lakes Region." *International Journal of African Historical Studies* 5, no. 4 (1972): 543–86.

Goodwyn, Lawrence. *The Populist Moment: A Short History of the Agrarian Revolt in America.* New York: Oxford University Press, 1978.

Gordon, Linda, and Allen Hunter. "Not All Male Dominance Is Patriarchal." *Radical History Review* no. 71 (Spring 1998): 71–83.

Gottlieb, Robert. *Forcing the Spring: The Transformation of the American Environmental Movement.* Washington, D.C.: Island Press, 1993.

Graf, William L. *Wilderness Preservation and the Sagebrush Rebellions.* Savage, Md.: Rowman and Littlefield, 1990.

Gray, James R. *Ranch Economics.* Ames: Iowa State University Press, 1968.

Gregory, James. *American Exodus: The Dust Bowl Migration and Okie Culture in California.* New York: Oxford University Press, 1989.

Grosskopf, Linda A. *On Flatwillow Creek: The Story of Montana's N Bar Ranch.* Los Alamos, N.Mex.: Exceptional Books, 1991.

Guha, Ramachandra. *Environmentalism: A Global History.* New York: Longman, 2000.

Hadley, Diana, Scott Mills, and Richard V. N. Ahlstrom. *El Rio Bonito: An Ethnoecological Study of the Bonita Creek Watershed, Southeastern Arizona.* Phoenix: Arizona State Office of the Bureau of Land Management, 1993.

Hahamovitch, Cindy. *Fruits of Their Labor: Atlantic Coast Farmworkers and the Making of Migrant Poverty, 1870–1945.* Chapel Hill: University of North Carolina Press, 1997.

Hall, Stuart. "Ethnicity: Identity and Difference." *Radical America* 24 (1990): 9–20.

Hansen, John Mark. "Creating a New Politics: The Evolution of an Agricultural Policy Network in Congress, 1919–1980." New Haven, Conn.: Yale University Press, 1987.

Hardin, Garrett. "Tragedy of the Commons." *Science* 162 (1968): 1243–48.

Hargreaves, Mary W. M. "Land Use Planning in Response to Drought: The Great Plains Experience of the Thirties." *Agricultural History* 50 (October 1976): 561–82.

Harmon, Alexandra. *Indians in the Making: Ethnic Relations and Indian Identities around Puget Sound.* Berkeley: University of California Press, 1999.

Harvey, Brett. *The Fifties: A Women's Oral History.* New York: HarperCollins, 1993.

Hasselstrom, Linda. *Windbreak: A Woman Rancher on the Northern Plains.* Berkeley, Calif.: Barn Owl Books, 1987.

Hays, Samuel. *Conservation and the Gospel of Efficiency: The Progressive Conservation Movement, 1890–1920.* Cambridge, Mass.: Harvard University Press, 1959.

Hersey, Mark, and Lisa Brady. "New Directions in Environmental History." *American Historian* (September 2019). https://www.oah.org/tah/issues/2019/environmental-history/new-directions-in-environmental-history/.

Herron, John, ed. *Human/Nature: Biology, Culture and Environmental History.* Albuquerque: University of New Mexico Press, 1999.

Hess, Karl. *Visions upon the Land: Man and Nature on the Western Range.* Washington, D.C.: Island Press, 1992.

Hevly, Bruce William, and John Findlay, eds. *The Atomic West.* Seattle: University of Washington Center of the Study of the Pacific Northwest, 1998.

Hinds, Lynn Boyd. *The Cold War as Rhetoric: The Beginnings, 1945–1950.* New York: Praeger, 1991.

Hirt, Paul W. *A Conspiracy of Optimism: Management of the National Forests since World War Two.* Lincoln: University of Nebraska Press, 1994.

Hooks, Gregory Michael. *Forging the Military-Industrial Complex: World War II's Battle of the Potomac.* Urbana: University of Illinois Press, 1991.

Horowitz, Roger, ed. *Boys and Their Toys: Masculinity, Technology, and Class in America.* New York: Routledge, 2001.

Hunner, Jon. *Inventing Los Alamos: The Growth of an Atomic Community.* Norman: University of Oklahoma Press, 2004.

Hunt, Lynn. "Introduction: History, Culture, and Text." In *The New Cultural History,* edited by Lynn Hunt, 1–24. Berkeley: University of California Press, 1989.

Hurt, R. Douglas. *Agricultural Technology in the Twentieth Century.* Manhattan: Sunflower University Press, 1991.

——. *American Agriculture: A Brief History.* Ames: Iowa State University Press, 1994.

——. *The Dust Bowl: An Agricultural and Social History.* Chicago: Nelson-Hall, 1981.

——, ed. *The Rural West since World War II.* Lawrence: University Press of Kansas, 1998.

Hyde, Anne. *An American Vision: Far Western Landscape and National Culture.* New York: NYU Press, 1990.

——. "From Stagecoach to Packard Twin Six: Yosemite and the Changing Face of Tourism, 1880–1930." *California History* 69, no. 2 (Summer 1990): 154–69.

Igler, David. *Industrial Cowboys: Miller and Lux and the Transformation of the Far West, 1850–1920.* Berkeley: University of California Press, 2001.

Ingold, Tim. *The Perception of the Environment: Essays in Livelihood, Dwelling, and Skill.* New York: Routledge, 2000.

Iverson, Peter. *When Indians Became Cowboys: Native Peoples and Cattle Ranching in the American West.* Norman: University of Oklahoma Press, 1994.

Jackson, T. J., ed. *The Culture Consumption: Critical Essays in American History, 1880– 1980.* New York: Pantheon Books, 1983.

Jacobs, Lynn. *The Waste of the West: Public Lands Ranching.* Tucson, Ariz.: L. Jacobs, 1991.

Jacobs, Margaret. *Engendered Encounters: Feminism and Pueblo Cultures, 1879–1934.* Lincoln: University of Nebraska Press, 1999.

Jacoby, Karl. *Crimes against Nature: Squatters, Poachers, Thieves, and the Hidden History of American Conservation.* Berkeley: University of California Press, 2001.

Jakle, John. *The Tourist: Travel in Twentieth-Century North America.* Lincoln: University of Nebraska Press, 1985.

Jameson, Elizabeth, ed. *The Women's West.* Norman: University of Oklahoma Press, 1987.

——, ed. *Writing the Range: Race, Class, and Culture in the Women's West.* Norman: University of Oklahoma Press, 1997.

Jellison, Katherine. *Entitled to Power: Farm Women and Technology, 1913–1963.* Chapel Hill: University of North Carolina Press, 1993.

Jemison, R., and C. Raish. *Livestock Management in the American Southwest: Ecology, Society and Economics.* Amsterdam: Elseveir, 2000.

Jenkins, J. Craig. *The Politics of Insurgency: The Farm Worker Movement in the 1960s.* New York: Columbia University Press, 1985.

Jensen, Joan. *Loosening the Bonds: Mid-Atlantic Farm Women, 1750–1850.* New Haven, Conn.: Yale University Press, 1986.

———. *Promise to the Land: Essays on Rural Women.* Albuquerque: University of New Mexico Press, 1991.

Johnson, Susan Lee. "'A Memory Sweet to Soldiers': The Significance of Gender." In *A New Significance: Re-Visioning the History of the American West,* edited by Clyde Milner, 255–79. New York: Oxford University Press, 1996.

———. *Roaring Camp: The Social World of the California Gold Rush.* London: Norton, 2000.

Johnston, Robert D., and Catherine McNicol Stock, eds. *The Countryside in the Age of the Modern State: Political Histories of Rural America.* Ithaca, N.Y.: Cornell University Press, 2001.

Johnstone, Steve. "Virtuous Toil, Vicious Work: Xenophon on Aristocratic Style." *Classical Philology* 89, no. 3 (1994): 219–40.

Jones, Jacqueline. "Tore Up and a Movin': Perspectives on the Work of Black and Poor White Women in the Rural South, 1865–1940." In *Women and Farming: Changing Roles, Changing Structures,* edited by Wava G. Haney. Boulder, Colo.: Westview Press, 1988.

Jordan, Teresa. *Cowgirls: Women of the American West.* Lincoln: University of Nebraska Press, 1982.

Jordan, Terry. *North American Cattle-Ranching Frontiers: Origins, Diffusion, and Differentiation.* Albuquerque: University of New Mexico Press, 1993.

Kaledin, Eugenia. *Mothers and More: American Women in the 1950s.* Boston: Twayne, 1984.

Kammen, Michael. *Mystic Chords of Memory: The Transformation of Tradition in American Culture.* New York: Knopf, 1991.

Kaplan, Flora E. S., ed. *Museums and the Making of Ourselves: The Role of Objects in National Identity.* London: Leicester University Press, 1994.

Kelley, Robin D. G. *Hammer and Hoe: Alabama Communists during the Great Depression.* Chapel Hill: University of North Carolina Press, 1990.

Kelly, Joan. *Women, History, and Theory.* Chicago: University of Chicago Press, 1984.

Kennedy Michael S., ed. *Cowboys and Cattlemen: A Roundup from Montana: The Magazine of Western History.* New York: Hastings House, 1964.

Klemme, Marvin. *Home Rule on the Range: Early Days of the Grazing Service.* New York: Vantage Press, 1984.

Knight, Richard, Wendell C. Gilgert, and Ed Marston, eds. *Ranching West of the 100th Meridian: Culture, Ecology, and Economics.* Washington, D.C.: Island Press, 2002.

Knobloch, Frieda. *The Culture of Wilderness: Agriculture as Colonization in the American West.* Chapel Hill: University of North Carolina Press, 1996.

Koistenen, Paul A. C. *The Military-Industrial Complex: A Historical Perspective.* New York: Praeger, 1980.

Kolodny, Annette. *The Land before Her: Fantasy and Experience of the American Frontiers, 1630–1860.* Chapel Hill: University of North Carolina Press, 1984.

——. *The Lay of the Land: Metaphor as Experience and History in American Life and Letters.* Chapel Hill: University of North Carolina Press, 1975.

LaCapra, Dominick. *Rethinking Intellectual History: Texts, Contexts, Language.* Ithaca, N.Y.: Cornell University Press, 1983.

Lamar, Howard. *The Far Southwest, 1846–1912: A Territorial History.* New Haven, Conn.: Yale University Press, 1966.

——. "Westering in the Twenty-First Century: Speculations on the Future of the Western Past." In *Under an Open Sky: Rethinking America's Western Past,* edited by William Cronon, George A. Miles, and Jay Gitlin, 257–75. New York: Norton, 1992.

Lamm, Richard, and Michael McCarthy. *The Angry West: A Vulnerable Land and Its Future.* Boston: Houghton Mifflin, 1982.

Latour, Bruno. *Pandora's Hope: Essays on the Reality of Science Studies.* Cambridge, Mass.: Harvard University Press, 1999.

——. *The Politics of Nature: How to Bring the Sciences into Democracy.* Cambridge, Mass.: Harvard University Press, 2002.

Lauenroth, W. K., D. G. Milchunas, J. L. Dodd, R. H. Hart, R. K. Heitschmidt, and L. R. Rittenhouse. "Effects of Grazing on Ecosystems of the Great Plains." In *Ecological Implications of Livestock Herbivory in the West,* edited by Martin Vavra, William A. Laycock, and Rex D. Pieper. Denver: Society for Range Management, 1994.

Lawrence, Amy, et al. "Wyoming Memories: Blizzard of 1949." *Annals of Wyoming: The Wyoming History Journal* 76, no. 1 (Winter 2004): 31–38.

Lears, T. J. Jackson. "The Concept of Cultural Hegemony: Problems and Possibilities." *American Historical Review* 90, no. 3 (1985): 567–93.

Leonard, Kevin Allen. "Migrants, Immigrants, and Refugees: The Cold War and Population Growth in the American West." In Fernlund, *The Cold War American West,* 29–51.

Libecap, Gary. *Locking Up the Range: Federal Land Controls and Grazing.* Cambridge, Mass.: Ballinger, 1981.

Lichtenstein, Nelson. *Labor's War at Home: The CIO in World War II.* Cambridge: Cambridge University Press, 1982.

Limerick, Patricia Nelson, Clyde A. Milner II, and Charles E. Rankin, eds. *Trails: Toward a New Western History.* Lawrence: University Press of Kansas, 1991.

Liu, Tessie P. *The Weaver's Knot: The Contradictions of Class Struggle and Family Solidarity in Western France, 1750–1914.* Ithaca, N.Y.: Cornell University Press, 1994.

Lowenthal, David. *The Heritage Crusade and the Spoils of History.* New York: Viking, 1996.

Lubar, Steven. "Men/Women/Production/Consumption." In *His and Hers: Gender, Consumption, and Technology,* edited by Roger Horowitz, 7–39. Charlottesville: University of Virginia Press, 1998.

MacKenzie, John M. *The Empire of Nature: Hunting, Conservation, and British Imperialism.* Manchester: Manchester University Press, 1988.

MacLean, Nancy. *Behind the Mask of Chivalry: The Making of the Second Ku Klux Klan.* New York: Oxford University Press, 1994.

Makley, Michael. *Open Space, Open Rebellions: The War over America's Public Lands.* Boston: University of Massachusetts, 2018.

Malone, Michael P., and Richard W. Etulain. *The American West: A Twentieth-Century History.* Lincoln: University of Nebraska Press, 1989.

Mather, Eugene. "The Production and Marketing of Wyoming Beef Cattle." *Economic Geography* 26, no. 2 (1950): 81–93.

May, Elaine Tyler. *Homeward Bound: American Families in the Cold War Era.* New York: Basic Books, 1988.

McChristian, Douglas C. *Ranchers to Rangers: An Administrative History of Grant-Kohrs National Historic Site.* Denver: Rocky Mountain Cluster, National Park Service, 1977.

McEnaney, Laura. *Civil Defense Begins at Home: Militarization Meets Everyday Life in the Fifties.* Princeton, N.J.: Princeton University Press, 2000.

McEvoy, Arthur. *The Fisherman's Problem: Ecology and Law in the California Fisheries, 1850–1980.* New York: Cambridge University Press, 1986.

McGerr, Michael. "Is There a Twentieth-Century West?" In *Under an Open Sky: Rethinking America's Western Past,* edited by George Miles, William Cronon, and Jay Gitlin, 239–57. New York: Norton, 1992.

McMath, Robert. *American Populism: A Social History, 1877–1898.* New York: Hill and Wang, 1992.

———. *Populist Vanguard: A History of the Southern Farmers' Alliance.* Chapel Hill: University of North Carolina Press, 1975.

McMurry, Sally. *Transforming Rural Life: Dairying Families and Agricultural Change, 1820–1885.* Baltimore: Johns Hopkins University Press, 1995.

Medhurst, Martin J., ed. *Cold War Rhetoric: Strategy, Metaphor, and Ideology.* New York: Greenwood Press, 1990.

Mendoza, Mary. "Treacherous Terrain: Racial Exclusion and Environmental Control at the U.S.-Mexico Border," *Environmental History* 23, no. 1 (January 2018): 117–26. doi.org/10.1093/envhis/emx124.

Merchant, Carolyn. *Ecological Revolutions: Nature, Gender, and Science in New England.* Chapel Hill: University of North Carolina, 1989.

———. *Reinventing Eden: The Fate of Nature in Western Culture.* New York: Routledge, 2003.

Merrill, Karen. *Public Lands and Political Meaning: Ranchers, the Government, and the Property between Them.* Berkeley: University of California Press, 2002.

Meyerowitz, Joanne, ed. *Not June Cleaver: Women and Gender in Postwar America, 1945–1960*. Philadelphia: Temple University Press, 1994.

Milner, Clyde A., ed. *A New Significance: Re-Envisioning the History of the American West*. Essays by Alan Bogue. New York: Oxford University Press, 1996.

Milner, Clyde A., Carol O'Conner, Martha Sandweiss, eds. *The Oxford History of the American West*. New York: Oxford University Press, 1994.

Montgomery, David. *The Fall of the House of Labor: The Workplace, the State, and American Labor Activism, 1865–1925*. New York: Cambridge University Press, 1987.

Montoya, Maria. "Landscapes of the Cold War West." In *The Cold War American West, 1945–1989*, edited by Kevin J. Fernlund, 9–29. Albuquerque: University of New Mexico Press, 1998.

Mooney, Patrick H., ed. *Farmers' and Farm Workers' Movements: Social Protest in American Agriculture*. New York: Twayne Publishers, 1995.

——. *My Own Boss? Class, Rationality, and the Family Farm*. Boulder, Colo.: Westview Press, 1988.

Moore, Jacqueline. *Cow Boys and Cattle Men: Class and Masculinities on the Texas Frontier, 1865–1900*. New York: New York University Press, 2009.

Morris, Peter. "Disturbed Belt or Rancher's Paradise? Frontier Exploration and Place-Making in a Western Canadian-American Borderland." In *Farming across Borders: A Transnational History of the North American West*, edited by Sterling Evans, 169–98. Chapel Hill: University of North Carolina Press, 2017.

Morrissey, Katherine. *Mental Territories: Mapping the Inland Empire*. Ithaca, N.Y.: Cornell University Press, 1997.

Mukerji, Chandra, and Michael Schudson, eds. *Rethinking Popular Culture: Contemporary Perspectives in Cultural Studies*. Berkeley: University of California Press, 1991.

Nash, Gerald D. *The American West Transformed: The Impact of the Second World War*. Bloomington: Indiana University Press, 1985.

——. *The Federal Landscape: An Economic History of the Twentieth-Century West*. Tucson: University of Arizona Press, 1999.

——. *World War II and the West: Reshaping the Economy*. Lincoln: University of Nebraska Press, 1990.

Nash, Linda. "The Agency of Nature or the Nature of Agency?" *Environmental History* 10, no. 1 (January 2005): 67–69.

——. *Inescapable Ecologies: A History of Environment, Disease, and Knowledge*. San Francisco: University of California Press, 2007.

Nash, Roderick. *Wilderness and the American Mind*. New Haven, Conn.: Yale University Press, 1967.

Needham, Andrew. *Power Lines: Phoenix and the Making of the Modern Southwest*. Princeton, N.J.: Princeton University Press, 2014.

Nelson, Paula. *After the West Was Won: Homesteaders and Townbuilders in Western South Dakota, 1900–1917*. Iowa City: University of Iowa Press, 1986.

Neth, Mary. *Preserving the Family Farm: Women, Community, and the Foundations of Agribusiness in the Midwest, 1900–1940*. Baltimore: Johns Hopkins University Press, 1995.

Nixon, Rob. *Slow Violence and the Environmentalism of the Poor*. Cambridge, Mass.: Harvard University Press, 2011.

Oakes, Guy. *The Imaginary War: Civil Defense and American Cold War Culture*. New York: Oxford University Press, 1994.

O'Conner, Carol A. "A Region of Cities." In *The Oxford History of the American West*, edited by Clyde A. Milner, Carol O'Conner, and Martha Sandweiss. New York: Oxford University Press, 1994.

Odum, Eugene P. *Fundamentals of Ecology*. Philadelphia: Saunders, 1953.

Olson, Mancur. *The Logic of Collective Action*. Cambridge, Mass.: Harvard University Press, 1965.

Osterud, Nancy Grey. "'She Helped Me Hay It as Good as a Man': Relations among Women and Men in an Agricultural Community." In Groneman and Norton, *"To Toil the Livelong Day,"* 87–98.

Peck, Gunther. "The Nature of Labor: Fault Lines and Common Ground in Environmental and Labor History." *Environmental History* 11, no. 2 (April 2006): 212–38.

Peffer, E. L. *The Closing of the Public Domain: Disposal and Reservation Policies, 1900–1950*. Stanford, Calif.: Stanford University Press, 1951.

Pena, Devon. *Chicano Culture, Ecology, and Politics*. Tucson: University of Arizona Press, 1998.

Petracca, Mark P., ed. *The Politics of Interest: Interest Groups Transformed*. Boulder, Colo.: Westview Press, 1992.

Phillips, Steven J., and Patricia Wentworth Comus, eds. *A Natural History of the Sonoran Desert*. Berkeley: University of California Press, 2000.

Pincus, J. "Pressure Groups and the Pattern of Tariffs." *Journal of Political Economy* 83, no. 4 (August 1975): 757–78.

Pisani, Donald J. *To Reclaim a Divided West: Water, Law, and Public Policy, 1848–1902*. Albuquerque: University of New Mexico Press, 1992.

———. *Water and American Government: The Reclamation Bureau, National Water Policy, and the West, 1902–1935*. Berkeley: University of California Press, 2002.

Pomeroy, Earl. *In Search of the Golden West: The Tourist in Western America*. New York: Knopf, 1957.

Price, Jennifer. *Flight Maps: Adventures with Nature in Modern America*. New York: Basic Books, 1999.

Pulido, Laura. *Environmentalism and Economic Justice: Two Chicano Struggles in the Southwest*. Tucson: University of Arizona Press, 1998.

Rasmussen, Wayne David. *Taking the University to the People: Seventy-Five Years of Cooperative Extension*. Ames: Iowa State University Press, 1989.

Rasmussen, Wayne D., and Gladys L. Baker. *Price-Support and Adjustment Programs from 1933 through 1978: A Short History.* Agriculture Information Bulletin No. 424. Washington, D.C.: U.S. Department of Agriculture, 1978.

Reiger, John F. *American Sportsmen and the Origins of Conservation.* Corvallis, Ore.: Oregon State University Press, 2001.

Reisner, Marc. *Cadillac Desert: The American West and Its Disappearing Water.* New York: Viking, 1986.

Remley, David. *Bell Ranch: Cattle Ranching in the Southwest, 1824–1947.* Albuquerque: University of New Mexico Press, 1993.

Rifkin, Jeremy. *Beyond Beef: The Rise and Fall of the Cattle Culture.* New York: Dutton, 1992.

Ringholz, Raye Carleson. *Uranium Frenzy: Boom and Bust on the Colorado Plateau.* Albuquerque: University of New Mexico Press, 1991.

Robbins, Roy M. *Our Landed Heritage: The Public Domain, 1776–1970.* Lincoln: University of Nebraska Press, 1976.

Rogers, Jedediah. *Roads in the Wilderness: Conflict in Canyon Country.* Salt Lake City: University of Utah Press, 2013.

Rogers, Thomas D., *The Deepest Wounds: A Labor and Environmental History of Sugar in Northeast Brazil.* Durham: University of North Carolina Press, 2010.

Roediger, David. *The Wages of Whiteness: Race and the Making of the American Working Class.* New York: Verso, 1991.

Rothman, Hal. *Devil's Bargains: Tourism in the Twentieth-Century American West.* Lawrence: University of Kansas Press, 1998.

———. *Saving the Planet: The American Response to the Environment in the Twentieth Century.* Chicago: Ivan R. Dee, 2000.

Rowell, Andrew. *Green Backlash: Global Subversion of the Environmental Movement.* London: Routledge, 1996.

Rowley, William D. *U.S. Forest Service Grazing and Rangelands: A History.* College Station: Texas A&M University Press, 1985.

Rupp, Leila, ed. *Survival in the Doldrums: The American Women's Rights Movement 1945–1960s.* New York: Oxford University Press, 1987.

Russell, Edmund. "'Speaking of Annihilation': Mobilization for War against Human and Insect Enemies, 1914–1945." *Journal of American History* 82, no. 4 (1996): 1505–29.

Sachs, Carolyn. *Invisible Farmers: Women in Agricultural Production.* Totowa, N.J.: Rowman and Allanheld, 1983.

Sayre, Nathan. *The Politics of Scale: The History of Rangeland Science.* Chicago: University of Chicago Press, 2017.

———. *Ranching, Endangered Species, and Urbanization in the Southwest: Species of Capital.* Tucson: University of Arizona Press, 2002.

Scanlon, Jennifer. *Inarticulate Longings: The Ladies Home Journal, Gender, and the Promises of Consumer Culture.* New York: Routledge, 1995.

Scharff, Virginia, ed. *Seeing Nature through Gender.* Lawrence: University of Kansas Press, 2003.

——. *Taking the Wheel: Women and the Coming of the Motor Age.* New York: Maxwell Macmillan, 1991.

Schlebecker, John T. *Cattle Raising on the Plains, 1900–1961.* Lincoln: University of Nebraska Press, 1963.

——. "Grasshoppers in American Agricultural History." *Agricultural History* 27, no. 3 (July 1953): 85–93.

Schlosser, Eric. *Fast Food Nation: The Dark Side of the All-American Meal.* Boston: Houghton Mifflin, 2001.

Schwantes, Carlos A. "No Aid and No Comfort: Early Transportation and the Origins of Tourism in the Northern West." In Wrobel and Long, *Seeing and Being Seen,* 125–42.

Schwartz, Marvin. *J. B. Hunt: The Long Haul to Success.* Fayetteville: University of Arkansas Press, 1992.

Scott, Joan Wallach. *Gender and the Politics of History.* New York: Columbia University Press, 1988.

Sellers, Christopher. *Hazards of the Job: From Industrial Disease to Environmental Health Science.* Chapel Hill: University of North Carolina Press, 1997.

——. "Thoreau's Body: Towards an Embodied Environmental History." *Environmental History* 4 (1999): 486–514.

Shaiko, Ronald, ed. *The Interest Group Connection: Electioneering, Lobbying, and Policymaking in Washington.* Chatham, Md.: Chatham House, 1998.

Sharp, Robert L. *Big Outfit: Ranching on the Baca Float.* Tucson: University of Arizona Press, 1974.

Sheflin, Douglas. *Legacies of Dust: Land Use and Labor on the Great Plains.* Lincoln: University of Nebraska Press, 2019.

Sherow, James E., ed. *A Sense of the American West: An Environmental History Anthology.* Albuquerque: University of New Mexico Press, 1998.

Shivik, John. *The Predator Paradox: Ending the War with Wolves, Bears, Cougars, and Coyotes.* New York: Beacon Press, 2014.

Skaggs, Jimmy M. *The Cattle-Trailing Industry: Between Supply and Demand, 1866–1890.* Lawrence: University Press of Kansas, 1973.

——. *Prime Cut: Livestock Raising and Meatpacking in the United States, 1607–1983.* College Station: Texas A&M University Press, 1986.

Skillen, James R. *This Land Is Your Land: Rebellion in the West.* New York: Oxford University Press, 2020.

Slotkin, Richard. *The Fatal Environment: The Myth of the Frontier in the Age of Industrialization, 1800–1890.* New York: Atheneum, 1985.

Smith, Henry Nash. *Virgin Land: The American West as Symbol and Myth.* Cambridge, Mass.: Harvard University Press, 1950.

Smith, Richard K. *Agricultural Statistics 1949*. Washington, D.C.: U.S. Department of Agriculture, 1949.

Solinger, Rickie. *Beggars and Choosers: How the Politics of Choice Shapes Adoption, Abortion, and Welfare in the United States*. New York: Hill and Wang, 2001.

Sparrow, Bartholomew H. *From the Outside In: World War II and the American State*. Princeton, N.J.: Princeton University Press, 1996.

Spence, Mark David. *Dispossessing the Wilderness: Indian Removal and the Making of the National Parks*. New York: Oxford University Press, 1999.

Starrs, Paul. *Let the Cowboy Ride: Cattle Ranching in the American West*. Baltimore, Md.: Johns Hopkins University Press, 1998.

Steen, Harold K. *The U.S. Forest Service: A History*. Seattle: University of Washington Press, 1976.

Steiner, Michael, and David Wrobel, eds. *Many Wests: Place, Culture, and Regional Identity*. Lawrence: University Press of Kansas, 1997.

Stewart, Mart A. *"What Nature Suffers to Groe": Life, Labor, and Landscape on the Georgia Coast, 1680–1920*. Athens: University of Georgia Press, 1996.

Strasser, Susan. *Never Done: A History of American Housework*. New York: Henry Holt, 2000.

Sturgeon, Noel. *Environmentalism in Popular Culture: Gender, Race, Sexuality, and the Politics of the Natural*. Tucson: University of Arizona Press, 2009.

Sutter, Paul. *Driven Wild: How the Fight against Automobiles Launched the Modern Wilderness Movement*. Seattle: University of Washington Press, 2002.

Switzer, Jacqueline Vaughn. *Green Backlash: The History and Politics of Environmental Opposition in the U.S.* Boulder, Colo.: Lynne Rienner Publishers, 1997.

Taylor, Joseph E. *Persistent Callings: Seasons of Work and Identity on the Oregon Coast*. Corvallis: Oregon State University Press, 2019.

——. "As though Bunkerville and Malheur Are the West." H-Net Reviews in the Humanities and Social Sciences, November 2021. https://www.h-net.org /reviews/showpdf.php?id=56763.

Thompson, Charles Dillard, ed. *The Human Cost of Food: Farmworkers' Lives, Labor, and Advocacy*. Austin: University of Texas Press, 2002.

Thompson, E. P. "Folklore, Anthropology, and Social History." *Indian Historical Review* 3 (1977): 247–66.

——. *The Making of the English Working Class*. New York: Vintage Books, 1966.

Thompson, Jonathan. "The First Sagebrush Rebellion: What Sparked It and How It Ended." *High Country News*, January 14, 2016. https://www.hcn.org/articles/a -look-back-at-the-first-sagebrush-rebellion.

Tobey, Ronald C. *Saving the Prairies: The Life Cycle of the Founding School of American Plant Ecology, 1895–1955*. Berkeley: University of California Press, 1981.

Truman, David. *The Governmental Process*. New York: Knopf, 1951.

Tuan, Yi Fu. *Topophilia: A Study of Environmental Perception, Attitudes, and Values*. New York: Columbia University Press, 1990.

Turner, Frederick. *Of Chiles, Cacti, and Fighting Cocks: Notes on the American West.* San Francisco: North Point Press, 1990.

Udall, Stewart. *The Myths of August: A Personal Exploration of Our Tragic Cold War Affair with the Atom.* New York: Pantheon Books, 1994.

U.S. Department of Agriculture. *Agricultural Statistics.* Washington, D.C.: GPO, 1949.

——. *Agricultural Statistics.* Washington, D.C.: GPO, 1957.

——. *Agricultural Statistics.* Washington, D.C.: GPO, 1963.

U. S. Forest Service. *The Western Range. Letter from the Secretary of Agriculture Transmitting in Response to Senate Resolution No. 289: A Report on the Western Range—a Great but Neglected Natural Resource.* Washington, D.C.: U.S. Printing Office, 1936.

Utley, Robert. *The Indian Frontier of the American West, 1846–1890.* Albuquerque: University of New Mexico Press, 1984.

Vail, David. *Chemical Lands: Pesticides, Aerial Spraying, and Health in North America's Grasslands since 1945.* Tuscaloosa: University of Alabama Press, 2018.

Vavra, Martin, ed. *Ecological Implications of Livestock Herbivory in the West.* Denver, Colo.: Society for Range Management, 1994.

Veracini, Lorenzo. *Settler Colonialism: A Theoretical Overview.* London: Palgrave Macmillan, 2010.

Walton, John. *Western Times and Water Wars: State, Culture, and Rebellion in California.* Berkeley: University of California Press, 1992.

Wander, Philip. "Political Rhetoric and the Un-American Tradition." In *Cold War Rhetoric: Strategy, Metaphor, and Ideology,* edited by Martin J. Medhurst, 185–200. New York: Greenwood Press, 1990.

Warren, Louis. *The Hunter's Game: Poachers and Conservationists in Twentieth-Century America.* New Haven, Conn.: Yale University Press, 1997.

Webb, Walter Prescott *The Great Frontier.* Boston: Hougton Mifflin, 1952.

Weiner, Douglas. "Presidential Address American Society for Environmental History." Houston, Texas, 2005.

Weisiger, Marsha. *Dreaming of Sheep in Navajo Country.* Seattle: University of Washington Press, 2009.

Welsh, Michael. *Dunes and Dreams: A History of White Sands National Monument.* Santa Fe, N.Mex.: National Park Service Intermountain Cultural Resources Center, 1995.

White, Hayden. *Tropics of Discourse: Essays in Cultural Criticism.* Baltimore: Johns Hopkins University Press, 1978.

White, Richard. "Are You an Environmentalist or Do You Work for a Living?" In *Uncommon Ground: Toward Reinventing Nature,* edited by William Cronon, 171–86. New York: Norton, 1995.

——. *"It's Your Misfortune and None of My Own": A History of the American West.* Norman: University of Oklahoma Press, 1991.

——. *The Roots of Dependency: Subsistence, Environment, and Social Change among the Choctaws, Pawnees, and Navajos.* Lincoln: University of Nebraska Press, 1983.

Whyte, William Hollingworth. *The Organization Man.* Garden City, N.Y.: Doubleday, 1956.

Wilbur-Cruce, Eva Antonia. *A Beautiful, Cruel Country.* Tucson: University of Arizona Press, 1987.

Wilcox, Robert W. "Zebu Elbows: Cattle Breeding and the Environment in Central Brazil, 1890–1960." In *Territories, Commodities and Knowledges: Latin American Environmental History in the Nineteenth and Twentieth Centuries,* edited by Christian Brannstrom, 34–56. London: Institute for the Study of the Americas, 2004.

Wilentz, Sean. *Chants Democratic: New York City and the Rise of the American Working Class, 1788–1850.* New York: Oxford University Press, 1984.

Williams, James. "Getting Housewives the Electric Message: Gender and Energy Marketing in the Early Twentieth Century." In *His and Hers: Gender, Consumption, and Technology,* edited by Roger Horowitz, 95–115. Charlottesville: University of Virginia Press, 1998.

Williams, Robert C. *Fordson, Farmall, and Poppin' Johnny: A History of the Farm Tractor and Its Impact on America.* Urbana: University of Illinois Press, 1987.

Williams, Terry Tempest. *Refuge: An Unnatural History of Family and Place.* New York: Pantheon Books, 1991.

Winkler, Allan M. *The Politics of Propaganda: The Office of War Information, 1942–1945.* New Haven, Conn.: Yale University Press, 1978.

Winner, Langdon. *The Whale and the Reactor: A Search for Limits in an Age of High Technology.* Chicago: University of Chicago Press, 1989.

Wirth, John. *Smelter Smoke in North America: The Politics of Transborder Pollution.* Lawrence: University Press of Kansas, 2000.

Worster, Donald. *Dust Bowl: The Southern Plains in the 1930s.* New York: Oxford University Press, 1979.

——. *Nature's Economy: A History of Ecological Ideas.* New York: Cambridge University Press, 1977.

——. *Rivers of Empire: Water, Aridity, and the Growth of the American West.* New York: Pantheon, 1985.

——. "Transformations of the Earth: Toward an Agroecological Perspective in History." *Journal of American History* 76, no. 4 (1990): 1087–1106.

——. *Under Western Skies: Nature and History in the American West.* New York: Oxford University Press, 1992.

Wrobel, David. *Promised Lands: Promotion, Memory, and the Creation of the American West.* Lawrence: University Press of Kansas, 2002.

Wrobel, David, and Patrick Long, eds. *Seeing and Being Seen: Tourism in the American West.* Lawrence: University Press of Kansas, 2001.

Wuerthner, George, and Mollie Yoneko Matteson, eds. *Welfare Ranching: The Subsidized Destruction of the American West.* Sausalito, Calif.: Foundation for Deep Ecology, 2002.

Wunder, John R., and Frances W. Kaye, eds. *Americans View Their Dust Bowl Experience.* Niwot: University of Colorado Press, 1999.

Yoshiie Yoda, and Kurt W. Radtke. *The Foundations of Japan's Modernization: A Comparison with China's Path toward Modernization.* Leiden: E. J. Brill, 1996.

Young, James A., and B. Abbott Sparks. *Cattle in the Cold Desert.* Logan: Utah State University Press, 1985.

Zinnemann, Fred, dir. *High Noon.* Los Angeles: United Artists, 1952.

Index

wage disparities and hierarchies, 63–65
Wallins, Shorty, 61–64
Warren, Con, 63, 83, 137–39, 168–70
Warren, Fred, 164
Warren, Louis, 34, 38
Warren, Nell (Con's wife), 138, 168–69
water conservation, 96–97
weather as bonding commonality, 205–6
weather extremes. *See* blizzards,
    noteworthy; droughts
"West, the" (definition of), 213–14n2
West (American), mythologies of, 13, 217n19
Western Livestock Journal, 61–62, 138
wheatgrasses, 92, 95, 97
White, Richard, 8, 34, 81
White Sands Proving Ground, N.Mex.,
    25–27
wildfires, 32–33, 85
wildlife control issues: carnivores in
    ecological systems, 101–2; game species
    and hunting, 35, 36–37, 38–39, 116;
    nuisance plants and insects, 71, 73,
    85–90, 98–99, 104; predator suppression
    and consequences, 12, 116–19. *See also*
    competitive species for grass resources
wildlife refuges, 35
Willey, William, 33
Winner, Langdon, 172
winter cow work, overview, 54
Woman in Levi's (Bourne), 101
women. *See* ranchwomen
Workman, Jack, 90

World War II, impact and influence of,
    216n15; economic fluctuations, 9–10, 48,
    216n15; military facility construction,
    26–27; modernization, 20–21, 60–61, 88;
    road construction, 29–30
Worster, Donald, 48
Wrobel, David, 154
Wyatt Manufacturing Company, 49
Wyoming: blizzard of 1949, 163–64; conflicts
    with hunters in, 40; Cowbelles in, 142,
    149; government sponsored ecology field
    day, 92, *94*; grasshopper eradication
    program, 99; heroization of cow work
    and ranch culture, 193–95; property
    values in, 27; road development in, 30;
    severe drought in, 131; wages profile,
    63–64. *See also* Wyoming Stock Growers
    Association (WSGA)
Wyoming Fish and Game Department, 40
Wyoming Natural Resource Board, 92
Wyoming Stock Growers Association
    (WSGA), *69*; blizzard relief efforts, 164;
    histories published by and memory
    construction, 154, 157–62, 245n6;
    leadership positions, 132, 170, 184;
    material culture preservation, 171;
    postwar profile of, 185–86; survey about
    impact of hunters, 39–40. See also *Cow
    Country* (WSGA publication)

Xanthium spp. (cockleburs), 71, 73, 87–90,
    104

Printed in the USA
CPSIA information can be obtained
at www.ICGtesting.com
CBHW032124250524
9109CB00002B/44